DUDLEY CARLETON

to

JOHN CHAMBERLAIN
1603–1624

Sir Dudley Carleton. *Courtesy of the National Portrait Gallery, London.*

DUDLEY CARLETON
to
JOHN CHAMBERLAIN
1603–1624
JACOBEAN LETTERS

Edited with an introduction by
MAURICE LEE, Jr.

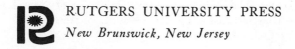

RUTGERS UNIVERSITY PRESS
New Brunswick, New Jersey

By the Same Author

Selections from Bayle's Dictionary, with E. A. Beller (1952)

James Stewart, Earl of Moray (1953)

Political Community and the North Atlantic Area,
with K. W. Deutsch *et al.* (1957)

John Maitland of Thirlestane (1959)

The Cabal (1965)

James I and Henri IV (1970)

Library of Congress Cataloging in Publication Data

Dorchester, Dudley Carleton, 1st Viscount, 1573–1632.
  Dudley Carleton to John Chamberlain, 1603–1624.

  1. Gt. Brit.—Foreign relations—1603–1625.
I. Chamberlain, John, 1554?–1628. II. Title.
DA46.D65A43   320.9′42′061   76-185391
ISBN 0-8135-0723-5

To J. and G.

Over the years my favorite correspondents

CONTENTS

WORKS REFERRED TO MORE THAN
ONCE IN THE NOTES

Ashton, *Money Market*   R. S. Ashton, *The Crown and the Money Market 1603–1640* (Oxford, 1960)

Bouwsma, *Venice*   W. J. Bouwsma, *Venice and the Defense of Republican Liberty* (Berkeley, 1969)

Carter, *Secret Diplomacy*   C. H. Carter, *The Secret Diplomacy of the Habsburgs 1598–1625* (New York, 1964)

C. S. P. Domestic   Calendar of State Papers, Domestic series, ed. M. A. E. Green *et al.* (London, 1857 ff.)

C. S. P. Venetian   Calendar of state papers and manuscripts relating to English affairs existing in the archives of Venice, ed. H. F. Brown and A. B. Hinds, vols. 10–18 (1603–1625) (London, 1907 ff.)

Dick, *Lives*   O. L. Dick, ed., *Aubrey's Brief Lives* (London, 1949)

Gardiner, *History*   S. R. Gardiner, *History of England from the Accession of James I to the Outbreak of the Civil War 1603–1642,* 10 vols. (London, 1887–1891)

Letters, Holland   Philip Yorke, second earl of Hardwicke, ed. *Letters to and from Sir Dudley Carleton During His Embassy in Holland from January 1615/–16 to December 1620,* 2nd ed. (London, 1775)

L. J. C.   N. E. McClure, ed., *The Letters of John Chamberlain,* 2 vols. (Philadelphia, 1939)

Lythe, *Economy*   S. G. E. Lythe, *The Economy of Scotland in Its European Setting, 1550–1625* (Edinburgh, 1960)

P. R. O., S. P.   Public Record Office, State Papers

Smith, *Wotton*   L. P. Smith, *The Life and Letters of Sir Henry Wotton,* 2 vols. (Oxford, 1907)

Steele, *Proclamations* R. R. Steele, ed., *Tudor and Stuart Proclamations, 1485–1714,* 2 vols. (Oxford, 1910)

Stoye, *Travellers*   John W. Stoye, *English Travellers Abroad, 1604–1667* (London, 1952)

Willson, *Bowyer*   D. H. Willson, ed., *The Parliamentary Diary of Robert Bowyer, 1606–1607* (Minneapolis, 1931)

Winwood, *Memorials* E. Sawyer, ed., *Memorials of Affairs of State in the reigns of Queen Elizabeth and King James I, collected chiefly from the original papers of Sir Ralph Winwood,* 3 vols. (London, 1725)

DUDLEY CARLETON

to

JOHN CHAMBERLAIN

1603–1624

INTRODUCTION

The name of John Chamberlain is known to every student of Jacobean England. A. L. Rowse, himself a distinguished stylist, calls Chamberlain "the best letter writer of his time"; his letters, published in a two-volume edition by Norman E. McClure, are a major historical source for the first quarter of the seventeenth century.[1] Chamberlain has been the subject of commentary, mostly favorable, by literary scholars and historians alike; the best and most perceptive study is the long and graceful essay by Wallace Notestein in his *Four Worthies*. It is, in fact, just about impossible to write about any aspect of the Jacobean period without quoting Chamberlain at least once.

No such scholarly attention or celebrity has come to the man to whom the vast majority of Chamberlain's surviving letters are addressed. Dudley Carleton was a young man in his early twenties casting about for a career for himself when the correspondence began, in the middle of the 1590s; when it ended, early in the reign of Charles I, Carleton was a highly successful diplomatist, on the verge of a peerage. In 1628, the year of Chamberlain's death, Carleton rose to the top of his profession, becoming Secretary of State; he had but four years to live and died in office. He left behind him an enormous mass of correspondence, almost none of which has been published, except for an eighteenth-century collection of some of his dispatches from The Hague during the first five years of his embassy there.[2] The great majority of the letters are in the Public Record Office, London, where they bulk very large, not only in the appro-

[3]

priate collections of *State Papers, Foreign,* but also in the *State Papers, Domestic.* We would know much less about the reign of James I than we do had Carleton been less of a magpie about his papers. Much of the correspondence was official, but by no means all of it; there are a number of letters to and from his relatives and friends, among them John Chamberlain. When Carleton was in England the two men corresponded sporadically; when Carleton was out of the country, which was most of the time, they wrote regularly, two or three times a month. The letters in this book constitute the first systematic publication of a part of the other side of the most interesting private correspondence of Jacobean England.

Only a small fraction of Carleton's letters to his friend are included in this volume. The first limitation imposed is chronological: all the letters are taken from the reign of James I. Those written before and after the tenure of the Scottish Solomon are certainly not devoid of interest, but they illustrate nothing which cannot be shown from the letters written between 1603 and 1625. The second criterion of selection, a necessarily vague one, is that each letter should be of as much general interest as possible. This meant the exclusion of certain types of letters: those which deal purely with the private affairs of the two men's wide circle of relatives and friends; those which are chiefly concerned with Carleton's money problems or his prospects of promotion; those which are merely a rehash of the dispatch which the busy ambassador had just composed for his superiors in London—the number of this sort increases as the years go by. One further group is excluded, those letters which are in large part an answer to Chamberlain's and which would not be intelligible without a reading of the Chamberlain text. The selection made from the remaining letters is intended to illustrate as many facets as possible of the Jacobean world and of the life of one of the upwardly mobile members of its Establishment. This selection is not designed to provide in any systematic way material for a history of James's foreign policy, or of his foreign service, or of Jacobean society, though the letters do shed light on all these things. For the would-be biographer of Carleton they are merely the tip of the iceberg.

The selection is designed to illuminate that indefinable thing, the temper of the times, both in England and in Europe, as seen through the eyes of a perceptive, witty, and increasingly unhopeful observer of a complex and not always intelligible scene.

II

Dudley Carleton was born in 1573 into a large family of lesser gentry in Oxfordshire. He had two brothers and five sisters and assorted uncles, aunts, and cousins. John Chamberlain was among his connections; Carleton's mother's sister was the wife of Chamberlain's nephew Thomas Stukely. This would suggest a greater disparity in age between the two than in fact existed; Chamberlain was about twenty years older than his friend. Carleton went to Westminster School and to Christ Church, Oxford, where he took his B.A. in 1595. He then faced the question of how to make his way in the world. Unlike Chamberlain's, his private means were too small to provide him with enough income to be a gentleman of leisure. The diplomatic service seemed to him to be a hopeful possibility from the beginning; in 1596 he was anxious to be employed by Sir Anthony Mildmay, who was then ambassador in France. He went twice to France in 1596 and 1597, but without getting any job, which, in view of Mildmay's short, inglorious diplomatic career, was perhaps just as well. Carleton's first significant employment was not really public service at all; he was taken on by the Norris family, thanks in part, perhaps, to Mildmay and in part to his cousin Michael Dormer, one of Chamberlain's close friends, whose house at Ascot was one of Chamberlain's regular stopping-places when he was on one of his "progresses" through the countryside. In the spring of 1598 Carleton went to Ostend as secretary and general factotum to the governor, Sir Edward Norris, son of Henry, Baron Norris of Rycote. Over the next few years he spent considerable time in Ostend and at the various Norris properties in England: Rycote, Sir Edward's country house at Englefield, and his city house at Puddlewharf.

Employment by the Norrises had its drawbacks, however. In the first place, the family's interests were military, and Carleton had neither the desire nor the aptitude for a military life. In the

[5]

second place, the future looked questionable. Old Baron Henry died in 1601, having outlived all of his sons but Sir Edward; the latter's own health began to break in the year of his father's death, and he died in the first year of the new reign. The new head of the family, Sir Edward's nephew, was a strange young man, moody and violent, who was ultimately to commit suicide in a most bizarre fashion, by shooting himself with a crossbow after brooding over the humiliation of a brief imprisonment for scuffling with a fellow peer in the presence of Prince Charles. So Carleton began to cast about again. In July 1601 the first suggestion of the possibility of a post with the earl of Northumberland was made. Nothing came of this for the moment, however, and in the following year a much more attractive opportunity presented itself, in the form of a secretaryship to the newly appointed ambassador to France, Sir Thomas Parry. So in April 1602 Carleton arrived in Paris to prepare the way for the new tenant of the embassy; in the process, he got well acquainted with the old, Ralph Winwood, a friend of Chamberlain's whom Carleton had not known well prior to this time. He and Winwood became close friends, a friendship which was crucial to Carleton's future.

Parry took his time about getting to Paris; he did not arrive until August 1602. After six weeks Carleton's disenchantment with his superior was apparent; six weeks more saw an open breach between them. Carleton hung on unhappily in the job for lack of anything else to do; his friends and relatives were all alerted to his situation. The line to Northumberland was reopened, especially by Carleton's brother George and by another friendly diplomatist, Thomas Edmondes, who had been instrumental in getting Carleton his job with Parry. But the dawn of the new reign saw Carleton still in France; the first letter in this collection describes the initial French reaction to the smooth change of dynasty.

In most ways Carleton's letters to his older friend during the years before 1603 exhibit the characteristics to be found in the Jacobean letters; in two respects they are different. They are the letters of a young man in his twenties, sometimes cocksure, sometimes immature, sometimes parroting the views of others. There is also a certain stiffness of manner: the younger man was still aware of the difference in their ages, though by the turn of the century this formalism had just about vanished. The acutely observant eye is there already, and so is the ability to report and express an opinion simultaneously and briefly. For example, here is what he has to say about Dutch reaction to the execution of Lord Essex: "The earl's fall is generally bewailed, but his fault so ill understood by the people, that no reason can beat into their maudlin drunken heads, but that he lost his head wrongfully." [3] Also present is the bawdy and playful wit. Shortly after the treaty of Vervins he wrote of Henri IV, "Though he hath laid by all other arms, he lays about him with his truncheon, for his mistress is again with child before the last be christened." [4] He also had the ability to write the theatrical set piece, which can be seen in the two letters of November 27 and December 11, 1603, given below, on the trial of Sir Walter Raleigh; his letter of July 31/August 10, 1602, on the last hours of Marshal Biron is a beautifully constructed narrative.[5] And finally, there is the style: in this writer's view, every bit as clear and polished as that of his older friend. "The ague," he wrote, "dealt fairly with me: it came every third day, held me three hours hot and three cold, lasted three fits, left me three weeks ago, and so in fine, proved a right Tertian." [6]

III

For all his gifts, Carleton was still nothing more than a promising young man of thirty with a circle of useful friends in the middle echelons of government service when the Stuart era dawned in March 1603. He disliked his employer and although he admired Henri IV he did not like the French. "I once saw in this realm the very face of misery, when I longed to see it restored and in the best beauty," he wrote in April 1602, "and now having taken a surfeit of the plenty which is accompanied with such pride and insolency, it would not grieve me much to see it *in statu quo prius.*" [7] His venture into diplomacy seemed to have been a failure. He therefore returned home, at the urging of his brother George and some of his friends, and in September 1603 took employment as controller of the household to Henry Percy, ninth earl of Northumberland.

Carleton remained in Northumberland's service for a year and a half. His relations with the Percys were never close—"cool" was the word he later used to describe them—and in March 1605 he welcomed the chance to return to his old employers and accompany young Lord Norris to Spain. Norris was going as a member of the entourage of Charles Howard, earl of Nottingham, who was bearing James's ratification of the recently signed Anglo-Spanish peace treaty to Madrid. Carleton's service with Northumberland brought him to the fringes of the court, whose doings he chronicled with an amused and rather jaundiced eye. Carleton was both prudish and penurious; the extravagant, somewhat raffish camarilla which surrounded King James he found rather undesirable—and, like most of his fellow-countrymen, Carleton did not like Scots. Carleton was not a Puritan in any theological sense, though he was always a staunch Protestant, but he had many of the qualities associated with what some scholars have called the Puritan, bourgeois ethic. At this stage of his career he much preferred austere, hard-working bureaucrats like Winwood, or Salisbury himself. Because of his friends at court Carleton was elected to Parliament in 1604, for the Cornish borough of St. Mawes, which habitually returned court-connected candidates: in the house he was a steady supporter of the government. Carleton evidently enjoyed Parliament, and he was an entertaining reporter of its doings. But his career did not lie that way.

In fact, Carleton came close to having no career at all. One of Northumberland's cousins, Thomas Percy, was one of the major figures in the Gunpowder Plot; Carleton, quite innocently, was involved in the negotiations for the transfer of the vault in which the conspirators placed their deadly charge. At the time of the discovery of the plot Carleton was in Paris, on his way back from Spain; Lord Norris had fallen ill, and Carleton was looking after him. Carleton's first reaction to the plot was one of incredulity; unaware of the fact that his name had been mentioned in connection with it, he stayed on in Paris with Norris. Finally he was ordered home and taken into custody. It did not take a long investigation to convince Salisbury that Carleton was innocent; his imprisonment was brief, and by the end of 1606 the all-powerful Secretary had assented to his petition to be allowed to resume his seat in Parliament. But public employment was another matter. His principal reliance was on the good will of Sir Walter Cope, one of Salisbury's intimates, who ultimately became chamberlain of the exchequer and master of the court of wards. Cope was distantly connected by marriage to Carleton, who occasionally refers to him in the letters as his "cousin." Carleton was not overfond of Cope, whom he thought self-important and fussy; but Cope had gotten him released from custody and could perhaps do more. In the meantime, Carleton appealed to Northumberland, who was himself in the Tower and could do little for him, and lived with his relatives and friends, principally his brother George, his brother-in-law Alexander Williams, his cousin Sir Rowland Lytton (Cope's brother's nephew), his cousin by marriage Sir Michael Dormer—all of these good friends of Chamberlain's—and, increasingly, Sir Henry Savile, Provost of Eton. Savile had a stepdaughter, Anne, recently widowed; Carleton courted her, married her in November 1607, and settled down to help his father-in-law with his great edition of St. Chrysostom. The marriage was a happy one. Carleton was not a wencher, and there is no evidence of marital discord, although his wife did not always get along with Carleton's large brood of relatives. Carleton seems to have had no in-law problems, and, indeed, he liked and admired Savile. The only pall cast over the marriage was that none of the children survived infancy; Carleton's peerage was to die with him.

St. Chrysostom and the academic life did not appeal very much to Carleton either—though in later years he was to canvass very earnestly to succeed his father-in-law at Eton—and he kept hoping for better things. The hope seemed needlessly deferred. Carleton was resilient—within a few months of his imprisonment he was able to make jokes about the Gunpowder Plot in describing an accident during the visit of King Christian of Denmark to England—but the implication of guilt by association was slow to vanish. In the summer of 1607 he was planning to accompany Cope on a semiofficial mission to the Continent, which Salisbury cancelled at the last minute. In the autumn there was some discussion of a mission to Florence which never materialized. In the summer of 1608 Salisbury asked Carleton to go to Bath to talk to his friend Lord Norris and persuade him not to disinherit his daughter—Norris's estranged wife was Salisbury's niece. Carleton went and thus encouraged, appealed once more to Salisbury, both directly and through Cope, asking for foreign employment. He left Eton and moved to Westminster, so as to be able to further his suit with the powers-that-be in person. This time Salisbury's response was favorable; the fumes of the powder treason had at last blown away sufficiently for the king to be persuaded to give employment to a man whose name had been mentioned in connection with it. A major diplomatic reshuffle was in prospect in 1609; Carleton was most anxious to succeed his friend Winwood as ambassador at The Hague. As it turned out, Winwood was not transferred, and as the reshuffle went on Carleton's hopes sank lower and lower, until by September he was willing to settle for a position in Ireland. The formal appointment to an Irish secretaryship was made in January 1610, and Carleton, glad for this crumb, was effusive in his thanks to Sir Walter Cope. Then, all at once, in May 1610, the skies brightened. He was not to go to Ireland after all—he would go to Brussels, to succeed his friend Sir Thomas Edmondes as ambassador to the court of "the Archdukes": Archduke Albert, the emperor's brother, and his wife the Infanta Isabella Clara Eugenia, sister of Philip III of Spain. Carleton was delighted, and flooded Edmondes, who had been transferred to the embassy in Paris, with a spate of letters asking for advice on how to conduct himself. Then, very suddenly, the picture changed once more. As Carleton wrote Edmondes on July 25, "My course to Brussels was so far advanced, that both my privy seal was drawn for that employment, and I had order for my plate. . . . having my hour assigned to be presented to the king, a consideration of the archduke's slackness to send hither (who first revoked his ambassador and should therefore first send), diverted my course, and I was at the same instant, as I should have taken leave for that service, assigned to Venice." [8] So to Venice Carleton, now Sir Dudley, went, taking his wife and sister with him. Among his travelling companions was Chamberlain, who stayed with him for several months after his arrival, not leaving Venice till the late summer of 1611. Carleton's diplomatic career was beginning; for the remainder of the reign of James I he would see very little of his native land.

During these years of waiting and uncertainty and frustration—and, indeed, in subsequent years too—Carleton's first purpose in his letters to Chamberlain was to provide information for his friend. All sorts of information provided grist for Chamberlain's mill; so Carleton described with equal care Henri IV's progress to Metz, a masque or a wedding at court, Sir Walter Raleigh's trial, the doings of Parliament, and academic disputes at Oxford. Carleton was not just a sobersided reporter, however; the amusing trivia are here too—the story of the alcoholic shipboard party given for Christian of Denmark, for instance, or the narrow escape of the king's physician Sir William Paddy from a fate worse than death. One of the bonds between the two men was that they had the same sort of sense of humor: a drily understated wit flavored with bawdiness.

Carleton's tone throughout his letters is an even one, never heavy-handed, never really revealing the anxieties he must have felt. Chamberlain was his friend; Carleton obviously felt great affection for him, and greatly enjoyed his company. But he very quickly came to appreciate what sort of man Chamberlain was: a man who, as Chamberlain himself put it, aimed at "nothing but how to live *suaviter* and in plenty." [9] He would not run any risks, financial or otherwise; he would not put himself out unduly—which helps, perhaps, to explain why he never married. He was willing to serve as a go-between, to transmit messages, to give advice, but not to commit himself to anything which might involve difficulties. So Carleton treated him as though he were an affectionate, charming, lazy, sensible old uncle. He gave Chamberlain information, told him the gossip, and received the gossip in return and hard information too. Nothing ever disturbed the friendship of the two men, perhaps because it was never subjected to any serious strain. Chamberlain had nothing to ask of his younger friend; Carleton was too perceptive to ask of Chamberlain what he was unwilling or unable to give.

IV

Of the half-dozen or so permanent posts in the Jacobean diplomatic service, the embassy at Venice was the least important. The Serene Republic no longer held the gorgeous East in fee; she had, in fact, begun on the long, slow, downward path to extinction. At the time of Carleton's arrival she had just emerged from a serious quarrel with the Papacy which had led to the imposition of a papal interdict. The growth of English and Dutch commerce in the Mediterranean, the latter accelerated by the Spanish-Dutch truce of 1609, confronted her with an economic crisis which she chose to meet by a policy of protectionism that ultimately hastened her decline. The assassination of Henri IV alarmed her, since only Spain would profit, and in Italy, Spain and a still-hostile Papacy were firm allies. In these circumstances Venetian foreign policy aimed at avoiding a major entanglement at all costs. She threatened to join an anti-Habsburg league, but never quite committed herself. She sometimes encouraged other Italian quarrels, so that Spain would be occupied elsewhere. The Austrian branch of the Habsburg family was in some ways more menacing to the Republic than Spain, owing to the Archduke Ferdinand's patronage of the Uskoks, a band of Dalmatian-based pirates. Venice was finally goaded into war against them in 1615, a war which, by its very existence, marked a failure for Venetian policy and was not very successful.

English policy toward Venice and toward Italian affairs generally was ambivalent. King James was sympathetic to Venice on account of the Republic's antipapal attitude and her hostility to Jesuits. He wanted the peace to be kept in Italy, if peace did not mean Spanish domination; at the same time he saw that it was potentially useful for England that Spain be kept busy in Italy. But basically Italy counted for little in the affairs of Europe as seen from London. The chief function of the ambassador at Venice, then, was not so much to deal in great events as to look after the interests of English merchants, who were doing more and more business in the Mediterranean—their problems occupy a great deal of space in Carleton's official dispatches—and to keep an eye on English travellers there. Two sorts of travellers in particular were important. First, there were the V.I.P.s, of which there were a large number—some of them young men travelling with tutors, like the earl of Devonshire's son, some of them great nobles like the earl of Arundel, the famous art collector. When such people came to Venice it was the ambassador's job to look after them, present them to the authorities, and see that they saw the sights in which they were interested. An Italian visit was now a part of the nascent "Grand Tour," and the English ambassador in Venice was his country's most important representative in the peninsula. The second class of traveller was more difficult to watch and therefore more worrying. It consisted of Catholics, actual and potential; they were bothersome because they might be, or become, conspirators. King James was always highly nervous about the possibilities of an assassination plot. In order to keep watch on such people and for general purposes of information-gathering, each ambassador was allotted a certain sum of money (not large and usually in arrears) for "intelligence," the employment of informers, who were about as rascally and unreliable as such people usually are.

Carleton did not enjoy his years in Venice. His command of the language never became as thorough as he wished. The climate bothered him. He was beginning to suffer from bad health, particularly the stone, which was to trouble him for the rest of his life. He was fond of his sister, but she and Lady Carleton squabbled from time to time, and the presence in his household during the last part of his stay of his alcoholic young cousin Philip Lytton created problems too. And, above all, he was bored. The job was both trivial and dull. He took an immediate dislike to his predecessor, Sir Henry Wotton, an elegant and incompetent dilettante to whom he and Chamberlain habitually referred as *Fabritio;* it was galling to Carleton to think that he was regarded by the powers-that-be as on a par with such a man. Carleton rather admired the administration of the Republic, and he applauded its antipapal stance. The Catholic religion as practiced in Venice,

[13]

however, filled him with disgust on account of its superstition: for example, the "new miraculous maid" he described in February 1612. He kept looking for converts among the clergy, and he continued to be hopeful even after he had, on one occasion at least, been spectacularly gulled. He was hopeful of being involved in a significant or useful negotiation, but this did not happen until the end of his stay, when, ironically, the crisis which developed between Spain and Savoy delayed for a year his departure for the new post he so much wanted. Most of the time he was reporting tempests in teapots like the dispute between Savoy and Mantua, which had its comic-opera aspects and which he once described to Chamberlain in theatrical terms.

It was not possible for Carleton to find compensation elsewhere for the boredom and triviality of his job, which was not improved by the money problems that afflicted all of King James's ambassadors and by the necessity of writing his wearisome and empty reports not only to London but also to his fellow ambassadors in Paris, Brussels, and elsewhere.[10] Venice was, as always, very attractive for the private tourist, whatever his tastes; but an ambassador had to be discreet, and a Protestant ambassador in a Catholic state doubly so. So Carleton saw but little of the people of Venice apart from official business with members of the government and his dealings with purveyors of books, art objects and luxury goods, and an occasional artist or so. These people provided him with items he was commissioned to buy (books for his father-in-law, for instance), with gifts for his friends and for the great back in London, and, increasingly, with items which he was buying on speculation, in the hope of turning a profit by resale to collectors, an aspect of his life which is rarely mentioned in his correspondence with Chamberlain. Apart from these people, however, his contacts were chiefly with English travellers, other ambassadors, and the occasional foreign resident, such as Jacques Asselinau, the "French doctor" mentioned in the letters.

Given the depressing and confining circumstances of his job, the tone of Carleton's letters to his friend became less and less light-hearted as the Venetian years wore on. He complained of being starved for news; in commenting on Chamberlain's relative neglect of the company of Lancelot Andrewes (whom Carleton greatly admired), he put it this way: "If you had been penned up for so many years together, as now I have been, from changing almost a word with any man of merit unless it be with a public minister (whose conversation consists only of compliments) or a straggling traveller (who hath no more for you than he gathers upon the highway) you would know what it was to lose so good an opportunity." He wanted books and almanacs from England, and he was always grateful for Chamberlain's letters. When he could, he went to Padua, ostensibly for his health but in large part because he felt more relaxed there, in the atmosphere of a university town with a fair number of English medical students in residence. It was not an exciting town, but Carleton seems to have preferred it to the combination of tension and idleness which was his lot in Venice.

Ambassadors could normally expect to be recalled and reassigned after a stint of about four years, though this was no more automatic than was prompt payment of their salaries and expenses. So by the beginning of 1614 Carleton's thoughts and hopes were focussed on getting a better post. What he really wanted, he said, was a "competent estate" at home, so that he could see his friends instead of having to write to them. From remarks occasionally dropped in his letters it seems fairly clear that Lady Carleton would have preferred this too, a preference which grew stronger with the passing years. But such a hope was not likely to be realized then; a much more practical possibility was that he might succeed Winwood at The Hague, since Winwood had been advanced to Secretary of State—a promotion which delighted Carleton, and which, he hoped and expected, would open the door to better things in the future. "Yet by the way of provision," he wrote Chamberlain, "when you have any idle talk with him, I pray you remember Eton college"—Carleton was hoping to succeed his father-in-law as Provost. He was willing to stay in the business of diplomacy for a while longer, but up to this point he had found it frustrating in the extreme, and he poured out his frustrations in reply to a letter of advice written by Chamberlain at the end of 1614.

Winwood's promotion brought Carleton what he wanted: recall

[15]

from Venice and transfer to The Hague. Henry Wotton was to return to Venice to replace him, having lived down the gaffe of his famous epigram. Then, in October 1614, after he had taken leave of the doge and was actually on his way home, he was met by letters which ordered him back to cope with the problem of the war between Spain and Savoy. He was assured that this meant no change in the contemplated arrangements, but he was alarmed by the possibility that it might: Wotton, who had been sent on a special mission to the Low Countries, was saying that he could stay in that job if he preferred it and that Carleton would then have to remain in Venice. Winwood, as Mr. Secretary, was much more difficult to deal with; he gave free rein to a disposition which was naturally morose and quarrelsome and vented his anger on Carleton for what Carleton said was the mere following of instructions. Winwood's disposition was notorious, but it is likely that the fault was not all on one side; both Chamberlain and Sir Henry Savile warned Carleton that he was neglecting to cultivate Winwood and that such neglect could be costly. Chamberlain did his best, and with some success, to smooth things over. In spite of Winwood's touchiness and quickness to take offense, he and Chamberlain always remained on the best of terms, possibly because Chamberlain's friendship was entirely private, unaffected by business dealings. Carleton continued to admire and respect Winwood, but their friendship never again became close.

The unexpected order to remain in Italy was not without its advantages for Carleton. At last he had a real diplomatic problem to work on, and he handled it well. His mediation was helpful in bringing about a settlement between Spain and the duke of Savoy, whom he came to admire: the Treaty of Asti, which was negotiated in the summer of 1615. Carleton still wanted to get out of Italy as soon as possible, but the tone of his letters from Savoy, the increased liveliness of the political detail, and its greater fullness, suggest that he got a good deal more satisfaction from his final months in Italy than from the first four years of his service there, in spite of his grumbling about the difficulties of the job and of his belief that it was beneficial to England to have Spain embroiled in Italy. By October 1615, with the treaty out of the way, Carleton was at last on his way home after five years away. He spent five months there with his friends and his family before departing in March 1616 for a very different sort of post at The Hague.

V

If the government of the Serene Republic seemed comparatively unimportant in the diplomatic calculations of King James and his advisers, just the reverse was true of that of their High Mightinesses the Estates-General of the United Provinces. In 1616, when Carleton arrived at The Hague, the Dutch were in the seventh year of their twelve-year truce with Spain and so were in theory at peace with all the world, but in fact a condition of cold war existed which threatened to turn hot at any time and which therefore required constant military preparations. It was a cold war on two major fronts. In Europe the most important threat to the peace lay in the complicated business of the Cleves-Julich succession, a problem which went back to the death in 1609 of the last duke of Cleves without male heirs and which had already produced two confrontations that had almost led to war. The Dutch position was dictated by geography and was simple enough: whoever got the duchies (the preferred candidate of the Dutch and their allies in the Protestant Union was the elector of Brandenburg), the Habsburgs should not. The Dutch were occupying some of the territory of the duchies in the interest of the lawful claimant; other territory, including the strategic fortress of Wesel, was in the hands of the armies of the Archduke Albert, ruler of the southern Netherlands, and commanded by Ambrogio Spinola. This situation could explode at any time.

The other major theater of cold war was the Far East, where the Dutch East India Company, steadily backed by the government, was intent on taking over the position once held by the Portuguese. This aim brought it into conflict with the English East India Company, which had the same ambition. The two governments realized that this was potentially a very dangerous situation, and they did their best to conquer the peril by coming to some kind of agreement. There was a good deal of discussion from time to time of merger of the two companies, but negotiations to this end never got very far. So the companies fell back on the idea of sharing the area and acting jointly against their common enemies. But the agreements reached at a negotiating table in Europe—notably that of July 1619—simply did not accord with the facts of the situation in the Indies, where the Dutch were the stronger and where their men on the spot, especially Jan Coen, were determined to brook no interference. The "massacre," so-called, of Amboina, which poisoned Anglo-Dutch relations for a long time, merely set the seal on a supremacy which had in fact been won years before.

English policy towards the Republic was complicated and occasionally contradictory. For years the English had had a financial stake in Dutch survival: they wanted repayment of the loans made by the government of Elizabeth. After a great deal of haggling the debt was about to be liquidated, at the time of Carleton's arrival, by the payment of a lump sum far less than the total debt, and the so-called Cautionary Towns turned over to Elizabeth as an earnest of repayment were to be handed back to the Dutch by their English garrisons. This transaction, of whose benefit to England Carleton was doubtful, was negotiated before Carleton arrived on the scene; his only responsibility was to help carry it out and to help pacify those soldiers who felt disgruntled about it. The loss of the Cautionary Towns deprived King James's government of a possible lever to use against the Dutch, a state of affairs which was partially balanced by the fact that, as the Spanish-Dutch truce came closer to expiration, the Dutch need for English friendship grew.

King James found the Dutch exasperating allies. They were rebels and republicans, which did not commend them to him, and they were ruthless commercial rivals to boot. Their federal system of government gave rise to all sorts of delays, some of which were genuine, in the transaction of business. But the Dutch were both Protestant and anti-Habsburg, and, after the ruin and execution of Johan van Oldenbarnevelt and the increased influence of the House of Orange which resulted, relations improved. Oldenbarnevelt was felt to be pro-French and was known to be sympathetic to the Arminians, though his personal views on the vexed question of predestination may have been more orthodox than is usually supposed. The king did not care for Arminians; so the whole weight of the English government was thrown behind the orthodox Calvinist faction and Prince Maurice in the dispute which led to Oldenbarnevelt's fall. Carleton had much to say about this dispute in his letters to Chamberlain from the end of 1616 until the tragic denouement in 1619. Carleton, whose duty it was to carry out the king's instructions in this matter, did so with enthusiasm. He was not at all sympathetic to Oldenbarnevelt, and he actively disliked some of Oldenbarnevelt's allies, notably Hugo Grotius.

The final stages of the transfer of the Cautionary Towns and the religious dispute were the two major issues Carleton had to deal with before the coming of the Thirty Years' War. He was not deeply involved in the East India negotiations, which were conducted mostly in London, though he tried to be as helpful as he could and was genuinely distressed at the accusation that he was pro-Dutch. As at Venice, there was a great deal of business involving English ships and English merchants, mostly accusations of piracy. The large number of English soldiers in the Netherlands supplied Carleton with many anecdotes for his letters and with occasional business, notably in connection with duels. Unemployed soldiers frequently make business for the authorities; once the war began in earnest, in 1621, Carleton reported these incidents much less frequently.

At the beginning the Thirty Years' War was rather peripheral to Carleton's duties and interest. In the opening phases he was far more preoccupied with the religious dispute, and he even expressed some cautious optimism. By the autumn of 1619, however, he was worried; by the turn of the year he was quoting with trepidation the Jesuits' prediction that Frederick of the Palatinate would be king only for a winter. With the arrival of the fugitive elector and his wife, King James's daughter, in the United Provinces in April 1621 and the simultaneous resumption of the war between the Dutch and Spain, Carleton became an immensely busy man, since he had to attend to the needs of the exiled court as well as to his regular duties and engage in various ceremonial functions such as the christenings of Elizabeth of Bohemia's annual offspring.

Carleton's letters to Chamberlain began to reflect the increasing burden of his work; they became less frequent, though often quite long, and were far more given to relations of public events which were, in effect, paraphrases of his official dispatches. Many are in the hand of one of his secretarial staff (often that of his nephew Dudley, George Carleton's son, at those times when Dudley was in The Hague with his uncle), which almost never happened before 1621; after 1623 they became almost entirely "official" and lost the personal quality which made them so attractive before.

Carleton, like so many others, became very attached to Elizabeth of Bohemia and was a staunch advocate of her cause. During his years as an ambassador Carleton seldom allowed himself to write critically of English policy to Chamberlain—one could never be sure of a letter's reaching its destination; hence the fact that so many of both men's letters begin by acknowledging receipt of, say, "yours of the 24th of the last." Still, even before the war began Carleton fretted at the passivity of English policy, and with the disaster in Bohemia his impatience at the dithering policy of King James began visibly to mount. It was not his place to suggest in detail what ought to be done, but he became more and more disenchanted with what was done. For example, he deplored the behavior of Mansfeld and, by implication, the English decision to employ him, and he was positively caustic respecting the will o' the wisp of the Spanish marriage and especially Prince Charles's idiotic adventure in Spain.

Carleton's views were no secret, of course; he was known as the friend and protégé of Sir Ralph Winwood, whose uncompromising hostility to Spain remained steadfast until his death in 1617. He was, therefore, *persona non grata* to the last of King James's favorites, the duke of Buckingham, as long as that disastrous man was pro-Spanish, and he had to suffer the humiliation of seeing himself passed over twice for the provostship of Eton, a post for which he was still hopefully canvassing. The second disappointment was by far the worst, because his successful rival was none other than the detested Wotton, who, Chamberlain wrote, went to Eton "so ill provided that the fellows were fain to furnish his bare walls and whatever else was wanting." [11] Not until the last year of the reign did Carleton's fortunes begin to change. Then, with Buckingham's metamorphosis into an enemy of Spain, it became possible for Carleton to find favor in the duke's eyes; he began to pay court to the great man, and a timely gift of marble statuary for the duke's new house did the trick. In 1625 Carleton became vice-chamberlain of the household; he was on his way, thanks to the favorite, to the peerage and the secretaryship of state, the office which was the goal of his ambition.

Carleton much preferred The Hague to Venice as a diplomatic post, though he developed no great enthusiasm for individual Dutchmen, who are rarely mentioned in his letters, and though after little more than a year he was ready to be transferred to the more prestigious embassy in Paris, if it could be arranged. He found it hard that all the negotiations with the Dutch which might improve the English image took place in London, while he received nothing but "commissions ruineuses," and he found the growing English hostility to the Dutch alarming. He had other difficulties as well. His health still bothered him. His trip to Spa in the summer of 1616 did alleviate his suffering from the stone, but he eventually began to suffer "with that which great persons call a defluction, and common people the gout," and he concluded that "when all is said, I find my poor mortal fabric go daily into ruin." [12] He had money problems: it was harder and harder to get his pay and allowances out of the treasury, and this was all the more disappointing in that he had hoped and expected to prosper in his new post as Winwood had done. The situation with respect to the money owed him did not improve until the early 1620s, when the effect of Lionel Cranfield's economies and reforms began to be felt. There is more complaint, in the aggrieved tone of a man who felt that others unjustly prospered while his service went unrewarded, and more correspondence about financial matters than before, and he went in more extensively for dealing in art objects than he had in Venice. In both fields he made greater use of his wife, who on her frequent visits to England (Carleton went only once, in the summer of 1618) busied herself with treasury officials and her husband's London men of business and went to sales to buy pictures for people at home. Carleton also began to acquire real estate, mostly on leases, as a way of building up an estate for himself. His ambition had not changed since his days in Venice: he wanted security and a post in England.

His letters to Chamberlain reflect his relative contentment in his new position and his pleasure in the company of his fellow-countrymen in The Hague—good Protestants, men of business and soldiers, instead of the Catholics and travelling lordlings who were the customary fare in Venice. His descriptions in the letters of the first year or two are much fuller; Chamberlain had accompanied him to Venice and knew the places there, but had not seen towns like Spa and Antwerp. After Carleton's visit to England in the summer of 1618, when, presumably, he satisfied his friend's visual curiosity, the letters became no more descriptive than those written from Italy. For a time Carleton continued to be interested in Italian affairs; the gazettes continued to come to him, and he sent them on to Chamberlain, along with pamphlets and books and, sometimes, letters he received from his correspondents in Italy and elsewhere, but as the crisis in central Europe mounted, Italy, though frequently mentioned, got less and less space in the letters. There is considerably more mention of France than there had been in the letters from Venice, since the policy of the Dutch had to take careful account of that of France, whose government was afflicted by most of the problems which arise during royal minorities.

The coolness between Carleton and Winwood continued and was in fact increased by a foolish letter of advice which Carleton left behind him on his departure for The Hague. Chamberlain did his best to heal the breach, but he could do no more than keep it from widening. Winwood's death, nevertheless, was a genuine blow to Carleton—"what I wanted of his love," he wrote, "I reposed in his honesty and sincerity. . . . he had small errors and imperfections, but many great virtues." [13] Not the least unfortunate aspect of Winwood's death was that Carleton had no friend left in the higher reaches of the diplomatic service. Carleton made a half-hearted and unsuccessful attempt to push his own candidacy for Winwood's post; the secretaries who emerged were nonentities, creatures of Buckingham's. For the first time Carleton was on his own; he had enough credit and experience to hold his own but not to gain until he had made his arrangements with Buckingham.

As an ambassador Carleton was more than competent. He was calm, he followed instructions, and he made a good impression on the governments of both Venice and the United Provinces. Dealing with the Dutch was often time-consuming, tricky, and difficult, but Carleton was willing to be patient and persistent because he, like his predecessor and patron, firmly believed in the value of the Dutch alliance. He had little opportunity to be creative and take initiatives, but he was always more concerned to follow instructions than to seize a chance for a dazzling personal coup, and he made no major errors. As a public figure Carleton was a success by the standards of his time, though he is of only secondary importance to its history. As an observer, however, he was acute, informed, amusing and perceptive, and he wrote as well as he observed. His interest and value to specialist and nonspecialist alike resembles that of Samuel Pepys, as an observer from a position of vantage within the Establishment, though not within its inner ring. From that position he chronicled an age which was in many ways like our own, an age of cold war and ideological conflict and defectors and ineptitude in high places, of shifting moral codes and violence and miscarriages of justice. It seems likely that Carleton and Chamberlain and their circle of friends would not find the Age of Aquarius especially enjoyable, but neither would they find it unfamiliar. On that point, however, each reader must judge for himself.

* * *

In preparing these letters for publication I have in most cases modernized the spelling, capitalization, and punctuation employed by Carleton, and have expanded the contractions which are so frequent in all seventeenth-century correspondence. I have occasionally—but infrequently—broken up one of Carleton's very long sentences. Carleton almost never paragraphed his letters; no paragraphing has been supplied. I have made no attempt to identify in the footnotes every individual mentioned in the letters; only those whom I consider to be interesting and/or important are singled out for mention. The text of all letters is complete.

When in England Carleton dated his letters according to the English calendar; when abroad, he used either English or Continental dating (according to the Gregorian Calendar, which was ten days ahead of that of England), save that he almost always followed the English practice of beginning the year on March 25. When he was on the Continent he usually indicated which system he was using, by adding *st. vet.* or *sto. no.* for the English and Continental systems, respectively; sometimes he simply wrote both dates—for example, March 4/14. Carleton almost invariably put his date and the place of writing at the end of the letter. I have supplied them at the beginning of the letter instead (both dates if Carleton used the Continental date) and have added the reference to the volume of State Papers in the Public Record Office, London, containing the original document. Only two letters, those of November 27 and December 11, 1603, are taken from a source other than the Public Record Office.

I owe thanks to many people and institutions for the completion of this work: the libraries of Douglass College, Princeton University, and the University of Illinois, the Folger Shakespeare Library, and, most obviously, the Public Record Office, London, and their efficient staffs; the membership of the S.F.A.; the Rutgers University Research Council; the secretariat of the Douglass College History Department, especially Mrs. Shirley Meinkoth and Miss Toby Shatzoff. Acknowledgement is gratefully made to the Controller of H. M. Stationery Office for permission to use Crown copyright material.

1. *L. J. C.* The comment by Rowse is in the preface to an abridged edition of the letters compiled by Elizabeth McClure Thomson, the original editor's daughter, and published in 1965 under the title *The Chamberlain Letters.*
2. *Letters, Holland.*
3. To Chamberlain, March 16, 1600/1601. P. R. O., S. P. 84/61, ff. 63–64.
4. To Chamberlain, August 7, 1598, P. R. O., S. P. 12/268, #18.
5. P. R. O., S. P. 78/46, ff. 218–21.
6. To Chamberlain, November 17, 1600. *C. S. P. Domestic, Addenda 1580–1625* (London, 1872), p. 377 (where the letter is misdated 1596).
7. To Chamberlain, April 26/May 6, 1602, P. R. O., S. P. 78/46, ff. 84–85.

8. Thomas Birch, *The Court and Times of James the First* (London, 1849) I, 130.

9. Chamberlain to Carleton, October 2, 1602, *L. J. C.* I, 163.

10. On these points see M. Lee, Jr., "The Jacobean Diplomatic Service," *American Historical Review,* LXXII (1966–67), 1264–82.

11. *L. J. C.* II, 575.

12. To Chamberlain January 6, 1625, P. R. O., S. P. 84/122, f. 12.

13. Letter of December 2, 1617; see below, p. 250.

I

THE ASPIRING BUREAUCRAT

1603–1610

Sample of Carleton's Handwriting. *Courtesy of the Public Record Office, London* (8736)

Paris, April 9/19–14/24, 1603

S. P. 78/49, ff. 50-51

Good Mr. Chamberlain, whilst the world is in labor with this great accident of our state and every man doth toil and torment himself, as if therein he had particular interest, we may (if it please you) roll on our tub in our wonted manner and salute one another with our accustomed caresses. For greater matters, since we see by this late experience that God can show us greater blessings than we have almost hearts to hope for and that his mercies are then greatest when they are nearest to be utterly despaired of, we may discharge ourselves of all care, as we have little part in any charge and only add the breath of our vows and good wishes to their sails, which in this perilous time have steered so right a course and brought us to so safe a harbor. You shall understand that the statists here who, in the depth of their judgments, presaged our ruin and confusion, shrink up their shoulders and allow as much to the wisdom and counsels of our great ones as they were wont to detract, and now they see we have so well shaped this fit, they begin to feel their own pulse and to cry with one voice, *"La France est bien malade."* Here have been many suitors for the charge to congratulate our king's happy success, as the duke of Guise, Monsieur le Grand, the duke of Nevers, Monsieur Vitry; but Monsieur Rosny is the man who hath taken it upon him and prepares to go with marvelous great equipage.[1] A world of people doth press to accompany him but he answereth all that the king hath undertaken to appoint him his train, save only two (which have done heretofore many friendly offices betwixt him and his mistresses), to whom yesternight he gave a resolute answer, that the women of that country were

[29]

coming enough of themselves without any need of their help. Here hath been a long strangeness betwixt the king and his mistress, [the marquise of Verneuil], for a humor took her upon the birth of her last daughter to shut up shop windows and to afford him no more of her ware, and he on the other side beat the market abroad and said he found as good or better in other places. Whilst he was at Metz she wrote him a long passionate letter, wherein she ripped up the beginning and progress of their loves, charged him with all manner of disloyalties, and concluded with an intention she had to retire herself out of his realm and to spend the rest of her days in banishment in the Low Countries. The king could hold out no longer, but upon this wrote her a relenting letter and of all loves desired her but to stay his coming. This day he is come hither in post from Fontainebleau, where he hath left the queen and court and is lighted at her lodging, but they say she maintains still her former resolution, and it will be at least [a] 50,000-crown matter to set all even betwixt them. Prince Joinville, in this breach, was tampering with her, which hastened his dispatch to Malta, whither he went about 3 weeks since. The duke of Nevers, with a great train of the most apparent *noblesse,* is preparing himself to go into Hungary. The wars at Strasburg are compounded for one year with these conditions, that such places as were possessed by the cardinal of Lorraine are committed to the guard of the Count Palatine and the duke of Bavaria as neuters till they see what this year will bring forth. Meantime the rents are equally divided betwixt the cardinal and the marquis of Brandenburg, and all things else remain in their wonted state.[2] There is some treaty at Geneva and commissioners are met on both parts at Saint-Julien to see how matters may be compounded with the duke [of Savoy]. Meantime there are blows dealt freely on both sides and the Genevois have taken in a pretty town, St. Genidotte [St. Genix d'Aoste] confining upon Dauphiné, which they make good, and the duke of Savoy's forces are drawing that way to recover.[3] The duke himself is gone to Nice to embark his sons for Spain. The duke of Bouillon is at this present with his brother-in-law at Anhalt by Frankfort, but is thought ere long will come down to Sedan. The Elector Palatine hath written to the king very effectually in his behalf, with great approbation of his government, of himself, and his courses since he came into Germany, withal declares what satisfaction he receives by the duke's relation of his procedure in these troubles and by his justification of the whole course of his life in as much as concerns the king's service. The king hath answered, if he be so innocent he should not fly from trial, for so doing, he doth condemn him of injustice. He willeth him though he be culpable yet not to despair of his mercy, for his own and his friends' sakes shall move him to much favor. He concludes that he gives him two months' time to bethink himself and to come to court, whereof if he fail he hopes his friends will think him unworthy of his favor and their further mediation. It stands now on the point what the duke will do, but we look for nothing less than his coming to court.[4] It were now too late to discourse unto you all particularities what I saw at Metz.[5] The entry was performed with much solemnity. The court was great in number but not in quality, for the principal personages were absent, as the count Soissons, the prince of Condé, Monsieur le Grand, the constable [Henri de Montmorency], the duke of Guise; but it was well helped out with strangers, especially the Lorrainois, as we had there the duke himself with the duke of Bar and the king's sister, the count of Vaudemont, his wife, and in a manner the whole *noblesse* of Lorraine, both male and female. The duke of Deux-Ponts was the only man of the German princes whom we saw there, and he came accompanied with 6 or 7 Dutch heers, his wife, and six or seven lusty Dutch wenches; but we had ambassadors from the two bishops of Cologne and Treves, from the landgrave of Hesse, from Count Philip, the governor of Luxemburg, from the administrator and town of Strasburg. The ambassador of Cologne (Louervallon, whose father lost his head with Egmont and Hoorn) bore away the bell from the rest in state and magnificency. He brought the queen an ebony cabinet from his master for a present which was valued at 500 crowns. The conceit on the top of it was a cupid archer-wise and his bow bent and drawn: by a device within, it had motion, which struck the ladies that were lookers on in great fear; but the king, to

[31]

encourage them willed them not to startle: *Il vient de la part d'un maître qui ne veut pas de mal aux dames,* to whom the ambassador could not deny his master to be as faithful a servant as the king himself. Two of the little ladies that were lookers on were in great dispute where this cabinet was made, and one of them affirmed it was d'Allemagne, the other said she heard with her own ears the ambassador say it was d'Ébène. The prettiest of the queen's Italian wenches did there get her a good husband, a rich financier's son who dwells by Caen in Normandy. The duke of Deux-Ponts' eldest son, who was at Metz with his father, is fianced to Monsieur de Rohan's younger sister. Sobole, the governor of the citadel at Metz, was cast out and disgraced before all the world for his tyrannies and extortions upon the people, and in his place was established Monsieur de Requien. The king hath given the government of the town to Monsieur Montigny, de Requien's brother, but they are both subaltern to Monsieur d'Espernon. Tuesday in Easter Week the king went from Metz towards Nancy; the same day I returned the ordinary post way and arrived here the next. I found your two letters of the 11th and last of February, for which I heartily thank you, and for your books, which were great novelties. At my departure from hence I sent you a letter by Mr. Day, our chaplain, enclosed in a packet to Mr. Gent.[6] Your next letters will be welcome hither, for I assure you save by the bruits of the town we understand of none of your doings in England, and, for aught we know, all is as it was wont without any alteration. For my particular, since the council of physicians prescribes me patience, I must be [paper torn] though it be an unproper remedy for a desperate disease. They fail in their judgments that think time can alter that which is grown into nature, but I will confess to you that time and use hath accustomed me to that which was intolerable in the beginning and hath taught me to pass it over with little molestation; and so I remain till God and good friends provide better for us, and for this present commit you to his holy protection. From Paris this 19th of April 1603 *sto. no.*

Yours most assured

I was long ere I wrote, and this letter hath stayed thus long for a messenger. I have in the interval received yours of the 30th of March, which came like a plentiful harvest after a long dearth. I owe you much in requital, but for this time will pay you with another man's purse and refer you to a letter I wrote yesterday to Mr. Winwood, as I will desire you to acquaint him with this if here be any thing which is wanting in his. I was beholden to my posting journey for headache, toothache, and as many aches as there are other letters in the Christ cross row [the alphabet]. They grew all together to the mumps and this last night to an impostume, which is broken this morning, and I am eased of a great torment. I meant to have made no brags of these indispositions till now that I hope the worst is past. I pray commend me to all my friends, to my brother in particular, and tell him I wrote to him about a week since and directed my letters to his old lodging enclosed in a cover to Otwell Smith the merchant. My cousin Cope shall hear from me as soon as I am well on foot again. I have not stirred out of the house these many days. *Iterum atque iterum vale.*

This 24th of April 1603
sto. no.

1. Rosny is better known by his subsequent title of duke of Sully. In addition to the formal congratulations to the new king, he was instructed to dissuade James from making peace with Spain, if he could, and to discuss the problem of aid to the Dutch rebels.

2. The "wars at Strasburg" had to do with possession of the bishopric; the claimants were the cardinal of Lorraine and the young son of the margrave of Brandenburg. The Catholics obtained possession in 1603, perhaps because the house of Brandenburg accepted a bribe. A Legrelle, *Louis XIV et Strasbourg,* (Paris, 1881), pp. 37–40.

3. Charles Emmanuel I of Savoy had made one of his numerous attempts to recover Geneva, by a surprise attack which failed—the famous "escalade" of December 11–13, 1602. Henri IV, who was in the process of turning Geneva into a French satellite, wanted no war at this stage and helped to bring about a peace between Savoy and Geneva, signed at St. Julien in July 1603.

4. Henri de La Tour d'Auvergne, duke of Bouillon, was one of the principal leaders of the Huguenot faction. He was suspected of complicity in the

conspiracy of Marshal Biron, who had been executed in 1602. He fled the country and at this point was trying to make terms with Henri IV. He succeeded eventually, at the cost of having to surrender his town of Sedan to the king. Henri ultimately restored it to him.

5. In addition to those mentioned by Carleton, one of Henri IV's purposes at Metz was to talk with representatives of the Jesuits. The order had been instrumental in persuading French Catholics to accept the Edict of Nantes. Henri was grateful for their attitude; his discussions in Metz were a preliminary to the re-establishment of the order in France, which was accomplished by an edict issued on September 1, 1603. H. Hauser, *La Prépondérance Espagnole (1555–1660)* (Paris, 1933), pp. 163–64.

6. William Gent, of Oxford, was a close friend of both Carleton's and Chamberlain's. Like Chamberlain he was a bachelor, had the same group of friends, and went on the same country-house circuit.

Windsor, July 4, 1603

S. P. 14/2, #33

Sir, I doubt not but court news keep their custom to be more rife in Paul's [1] than in the chamber of presence and therefore to give you occasion to write what you say there, you shall know from time to time particularly what we do here. The queen [Anne of Denmark] kept her day to be here on Thursday last; the young princess [Elizabeth] came before, accompanied with her governess the lady Kildare in litter with her and attended on with 30 horse; she had her trumpets and other formalities as well as the best. The queen had with her a court of ladies and many very fair and goodly ones which were never before seen *in rerum natura*. She had only two Scotchwomen of quality and both of them passable for their faces and fashions; and they say when she came out of Scotland and was pressed with many more she answered them that when she came out of Denmark they would not suffer her to bring above two women with her; and therefore because she could bring no more to them she would carry no more from them. She hath of herself a comely personage and an extraordinary good grace in her fashion, but for her favor she hath done it some wrong, for in all this journey she hath worn no mask. She hath been private since her coming hither till yesterday, when she rode abroad to the park, of which Sir Charles Howard hath the keeping and there dined. In the afternoon she killed a buck out of a standing, at which the king was so angry and discontented that she returned home without his company, not very well pleased. Our great ladies and the maids of honor are in a manner all sworn of the privy chamber, but the ladies of Bedford, Rich, and Essex especially in favor. There is great suit amongst our men for place and office about her, but as yet none admitted; yesterday the commissioners for that purpose sat long about settling her family, but we hear not what was resolved on. You have heard I am sure how my lords of Southampton and Grey played their prizes before her the first night she came hither; dared, and belied one another; were presently committed; heard the next day before the Council; condemned to be sent to the Tower; pardoned by the king; and made friends all with a breath.[2] The lord Murray and Mr. Somerset being at York with the queen went further than words and exchanged a blow upon a quarrel who should be most in favor with the queen's horse; on the way the earls of Sussex and Argyll were at hard words but came not to falling out.[3] We were much troubled here at first with certain wrangling Scots who, wheresoever they came, would have meat, drink, and lodging by strong hand; and one swaggerer amongst the rest, being beaten by certain footmen for a quarrel at dice, vowed to kill the first Englishman he met with and was so good as his word; for, meeting an old country fellow on the way, struck him such a blow with his short sword in the neck that he had like to have cut off his head. The man is since dead of his hurt and the Scot taken, whom, they say, we shall see hang before the court gate; many insolences are committed by them; and this remnant proves ten times worse than the first piece. Our Saint George's feast was performed with much solemnity. The Saturday, the prince, the duke, the earls of Southampton, Mar and Pembroke, were invested in their robes,[4] of which the king was only spectator. The next day the king was actor himself, sat out the whole service, went the procession, and dined in public with his fellow knights, at which sight every man was well pleased save some Scottish kirkmen, who said it sented too mikle of the Pape. The French ambassador [5] came to the dinner with great formality, to excuse his master's absence from that feast, to whom the king drank a health, the like to the knights, which was followed by the young prince. The Monday our late queen's ornaments were offered to the altar; the lord admiral and treasurer [6] bore the banner; the lords Cumberland and Shrewsbury the sword; the lords Northumberland and Worcester the helm. The king was not there present, nor the young prince. The queen did not give any grace to those solemnities by her presence, which we say was because the earl of Mar was one of the band, who hath small part in her good grace.[7] We hear out of France the king hath erected a new order of knighthood,[8] with which he hath yet only honored the lord Wemyss [James Colville, laird of Easter Wemyss] a Scotchman; the order is a white hatband with a *médaille* in which is graven an armed knight. Two English gentlemen that went from hence with my lord Wemyss are made knights by the French king but of the common sort. Créquy and Chambré were lately in the field to have made an end of their old quarrel but were interrupted by the marshal Boisdauphin, who hath made them friends. The French queen is gone in pilgrimage to *notre dame de vertu,* and as soon as the king hath done his diet they say he intends the like journey to *notre dame de liesse.*[9] Our king and queen have a purpose to make a petty progress to Oatlands, Hampton Court, and Nonesuch, but the household shall not stir. We have here at Eton an ambassador from Brunswick, who is defrayed and drinks the king out of debt; Sir Henry Neville is sent to meet the ambassador of Lorraine; the lord Wotton [10] is appointed to receive the Spaniard whom we long to see but doubt yet of his coming. The count of Aremberg lies in of his gout at Stanes; [11] his son with his troops have been present at all our solemnities. Sir Henry Wallop was here yesterday and is already vanished.[12] Sir Edward Norris comes hither this night. My brother is gone home, and after him I mean to go at the end of the week. I am set to school how to deal in the matter betwixt him and my sister Alice: for give it over I will not till I see what may be done to set them at peace, and in my manner of proceeding she suspects me; and he, since we met here, is half fallen out with me.[13] I pray you remember me to Mr. Winwood and let him know, if I knew anything more worth his knowledge than you may show him in this letter, I would not fail to write; and thus I commit you to God's protection,

Yours most assured

1. Chamberlain was known as a "Paul's walker": one of those who frequented the vicinity of St. Paul's Cathedral, which was a center of news and gossip for all Londoners.

2. Thomas, Baron Grey of Wilton, was one of the commission which condemned the earls of Essex and Southampton to death. The release of Southampton, whom he hated, embittered him and helped to lead him into the so-called Bye Plot. For this he was condemned to death, reprieved, and committed to the Tower, where he died in 1614. See the following two letters.

3. The quarrels between English and Scots which were to mark James's reign did not take long to start.

4. Of the Garter, of which Saint George is the patron. The "prince" was Prince Henry, James's eldest son; the "duke" was Ludovick Stuart, second duke of Lennox, James's cousin and close friend, the only duke in Great Britain.

5. Christophe de Harlay, count of Beaumont. Henri IV was a knight of the Garter.

6. The lord admiral was Charles Howard, earl of Nottingham, the victor of 1588. The lord treasurer was Thomas Sackville, Lord Buckhurst, who in 1604 became earl of Dorset.

7. Mar and Queen Anne had been at odds for some years, chiefly over the custody of Prince Henry; the custody of the heir to the Scottish throne was a traditional privilege of the head of the house of Erskine. The quarrel had recently broken out again, after James's departure for England. Anne suddenly decided she wanted to take Prince Henry south with her; Mar's deputies at Stirling—the earl himself was in England with James—would not surrender the boy without the king's approval. Anne was furious. James patched things up as best he could, and eventually gave the desired permission. See G. P. V. Akrigg, *Jacobean Pageant* (Cambridge, Mass., 1962), pp. 22–23.

8. This was a false report; Henri IV founded no knightly order.

9. Henri's usual secular shrine: *liesse* = gaiety.

10. Edward, Lord Wotton, was the older brother of Henry, who played so large a role in Carleton's career.

11. Aremberg was Archduke Albert's agent; his mission marked the beginning of the negotiations which led to the Anglo-Spanish peace treaty of 1604.

12. For Sir Henry Wallop see below, letter of August 20, 1606, n. 2.

13. Carleton was very fond of his unmarried sister Alice, as was Chamberlain, but she was occasionally a trial to him—she flirted with Catholicism, and she had a fierce temper. From the language Chamberlain used about her in his will and his substantial bequest to her, it has been surmised that at one time he intended to marry her. Neither ever married.

Winchester, November 27, 1603 [1]

Sir, I was taking care how to send unto you and little looked for so good a means as your man, who came to me this morning; and though he would in all haste be gone, I have stayed him this night to have time to discourse unto you these tragical proceedings.[2] I was not present at the first or second arraignment, wherein Brooke, Markham, Brookesby, Copley, and the two priests were condemned for practicing the surprise of the king's person, the taking of the Tower, the deposing of councillors, and proclaiming liberty of religion. They were all condemned upon their own confessions, which were set down under their own hands as declarations and compiled with such labor and care, to make the matter they undertook seem very feasible, as if they had feared they should not say enough to hang themselves. Parham was acquitted, being only drawn in by the priests as an assistant, without knowing the purpose; yet had he gone the same way as the rest (as it is thought) save for a word the Lord Cecil cast in the way, as his cause was in handling that the king's glory consisted as much in freeing the innocent as condemning the guilty. The commissioners for the trial were the lord chamberlain, lord of Devon, Lord Henry Howard, Lord Cecil, Lord Wotton, the vice-chamberlain, the two chief justices, Justice Gawdy, and Warburton.[3] Of the king's counsel, none were employed in that or the arraignment but the attorney [Sir Edward Coke], Hele, and Phelips;[4] and in effect none but the attorney. Sir Walter Raleigh served for a whole act and played all the parts himself. His cause was disjoined from the priests as being a practice only between himself and the lord Cobham to have brought in the Spaniard, to have raised rebellion in the realm by fastening money upon discontents, to have set up the lady Arabella, and to have tied her to certain conditions: as to have a perpetual peace with Spain, not to have bestowed herself in marriage but at the direction of the Spaniard, and to have granted liberty of religion. The evidence against him was only Cobham's confession, which was judged sufficient to condemn him; and a letter was produced, written by Cobham the day before, by which he accused Raleigh as the first practicer of the treason betwixt them, which served to turn against him, though he shewed, to countervail this, a letter written by Cobham and delivered to him in the Tower, by which he was clearly acquitted. After sentence given, his request was to have his answers related to the king and pardon begged, of which, if there were no hope, then that Cobham might die first. He answered with that temper, wit, learning, courage, and judgment that, save that it went with the hazard of his life, it was the happiest day that ever he spent. And so well he shifted all advantages that were taken against him that were not *fama malum gravius quam res* and an ill name half hanged, in the opinion of all men he had been acquitted. The two first that brought the news to the king were Roger Ashton [5] and a Scotchman, whereof one affirmed that never any man spake so well in times past nor would do in the world to come; and the other said, that whereas, when he saw him first, he was so led with the common hatred that he would have gone a hundred miles to have seen him hanged, he would, ere he parted, have gone a thousand to have saved his life. In one word, never was a man so hated and so popular in so short a time. It was thought the lords should have been arraigned on Tuesday last, but they were put off till Friday and Saturday and had their trials apart before the lord chancellor [Thomas Egerton, Lord Ellesmere] (as lord steward for both those days), eleven earls, nineteen barons. The duke [of Lennox] the earl of Mar, and many Scottish lords stood as spectators, and, of our ladies the greatest part, as the lady Nottingham, the lady of Suffolk, and the lady Arabella, who heard herself much spoken of these days. But, the arraignment before, she was more particularly remembered as by Sir Walter Raleigh for a woman with whom he had no acquaintance and one whom of all that he ever saw he never liked, and by Sergeant Hele as one that had no more right to the crown than himself; and for any claim that he had to it, he utterly disavowed it. Cobham led the way on Friday and made such a fasting day's piece of work of it that he discredited the place to which he was called; never was seen so poor and abject a spirit. He heard his indictment with much fear and trembling and would sometimes interrupt it by forswearing what he thought to be wrongly inserted; so as, by his fashion, it was known ere he spake what he would confess or deny. In his first answer, he said he had changed his mind since he came to the bar; for, whereas he came with an intention to have made his confession, without denying anything, now seeing many things inserted in this indictment with which he could not be charged, being not able in one word to make distinction of many parts, he must plead to all *not guilty*. For anything that belonged to the lady Arabella, he denied the whole accusation, only said she had sought his friendship, and his brother, Brooke, had sought hers. For the other purposes, he said, he had hammered in his brains some such imaginations; but never had purpose to bring them to effect. Upon Raleigh he exclaimed as one who had stirred him up to discontent and thereby overthrown his fortunes. Against him he said that he once propounded to him a means for the Spaniard to invade England, which was to bring down an army to the Groyne [Corunna] under pretense to send them into the Low Countries and land them at Milford Haven; that he had made himself a pensioner to Spain for 1500 crowns by the year to give intelligence, and, for an earnest of his diligence, had already related to the count of Aremberg the particularities of what passed in the States' audiences at Greenwich.[6] His brother's confession was read against him, wherein he accused him of a contract made with Aremberg for 500,000 crowns to bestow amongst discontents, whereof Raleigh was to have had 10,000, Grey as much, and Brooke 1000; the rest, as they should find fit men to bestow it on. He excepted against his brother as an incompetent accuser, baptizing him with the name of a viper, and laid to his charge (though far from the purpose) the getting of his wife's sister with child, in which it is thought he did young Coppinger some wrong.[7] A letter was produced which he wrote to Aremberg for so much money, and Aremberg's answer consenting for the furnishing of that sum. He then flew to his former retreat, that in this likewise he had no ill meaning, and excused Aremberg as one that meant only thereby to further the peace. When particularities were farther urged that in his intended travel he meant to have gone into the Low Countries to the archduke [Albert]; from thence into Savoy, so into Spain, then have returned by Jersey, and there to have met Raleigh; and to have brought some money from the well-spring, where it was to be had, he confessed imaginations, but no purposes, and still laid the fault upon his own weaknesses, in that he suffered himself to be misled by Raleigh. Being asked of his two letters to different purpose, the one excusing, the other condemning Raleigh, he said, the last was true, but the other was drawn from him by device in the Tower by young Harvey, the lieutenant's son,[8] whom Raleigh had corrupted and carried intelligence betwixt them (for which he is there committed and is likely to be arraigned at the King's Bench). Having thus accused all his friends and so little excused himself, the peers were not long in deliberation what to judge; and, after sentence of condemnation given, he begged a great while for life and favor, alleging his confession as a meritorious act. Grey, quite in another key, began with great assurances and alacrity; spake a long and eloquent speech, first to the lords, and then to the judges, and lastly to the king's council, and told them well of their charges, and spake effectually for himself. He held them the whole day, from eight in the morning till eight at night, in subtle traverses and scapes; but the evidence was too perspicuous, both by Brooke's and Markham's confessions, that he was acquainted with the surprise; yet the lords were long ere they could all agree and loath to come out with so hard censure against him. For, though he had some heavy enemies, as his old antagonist,[9] who was mute before his face but spake within very unnobly against him, yet most of them strove with themselves and would fain (as it seemed) have dispensed with their consciences to have shewed him favor. At the pronouncing of the opinion of the lords and the demand whether he had anything to say why sentence of death should not be given against him, these only were his words—"I have nothing to say"—there he paused long—"and yet a word of Tacitus comes in my mind. *Non eadem omnibus decora*—the house of the Wiltons had spent many lives in their prince's service, and Grey cannot beg his. God send the king a long and prosperous reign and to your lordships all honor." After sentence given, he only desired to have one Travers, a divine, sent for to come to him, if he might live two days. If he were to die before that, then he might have one Field, whom he thought to be near.[10] There was great compassion had of this gallant young lord, for so clear and fiery a spirit had not been seen by any that had been present at like trials. Yet the lord steward condemned his manner, terming it Lucifer's pride, and preached much humiliation, and the judges liked him as little, because he disputed with them against their laws. We cannot yet judge what will become of him or the rest, for all are not like to go one way. Cobham is of the surest side, for he is thought least dangerous, and the lord Cecil undertakes to be his friend. They say the priest shall lead the dance tomorrow, and Brooke next after, for he proves to be the knot that tied together the three conspiracies; the rest hang indifferent betwixt mercy and justice, wherein the king hath now subject to practice himself. The lords are most of them returned to the court. The lord chancellor and treasurer remain here till Tuesday to shut up the term. My lord[11] goeth from hence to Petworth, but I pick quarrel to stay behind to see an end of these matters. The court is like to Christmas at Windsor, and many plays and shows are bespoken to give entertainment to our ambassadors. The French king doth winter at Fontainebleau and is fallen into a new delight of the Italian comedians, of which I send you a conceit put upon M. Rosny. The queen is there made *chef du conseil* and grows very expert in dispatch of affairs. The marquis[e] is quite retired from court. Rosny and Soissons go up and down like two buckets, for they are not so reconciled but as one comes to the court the other is ever going away. They say we shall have here from thence ere long M. Zamet; I know not to what other purpose, unless it be to teach us to make good sauce and to show their variety of excellent men in all crafts.[12] The marquis of Luttin, ambassador of the duke of Savoy, is at Brussels and so far on his way hitherwards. The grand Chiaus is arrived at the French court and will likewise come hither to congratulate with our king from the Turk. The Venetian ambassadors [13] had audience at court on Sunday last. They were brought from Southampton to Salisbury by Mr. Allen Percy with two of the king's coaches and four pad horses and were welcomed with the foulest day that came this year and at night (as they came late) found but seven beds prepared for sevenscore. The day they were had to their audience there was an embargo of coaches before the court gate to bring them hither; but as soon as they arrived, every man departed with his own coaches for fear of the like arrest, so as the greatest part of them were forced to go home on foot and some of the best sort to stay till midnight for the return of their coaches. The knavish Frenchmen laugh at their disorders and say they are served like right pantaloons; but they deserve to be better styled, for they are come in best show and fashion of any I saw yet and do all things with as great magnificence. As to their captain that wafted them over, they gave forty crowns besides petty presents, whereas the Spanish ambassador gave Sir Robert Mansfield a leather jerkin and the count of Aremberg, a Parmesan cheese. A fortnight since there was a petty ambassador at court from the state of Stade, who came when no man looked for him and took the king as he found him, presently after sermon, and in the open presence set upon him with a long Latin oration. The king made him no long answer, but gave the honor of entertaining him to Secretary Herbert.[14] The agent of Geneva hath obtained a collection to be made in all the churches of England and Scotland for the space of three months; his masters in the meantime have fairly escaped another surprise on a Sunday as they were at service. The siege of Bolduc ['s Hertogenbosch] is raised, and the two generals retire to Brussels and The Hague. I send you a letter I received from Mr. Winwood of this summer's service in those parts, wherein I think you will marvel as well as I that the States are grown so curst-hearted to give away Grave because they cannot take Bolduc. The Spanish ambassador [Don Juan de Taxis, count of Villa Mediana] hath been with the king to expostulate some words he heard to be spoken at these arraignments in prejudice of his master, and to please him the attorney took occasion to make an open apology. The last week he feasted the French ambassador's wife, with many of our ladies, and he had music and dancing, at which the French ambassador and he were at half falling out who should lead the dance. They all returned very ill-satisfied for cheer or entertainment. The French ambassador at his last audience brought his companion d'Auval to take his leave, who is gone for good and all. The king knighted him and gave him a jewel of 150 crowns. Our ambassador in France [15] (they say) is busy in making a new French grammar and dictionary. One Walton, a man of his that has remained with him ever since his going over, is turned monk and hath put himself into a cloister at Compiègne. Fitzherbert, whom he took in my place, is come over to seek a new fortune. Out of Ireland here are come many captains and cashiered officers with their pockets full of brass and sue to have it made good silver, but the lord treasurer's skill is not that of alchemy. The coffers are so empty that household officers are unpaid and the pensioners and guard are ready to mutiny. There was a fortnight since, near Salisbury, a desperate combat betwixt Douglas, the master of the king's horse, and Lee, brother to the avener, who began their quarrel at Windsor. Douglas was left dead in the field with three hurts and was buried three days after in Salisbury Church with a kind of solemnity at which the duke, the Scottish lords and all other, scot and lot, were present. Lee was hurt in four places but lives and is like to escape. He is not much followed by the Scots, because they hold there was fair play between them. The younger Douglas has his brother's place, which doth somewhat help to appease the quarrel. Sir Thomas Jermyn hath got the reversion of Jersey, after Sir John Painton. Sir Philip Herbert and Sir James Hay have got betwixt them a grant of transport of cloths, worth £10,000 at the least. I do call to mind a pretty secret that the lady of Pembroke hath written to her son Philip and charged him of all her blessings to employ his own credit and his friends and all he can do for Raleigh's pardon; and though she does little good, yet she is to be commended for doing her best in showing *veteris vestigia flammae.*[16] And thus being come round where I began, it is time to leave you, desiring you to excuse me to my cousin Sir Roland Lytton for not writing; and so you well may, for you have enough for yourself and all my kindred and friends to make you all weary. My brother Carleton and brother [-in-law] Williams are both here and have left all well from whence they came, save only the little gentlewoman in Northamptonshire, who is so woebegone for lack of good company that she thinks the plague in London would not have hurt her so much as melancholy in the country. I supped this night with Sir Henry Fanshawe,[17] where you were kindly remembered. Sir Walter Cope is in this town, and Sir Hugh Beeston likewise, who often asks for you as your friend, and therefore you are the more to lament that he is untimely come to a nightcap.[18] Many marvel at his sudden breaking, but most ascribe it to a thought he took at a word which Sir Walter Raleigh spoke at his examination, who asked if Sir Hugh Beeston was not apprehended and tortured because he was always of his chiefest counsel. I shall never end, unless I abruptly bid you farewell.

Yours, etc.

1. The texts of this letter and the next are taken from Philip Yorke, second earl of Hardwicke, ed., *Miscellaneous State Papers from 1501 to 1726,* I (London, 1778), 378–93.

2. The "tragical proceedings" were the trials of the conspirators in the plots of 1603, one of which involved the seizure of the king, the other an intrigue with Aremberg, the archduke's agent, to set James's cousin Arabella Stuart on the throne. The principal figures in the first plot, the so-called Bye Plot, were the priests William Watson and William Clarke, Sir Griffin Markham, Anthony Copley, Bartholomew Brooksby, Thomas, Lord Grey of Wilton, and George Brooke. The latter's brother, Henry, Lord Cobham, and Sir Walter Raleigh, were the chief figures in the other conspiracy, the Main Plot. Sir Edward Parham was the acquitted man.

3. The lord chamberlain was Thomas Howard, earl of Suffolk; the vice

chamberlain, Sir John Stanhope; the chief justices, Sir John Popham of King's Bench and Sir Edmund Anderson of Common Pleas. Of the lay commissioners one of Raleigh's recent biographers remarks, "James could scarcely have assembled a less friendly collection." Willard M. Wallace, *Sir Walter Raleigh* (Princeton, 1959), p. 203.

4. Sir John Hele and Sir Edward Phelips were prominent lawyers; Phelips became Speaker of the Commons in 1604.

5. Roger Aston was an Englishman who had made his way successfully at the Scottish court and who benefitted from his master's largesse with his new wealth—among other things, he received the keeping of a park which on Cobham's conviction escheated to the crown (*C. S. P. Domestic 1603–1610,* p. 57). He eventually became master of the wardrobe.

6. A delegation from the United Provinces headed by Johan van Olden-barnevelt, the most important Dutch politician, had been trying to persuade King James to continue English aid to them and not to make peace with Spain.

7. Brooke was married to Elizabeth, daughter of Thomas, Lord Burgh. Her sister Frances was married to Francis Coppinger.

8. Sir George Harvey became lieutenant of the Tower on July 30.

9. The earl of Southampton. See the previous letter, n. 3.

10. Walter Travers was a well-known Puritan, an antagonist of Hooker's. Richard Field was more orthodox, an immensely learned theologian who became a great favorite with the king, who liked to discuss obscure points of divinity with him.

11. Henry Percy, ninth earl of Northumberland. Carleton had now been comptroller of the household for Northumberland for two months.

12. Sebastian Zamet, a naturalized Italian, was a close personal friend of Henri IV's; Henri frequently had supper parties with his mistresses at Zamet's house.

13. The Venetian ambassadors were Piero Duodo and Nicolo Molin; the latter stayed on as resident until 1606. Their escort was a brother of the earl of Northumberland.

14. John Herbert, who was appointed secretary in 1600. He was an unimportant man with no particular ability or political weight.

15. Sir Thomas Parry, whose service Carleton had left.

16. Lady Pembroke, the widow of Henry Herbert, earl of Pembroke, was the sister and literary executor of Sir Philip Sidney. The remark *veteris vestigia flammae* is obscure. John Aubrey says she was lascivious, but the evidence he gives is hardly reliable. See Dick, *Lives,* pp. 138–39. For her son Philip see below, letter of January 7, 1605, n. 3.

17. Sir Henry Fanshawe, remembrancer of the exchequer, was a close friend of Chamberlain's, who was a frequent visitor at Fanshawe's house at Ware Park.

18. Sir Hugh Beeston was a close friend of Cope's as well as of Chamberlain's. He figures in one of the more famous of Chamberlain's anecdotes, of Raleigh's execution. "As he went from Westminster Hall to the Gatehouse, he espied Sir Hugh Beeston in the thronge and calling to him prayed he wold see him dye to morow: Sir Hugh to make sure worke got a letter from Secretarie Lake to the sheriffe to see him placed connveniently, and meeting them as they came nere to the scaffold delivered his letter but the sheriffe by mishap had left his spectacles at home and put the letter in his pocket. In the mean time Sir Hugh beeing thrust by, Sir Walter bad him farewell and saide I know not what shift you will make, but I am sure to have a place." *L. J. C. II,* 177.

Salisbury, December 11, 1603

Sir, I know not when or how to send to you; yet here happening an accident worth your knowledge, I cannot but put it in record whilst the memory of it is fresh, and, for the rest, stand to the venture. But because I have taken a time of good leisure, and it is likely this letter will take his leisure ere it come to you, I may as well leap in where I left when I wrote you by your man and proceed in an order by narration, since this was a part of the same play and that other acts came betwixt to make up a tragical comedy. The two priests that led the way to the execution were very bloodily handled, for they were both cut down alive; and Clarke, to whom more favor was intended, had the worse luck, for he both strove to help himself and spake after he was cut down. They died boldly, both; and Watson (as he would have it seem) willing, wishing he had more lives to spend and one to lose, for every man he had by his treachery drawn into this treason. Clarke stood somewhat upon his justification and thought he had hard measure but imputed it to his function and therefore he thought his death meritorious, as a kind of martyrdom. Their quarters were set on Winchester gates and their heads on the first tower of the castle. Brooke was beheaded in the castle yard on Monday last and, to double his grief, had Saint Cross[1] in his

[47]

sight from the scaffold, which drove him first to discontent. There was no greater assembly than I have seen at ordinary executions nor no man of quality more than the lord of Arundel and young Somerset; only the bishop of Chichester, who was sent from the court two days before to prepare him to his end, could not get loose from him, but by Brooke's earnest entreaty was fain to accompany him to the scaffold and serve for his ghostly father. He died constantly (and to seeming religiously), spake not much, but what he said was well and assured. He did somewhat extenuate his offenses, both in the treasons and the course of his life, naming these rather errors than capital crimes and his former faults sins, but not so heinous as they were traduced, which he referred to the God of Truth and time to discover, and so left it, as if somewhat lay yet hid which would one day appear for his justification. The bishop went from him to the lord Cobham, and at the same time the bishop of Winchester was with Raleigh, both by express order from the king, as well to prepare them for their ends as likewise to bring them to liberal confessions and by that means reconcile the contradictions of the one's open accusation and the other's peremptory denial. The bishop of Chichester had soon done what he came for, finding in Cobham a willingness to die and readiness to die well, with purpose at his death to affirm as much as he had said against Raleigh; but the other bishop had more to do with his charge, for though for his conscience he found him well-settled and resolved to die a Christian and a good Protestant, for the point of confession he found him so strait-laced that he would yield to no part of Cobham's accusation; only the pension, he said, was once mentioned but never proceeded in. Grey, in the meantime, with his minister, Field, having had the like summons for death, spent his time in great devotions but with that careless regard of that with which he was threatened that he was observed neither to eat or sleep the worse or be any ways distracted from his accustomed fashions. Markham was told he should likewise die but, by secret message from some friends at court, had still such hope given him that he would not believe the worst news till the last day; and though he could be content to talk with the preacher which was assigned him, it was rather to pass time than for any good purpose, for he was Catholicly disposed; to think of death no way disposed. Whilst these men were so occupied at Winchester, there was no small doings about them at court, for life or death, some pushing at the wheel one way, some another. The lords of the council joined in opinion and advice to the king, now in the beginning of his reign, to show as well examples of mercy as severity and to gain the title of *Clemens* as well as *Justus;* but some others, led by their private spleen and passions, drew as hard the other way; and Patrick Galloway,[2] in his sermon on Tuesday, preached so hotly against remissness and moderation of justice in the head of justice as if it were one of the seven deadly sins. The king held himself upright betwixt two waters and first let the lords know that since the law had passed upon the prisoners and that they themselves had been their judges, it became not them to be petitioners for that but rather to press for execution of their own ordinances, and to others gave as good reasons to let them know that he would go no whit the faster for their driving but would be led as his own judgment and affections would move him, but seemed rather to lean to this side than the other by the care he took to have the law take its course, and the execution hasted. Warrants were signed and sent to Sir Benjamin Tichborne[3] on Wednesday last, at night, for Markham, Grey, and Cobham, who in this order were to take their turns, as yesterday being Friday, about ten of the clock. A fouler day could hardly have been picked out, or fitter for such a tragedy. Markham, being brought to the scaffold, was much dismayed and complained much of his hard hap to be deluded with hopes and brought to that place unprepared. One might see in his face the very picture of sorrow; but he seemed not to want resolution, for a napkin being offered by a friend that stood by to cover his face, he threw it away, saying he could look upon death without blushing. He took leave of some friends that stood near and betook himself to his devotions after his manner, and those ended, prepared himself to the block. The sheriff in the meantime was secretly withdrawn by one John Gib, a Scotch groom of the bedchamber; whereupon the execution was stayed and Markham left upon the scaffold to entertain

[49]

his own thoughts, which, no doubt, were as melancholy as his countenance, sad and heavy. The sheriff, at his return, told him that, since he was so ill prepared, he should yet have two hours' respite, so led him from the scaffold, without giving him any more comfort, and locked him into the great hall to walk with Prince Arthur.[4] The lord Grey, whose turn was next, was led to the scaffold by a troop of young courtiers and was supported on both sides by two of his best friends, and coming in this equipage had such gaiety and cheer in his countenance that he seemed a dapper young bridegroom. At his first coming on the scaffold, he fell on his knees, and his preacher made a long prayer to the present purpose, which he seconded himself with one of his own making, which, for the phrase, was somewhat affected and suited to his other speeches, but for the fashion, expressed the fervency and zeal of a religious spirit. In his confession he said, though God knew this fault of his was far from the greatest, yet he knew and could but acknowledge his heart to be faulty; for which he asked pardon of the king and thereupon entered into a long prayer for the king's good estate, which held us in the rain more than half an hour; but, being come to a full point, the sheriff stayed him and said he had received orders from the king to change the order of the execution and that the lord Cobham was to go before him; whereupon, he was likewise led to Prince Arthur's Hall, and his going away seemed more strange unto him than his coming thither, for he had no more hope given him than of an hour's respite; neither could any man yet dive into the mysteries of this strange proceeding. The lord Cobham, who was now to play his part and by his former actions promised nothing but *matière pour rire,* did much cozen the world, for he came to the scaffold with good assurance and contempt of death. He said some short prayers after his minister and so outprayed the company that helped to pray with him that a stander-by said he had a good mouth in a cry but was nothing single. Some few words he used to express his sorrow for his offence to the king and craved pardon of him and the world; for Sir Walter Raleigh he took it, upon the hope of his soul's resurrection, that what he had said of him was true, and with those words would have taken a short farewell of the world with that constancy and boldness that we might see by him it is an easier matter to die well than live well. He was stayed by the sheriff and told that there resteth yet somewhat else to be done, for that he was to be confronted with some other of the prisoners but named none. So as Grey and Markham, being brought back to the scaffold as they then were but nothing acquainted with what had passed no more than the lookers-on with what should follow, looked strange one upon the other, like men beheaded and met again in the other world. Now all the actors being together on the stage (as use is at the end of a play), the sheriff made a short speech unto them, by way of the interrogatory of the heinousness of their offences, the justness of their trials, their lawful condemnation, and due execution there to be performed, to all which they assented; then, saith the sheriff, see the mercy of your prince, who of himself hath sent hither a countermand and given you your lives. There was then no need to beg a plaudite of the audience, for it was given with such hues and cries that it went from the castle into the town and there began afresh, as if there had been some such like accident. And this experience was made of the difference of examples of justice and mercy, that in this last no man could cry loud enough, God save the king, and at the holding up of Brooke's head, when the executioner began the same cry, he was not seconded by the voice of any one man but the sheriff. You must think, if the spectators were so glad, the actors were not sorry, for even those that went best resolved to death were glad of life. Cobham vowed openly, if ever he proved traitor again, never so much as to beg his life, and Grey, that since he had his life without begging, he would deserve it. Markham returned with a merrier countenance than he came to the scaffold. Raleigh, you must think (who had a window opened that way), had hammers working in his head to beat out the meaning of this stratagem. His turn was to come on Monday next; but the king has pardoned him with the rest, and confined him with the two lords to the Tower of London, there to remain during pleasure. Markham, Brooksby, and Copley are to be banished the realm. This resolution was taken by the king without man's help, and no man can rob him of the praise of yesterday's action; for the lords knew no other but that execution was to go forward till the very hour it should be performed and then, calling them before him, he told them how much he had been troubled to resolve in this business, for to execute Grey, who was a noble, young spirited fellow, and save Cobham, who was as base and unworthy, were a manner of injustice. To save Grey, who was of a proud, insolent nature, and execute Cobham, who had shewed great tokens of humility and repentance, were as great a solecism, and so went on with Plutarch's comparisons in the rest till travelling in contrarieties but holding the conclusion in so indifferent balance that the lords knew not what to look for till the end came out, "and therefore I have saved them all." The miracle was as great there as with us at Winchester and it took like effect: for the applause that began about the king went from thence into the presence and so round about the court. I send you a copy of the king's letter, which was privately written the Wednesday night, and the messenger dispatched the Thursday about noon. But one thing had like to have marred the play, for the letter was closed and delivered him unsigned, which the king remembered himself and called for him back again. And at Winchester there was another cross adventure: for John Gib could not get so near the scaffold that he could speak to the sheriff but was thrust out amongst the boys and was fain to call out to Sir James Hay,[5] or else Markham might have lost his neck. There were other bypassages, if I could readily call them to mind; but here is enough already for *un petit mot de lettre* and therefore I bid you heartily farewell.

Yours, etc.

1. Brooke had been promised the mastership of the hospital of Saint Cross, near Winchester, by Queen Elizabeth. She died before making the appointment, however, and James bestowed it elsewhere. Brooke's disappointment was a factor in his becoming involved in the plot.

2. For Patrick Galloway see below, letter of January 15, 1604, n. 5.

3. The sheriff of Hampshire, whose duty it was to conduct the executions.

4. This is probably a reference to the fact that the alleged Round Table of King Arthur hangs on the wall of the great hall of Winchester Castle.

5. Sir James Hay, later Viscount Doncaster and earl of Carlisle, was a great favorite of the king's, who frequently employed him on special embassies. In an extravagant age his extravagance was pre-eminent.

Hampton Court, January 15, 1603/04
S. P. 14/6, #21

Sir, I perceived by Sir Rowland Lytton that in this time of your good leisure a small matter will serve for good entertainment, and therefore I send you such idle stuff as I received last out of France; but you must take the copies no otherwise than as lent, though you may keep them as long as you please; and for interest if they be worth it, I would gladly hear how you do in the country and with what contentment you pass your time; we have had here a merry Christmas and nothing to disquiet us save brabbles amongst our ambassadors, and one or two poor companions that died of the plague. The first holy days we had every night a public play in the great hall, at which the king was ever present and liked or disliked as he saw cause, but it seems he takes no extraordinary pleasure in them. The queen and prince were more the players' friends, for on other nights they had them privately and have since taken them to their protection. On New Year's night we had a play of Robin Goodfellow and a mask brought in by a magician of China. There was a heaven built at the lower end of the hall out of which our magician came down, and after he had made a long sleepy speech to the king of the nature of the country from whence he came, comparing it with ours for strength and plenty, he said he had brought in clouds certain Indian and China knights to see the magnificency of this court; and thereupon a traverse was drawn and the maskers seen sitting in a vaulty place with their torchbearers and other lights, which was no unpleasing spectacle. The maskers were brought in by two boys and two musicians, who began with a song, and whilst that went forward they presented themselves to the king. The first gave the king an impresa in a shield with a sonnet in a paper to express his device and presented a jewel of £40,000 value which the king is to buy of Peter van Lore.[1] But that is more than every man knew, and it made a fair show to the French ambassador's eye, whose master would have been well pleased with such a maskers' present, but not at that price. The rest in their order delivered their escutcheons with letters, and there was no great stay at any of them save only at one who was put to the interpretation of his device. It was a fair horse-colt in a fair green field, which he meant to be a colt of Bucephalus' race and had this virtue of his sire that none could mount him but one as great at least as Alexander. The king made himself merry with threatening to send this colt to the stable, and he could not break loose till he promised to dance as well as Banks his horse.[2] The first measure was full of changes and seemed confused but was well gone through withal, and for the ordinary measures they took out the queen, the ladies of Derby, Harford, Suffolk, Bedford, Susan Vere, Southwell the elder, and Rich. In the corantoes they ran over some other of the young ladies and so ended as they began, with a song; and, that done, the magician dissolved his enchantment and made the maskers appear in their likeness to be the earl of Pembroke, the duke [of Lennox], Monsieur d'Aubigny, young Somerset, Philip Herbert the young Bucephal, James Hay, Richard Preston, and Sir Henry Goodier. Their attire was rich but somewhat too heavy and cumbersome for dancers, which put them beside their galliards. They had loose robes of crimson satin embroidered with gold and bordered with broad silver laces, doublets and bases of cloth of silver, buskins, swords, and hats alike, and in their hats each of them an Indian bird for a feather, with some jewels. The twelfth day the French ambassador was feasted publicly, and at night there was a play in the queen's presence, with a masquerade of certain Scotchmen who came in with a sword dance, not unlike a matachin, and performed it cleanly; from thence the king went to dice into his own presence and lost £500, which marred a gamester, for since, he appeared not there, but once before was at it in the same place and parted a winner. The Sunday following was the great day of queen's mask, at which was present the Spanish and Polack ambassadors with their whole trains and the most part of the Florentines and Savoyards but not the ambassadors themselves, who were in so strong competition for place and precedence that to displease neither it was thought best to let both alone. The like dispute was betwixt the French and the Spanish ambassadors and hard hold for the greatest honor, which the Spaniard thinks he hath carried away by being first feasted (as he was the first holiday and the Polack the next) and invited to the greatest mask; and the French seems to be greatly discontented that he was flatly refused to be admitted to the last, about which he used unmannerly expostulations with the king and for a few days troubled all the court; but the queen was fain to take the matter upon her, who as a masker had invited the Spaniard as the duke before had done the French, and to have them both there could not well be without bloodshed. The hall was much lessened by the works that were in it, so as none could be admitted but men of appearance; the one end was made into a rock and, in several places, the waits placed, in attire like savages; through the midst from the top came a winding stair, of breadth for three to march, and so descended the maskers by three and three, which being all seen on the stairs at once was the best presentation I have at any time seen. Their attire was alike, loose mantles and petticoats, but of different colors, the stuffs embroidered satins and cloth of gold and silver, for which they were beholden to Queen Elizabeth's wardrobe. Their heads by their dressing did only distinguish the difference of the goddesses they did represent. Only Pallas had a trick by herself; for her clothes were not so much below the knee but that we might see a woman had both feet and legs, which I never knew before. She had a pair of buskins set with rich stones, a helmet full of jewels, and her whole attire embossed with jewels of several fashions. Their torchbearers were pages in white satin loose gowns, set with stars of gold, and their torches of white virgin wax gilded. Their *démarche* was slow and orderly; and first they made their offerings at an altar in a temple which was built on the left side of the hall towards the upper end; the songs and speeches that were there used I send you here enclosed. Then after the walking of two rounds fell into their measure, which for variety was nothing in-

ferior but had not the life as the former. For the common measures they took out the earl of Pembroke, the duke, the lord chamberlain, Lord Henry Howard, Southampton, Devonshire, Sidney,
Nottingham, Monteagle, Northumberland, Knollys, and Worcester. For galliards and corantoes they went by discretion, and the
young prince was tossed from hand to hand like a tennis ball.
The Lady Bedford and Lady Susan [3] took out the two ambassadors and they bestirred themselves very lively, especially the
Spaniard, for his Spanish galliard shewed himself a lusty old
reveller. The goddesses they danced with did their parts, and the
rest were nothing behindhand when it came to their turns; but of
all for good grace and good footmanship Pallas bore the bell away.
They retired themselves toward midnight in order as they came
and quickly returned unmasked but in their masking attire. From
thence they went with the king and the ambassadors to a banquet
provided in the presence, which was dispatched with the accustomed confusion; and so ended that night's sport with the end of
our Christmas gambols. Since, the Savoyard hath dined privately
with the king and after dinner was brought out into the great
chamber to see the prince dance and a nimble fellow vault; he
then took his leave but is not yet gone; and some doubt his leave
taking was but a cozenage to steal a dinner from the Florentine,
who expected to be first entertained. The Spaniard and Florentine
have not yet met, for they both stand upon terms, the one of his
greatness, the other upon custom that the first comer should salute
the other's welcome. The Polack doth this day feast the Spaniard;
he hath taken his leave and is presented with jewels and plate to
the value of £2000. The valuation of the king's presents, which
he hath made to ambassadors since his coming into England, comes
to £25,000. The constable of Castile is come to Brussels and hath
sent a dispatch to the Spanish ambassador with a letter to the king
from the king of Spain, by which he writes that he hath given
the constable absolute authority to treat and conclude of peace.[4]
So as we shall now fall to this work, for this ambassador doth
already begin to disgross the points of greatest difficulty, and
hath once had audience to this purpose and was met at his house
at Richmond on Friday last by the earls of Nottingham, Northum-

berland, and Devonshire, the lords Henry Howard and Cecil. We have here at this present the chief of our clergy in consultation about church matters;[5] yesterday the bishops with 4 or 5 of the deans were in privy chamber before the king and lords of the council, to whom the king made a speech with great respect to them and their callings and told them he sent not for them as persons accused but as men of choice, by whom he sought to receive instruction and chiefly sought to be satisfied in the points of confirmation, absolution, excommunication, and private baptism and insisted somewhat upon the disorders of bishops' chancellors, to which the archbishop of Canterbury, with the bishops of Winchester and Durham, made mild and good answers, and the bishop of London[6] spake well to the purpose but with too rough boldness; the deans, amongst whom was Westminster, were only hearers. In conclusion the king seemed to be reasonably satisfied, only did wish some alteration of scandalous words in the common prayer book but the substance to remain, upon which he willed the bishops to advise and return to him again on Wednesday next; meantime Patrick Galloway[7] and his crew shall have their turn, and tomorrow they appear before the king. These two companies as they differ in opinions so do they in fashions, for one side marches in gowns and rochets and the other in cloaks and nightcaps. Cartwright,[8] a ring leader of these reformed *palliati,* is lately dead. You have heard, I am sure, how Garter the King of Heralds, for behaving himself insolently in my lord Spencer's company, is ungartered and deposed. Lesieur is newly come out of Germany and Sir Anthony Standen out of Italy.[9] They parted at Canterbury as they went and there met in their return. Henry Wotton is come over with Sir Anthony Standen. Bulmer the alchemist is come out of Scotland and brings with him certain ore of the gold mine.[10] There is a pack of coiners discovered in London of certain old Low Country captains and some others, whereof two are taken and the rest fled the country; it were a fit match to set these new coiners a-work upon the new gold and so like to like; for there is little hope of this new discovery, though the Scotchmen compare it at least with the Indies, and the knights of the mine must needs go forward. The king hath honored his knights of the Bath with a difference from the rest, having given to certain of them that live hereabout the court crimson ribbons with *médailles* and leave to all other of that order that will be at the cost to come into the fashion. Young Peyton, the first of the king's knights, is the first disgraced gentleman of the privy chamber, for he is put out of his place for entertaining intelligence betwixt Cobham and Raleigh at their first coming into the Tower, and Sir Henry Neville, the lord treasurer's son-in-law, is sworn in his place.[11] Captain Kemys, a follower of Sir Walter Raleigh's who hath been kept close prisoner in the Tower from the beginning of those apprehensions, is set at liberty.[12] Brookesby is to pay Sir Robert Mansfield [13] £2500 to save his land, and it is thought the rest of the banished men will pass at like rates. The lords and Sir Walter have their lands and goods seized, and there is much ado to keep them in the king's hands undisposed. Sir John Ramsay hath gotten of the king a grant of Sir Walter's office of the wines, but the lord treasurer holds back to keep it for the king's use.[14] I have not heard from Mr. Winwood this many a day, but I hear of him by Captain Ogle, who came lately from thence,[15] that he holds up his horn and lives worshipfully. His excellency [Maurice of Nassau] hath been lately in the field upon some exploit which hath not succeeded, but we hear not what it is. Ostend is revictualed and the governor and garrison changed. Colonel Gistelles is there in place of Vandernode.[16] Sir Francis Vere [17] doth stand upon high points with the States and will either have absolute command of his English without subjection to his excellency or any other or return no more. The town of Geneva hath lately escaped a surprise, which was intended by the Savoyards with a ridiculous practice yet likely enough to have been effected. One John Bernard Lionois had provided certain bars with hooks and engines suddenly to have closed doors and had made sundry of his practice, when the *Génévois* were at their devotions and their church doors this cold weather close shut upon them, to have made them fast and there kept them sure, whilst the enemy by *scalado* might enter. He was discovered by one whom he sought to make of his party and, upon his own confession, condemned and executed.

I know not anything I have more to add either foreign or domestic, only I have omitted that we have new maids of honor: Mistresses Middlemore, Woodeose, and Carew, and three more we shall have as maids can be found fit for the purpose. The widow Norris is either married or made sure to Sir Thomas Erskine, the captain of the guard; [18] she lies at Denham at Sir Henry Bowyer's, who was the chief matchmaker, though Sir Thomas saith he takes the daughter upon the father's own tender and that within few days after her husband's death she was his to take or leave. I pray you let me hear by this bearer how you do, what you do, and when you mean to be at London, and I will not fail to meet you; meantime with my best wishes and commendations I commit you to God.

Yours most assured

1. Peter van Lore was one of those men who did a good deal of business with the court and made their profit from it, in the form of such things as fee-farms and the right to export cloth, duty free.

2. Banks was a famous showman, whose dancing horse, Morocco, was alleged to have climbed the steeple of Saint Paul's in 1600.

3. Vere. See below, letter of January 7, 1605.

4. Fernando Velasco, duke of Frias, constable of Castile, was the official head of the Spanish delegation at the forthcoming peace conference.

5. This refers to the Hampton Court conference.

6. John Whitgift was archbishop of Canterbury; he had but six weeks to live. His successor was Richard Bancroft, bishop of London, the principal anti-Puritan spokesman at the conference. Thomas Bilson was bishop of Winchester, Tobie Matthew of Durham.

7. Patrick Galloway, a Scottish clergyman of moderate views, was generally in favor with James, although not afraid to rebuke the king from the pulpit occasionally. At the conference he was acting as the medium of communication between James and the Edinburgh presbytery; his version of the conference was corrected by the king before it was sent north.

8. Thomas Cartwright, the Presbyterian. He died December 27, 1603.

9. Sir Stephen Lesieur, a Frenchman, became an English citizen and was employed on numerous diplomatic missions, mostly in Germany. He had just returned from an embassy to Rudolf II. Sir Anthony Standen had been sent to Italy by James. He was a Catholic, eager to promote the reconciliation of

England to Rome; he suggested to the Pope that Queen Anne might be a useful instrument to this end. The Pope gave him some consecrated objects for Anne; James, when he learned of this, imprisoned Standen in the Tower and returned the gifts. The king was always annoyed at any suggestion that his wife was anything other than a good Protestant. The fullest account of this business is by L. Hicks, S.J., "The Embassy of Sir Anthony Standen in 1605," *Recusant History* V (1959–60), 91–127, 184–222, VI (1961–62), 163–194, VII (1963–64), 50–81.

10. "Alchemist" is hardly an accurate word for Sir Bevis Bulmer; he was essentially a prospector and industrial speculator. His—and the king's—hope for a gold mine never materialized; later he did rather better with silver. See Lythe, *Economy,* pp. 53–57.

11. This Sir Henry Neville is not to be confused with the Sir Henry Neville who had been ambassador to France and was later, after Salisbury's death, to be a candidate for the secretaryship of state. This Sir Henry, the earl of Dorset's son-in-law, became Lord Abergavenny. Young Peyton was the son of Sir John Peyton, former lieutenant of the Tower and now governor of Jersey.

12. Lawrence Kemys was a close associate of Raleigh's and accompanied him on his fatal last voyage.

13. Sir Robert Mansell, the future treasurer of the navy.

14. Sir John Ramsay was one of James's great favorites; he killed the earl of Gowrie and his brother in 1600 at the time of the famous conspiracy. The office of the wines was the privilege of collecting £1 per annum from each vintner for a license to sell wine and one half of the fines imposed for infringement. It was worth £1,200 a year.

15. The Low Countries, where Winwood was the king's agent with the States-General. Sir John Ogle was an officer in the English forces there.

16. Jonkheer Pieter van Ghistelles had just replaced Colonel Charles von de Noot as governor of Ostend, which had been under siege by the archduke for some time. For its fall see below, letter September 21, 1604.

17. Sir Francis Vere, a brilliant soldier, was commander of the English forces in the Netherlands.

18. Sir Thomas Erskine, later first earl of Kellie, was educated with King James and always stood high in his favor. He married as his second wife the widow of Sir Edward Norris, Carleton's former employer.

London, August 10, 1604
S. P. 14/9, ff. 15–16

Sir: The rainy Sunday that stayed my journey did me no further hurt than to make me meet with my lord [the earl of Northumberland] just at Syon gates as he came from Petworth, where he was entertained with so good sports of fishing and hunting that he stayed two days longer than he purposed and now repents him that he made such haste away; for as it falls out his attendance might have been spared, since the great Spaniard[1] is not received with that great parade as was appointed. My lord Wotton took him at landing, and my lord of Northampton meets him with barges at Gravesend, and this night about six of the clock he comes up by water to Somerset stairs. The Spanish ambassador was very earnest to have him lodged and entertained as this night in the king's house at Greenwich that tomorrow with good ease he might come to Tower stairs and make a solemn entry through London at high noon-tide. But answer was made him that by reason of the king's absence the town was disfurnished of nobility and gentry fit for such a solemnity, which they give out as a respective consideration of their greatness and therefore seem to take the excuse in payment. The little French Monsieur [Beaumont] pries and spies out all advantages to make himself merry and saith he hath certain intelligence that this great man, partly for his ease and chiefly to save charges, had intention to have come by long seas as far as Gravesend and that the Spanish ambassador made him change that purpose in hope to have him received from town to town by lords of relay. He is not defrayed till his coming hither, but here he is like to have amends for all. For both the lodgings he shall use, at Somerset House and the banqueting house at Whitehall where he shall be feasted, is furnished as if it were for the king his master, and great care is taken that no curiosities for diet shall be wanting. His whole train is 220, of which there are gentlemen, besides officers, 80, but of Don Diegos of name, not above ten. The count of Aremberg with his fellow commissioners made a merry journey the last week to Theobalds,[2] where they were well entertained, and speak great wonders of the house. Two days after, they made the like journey to Wanstead and made appointment with my lord Cecil, there to surprise my lord of Devonshire, but he had a night's warning and so crammed their stomachs with all manner of dainties that now their mouths had no cause to envy their eyes. They mean ere they part to make the like visitations at Wimbledon, Hampton Court, and Windsor. The king was gone forward on his progress as far as my lord Mordaunt's and is now on his way hitherwards, but we shall not see him till Monday at the soonest. He hath had a merry hunting save for some mischances, as a fall he had by Huntingdon, which made him remember old sores, and Sir John Ramsay tumbled so long on the ground with his horse, one over the other, that at his feast day he was bedridden.[3] The king was much troubled with his Huntingdon stags that took [to] the fens and drowned land so as neither dog nor man could follow, and had it not been for the stilt-men of that country he had been there overmastered; but finding the use of their service he mustered a whole company of them and gave the chief command of these new soldiers to my lord Effingham.[4] Sunday last was celebrated by the lords of the council with a very solemn feast in the council chamber, where there were so many healths to king, queen, prince, duke, and princess that we think the good fashion of drinking will come again in request. The queen and her crew makes merry here at Whitehall. Sir James Hay is as good as sure to his young wife: for conditions are thus agreed on that Sir Edward Denny shall assure him £3000 land if he have no son, otherwise £1500 land; that in this consideration Sir Edward shall be made baron and the barony descend on his heir male if he have any; if not, on this new married couple. £1000 land shall be presently given them by the king, £100 old rent of Sir Edward's land, which was entitled on the crown, shall be released and £3000 debt paid.[5] So as we see the two immediate ways of a great fortune, which is a prince's favor and a good marriage, do both concur in this man. Your old acquaintance Mr. Thomas Lucas is secretly married to his old love Mrs. Leighton, wherein he is like to run another hazard of his father's disfavor.[6] I am sure you are little satisfied with these petty tidings when you are in expectation of great advertisements, but neither Sluys nor Ostend [7] afford any news [paper torn] than wagers upon the exchange, and the odds still go that Sluys will be first taken. If you hold appointment of coming hither, no doubt by that time we shall hear somewhat. The Spaniard's first audience will be on Wednesday next, his feast with the king tomorrow sevennight. I shall not need to pray you to remember my service to Sir Michael Dormer and my lady, for *cela s'entend,* but I pray you tell him that his journey hither at this time will be well bestowed, for he shall have Spanish *rodomontata* and *matière pour rire* all the summer after. If my lord goeth not the progress with the king I will see you safe again at Ascot; [8] if he do, I will be sure to meet you there, so as howsoever the carpes[?] will pay for it. I pray you commend me heartily to Mr. Gent, and so adieu till our next meeting.

Yours most assured

1. The constable of Castile, who was coming to England to be present at the final stages of the peacemaking.

2. Theobalds (Herts.) was Robert Cecil's house. King James became so attached to it that he later dragooned Cecil into exchanging it for the royal manor of Hatfield. Cecil thereupon rebuilt Hatfield House into essentially the building which exists today and which is still owned by his descendants.

3. Ramsay's "feast day" was, presumably, August 5, the anniversary of the Gowrie Conspiracy. See above, letter of January 15, 1604, n. 10.

4. William Howard, eldest son of the earl of Nottingham, who predeceased his father. The stilt-men were fen-dwellers who, according to William Camden, were "rude, uncivil, and envious to all others . . . who, stalking on high upon stilts, apply their mindes, to grasing, fishing and fowling." Quoted in H. C. Darby, *The Draining of the Fens* (Cambridge, 1940), p. 23.

5. Sir Edward was evidently reluctant to part with his daughter to a Scot. He did receive his barony; in the next reign he became earl of Norwich.

6. The marriage was evidently one of necessity, if the *Dictionary of National Biography* is correct in stating that their eldest son had already been born.

7. The Dutch forces were besieging Sluys, those of the archduke, Ostend.

8. Dormer lived at Ascot.

Sir: If this letter can come time enough to your Oxford carriers,
you shall have as much news as this place can afford you; but you
must remember where we are, neither in court nor city; and yet,
being as it were in the suburbs of both, happily we may catch
somewhat by the end before you remote countrymen. The king
comes tomorrow from Windsor to Hampton Court, where all his
little bairns do meet him; there is some mystery in this meeting
if a man knew what it were. The constable [of Castile] had a
foul passage homeward and was put into Calais, where both he
and his train was received with as much honor as could be shewed
them. The ambassador Taxis is returned to London and is seen
every day clad in green from the sole of the shoe to the top of
the feather, not so much as his sword excepted, hunting the wild-
goose chase betwixt Somerset House and the Swan, where his
horses stand. Little Beaumont sticks to the court like a burr, and
yet the king is half out of conceit both with him and his master
for certain jests and scorns they have made at our peace. On
Sunday last he made a feast at Eton College (where he is lodged)
to all, and only, the hunters, where were chief guests the duke [of
Lennox] the earls of Pembroke, Southampton, and Mar, the lord
Compton, and some ten others. They had many dainties, but one
of especial note, which was a red deer pie seasoned with garlic,
of which the king gave this commendation, that a garlic pie, tobacco, and surreverence [excrement] in a man's hose were a
dish for the Devil. The commissioners for the union [1] are sum-
moned by proclamation to meet the 20th of the next month at the
place appointed before; meantime the king goes down to Royston and with him only his hunting crew. Sir John Lee, for his good
service this summer, hath a gift of two of the Spanish ships, the
Mathew and the *Andrew,* and though they be half rotten and
of no use, yet methinks it is a suit of a strange nature. The States,
in their general mislike of our peace, do particularly quarrel at
one article by which we give liberty to the Spaniard to lodge his
ships of war in our ports. They are now at Sluys so busy in forti-

fying their island of Kadzand as if it were the rampart of their state, and indeed so it is held, for as long as they can keep the enemy play in Flanders they may hold themselves safe near at home. Ostend, after long drawing, on the 15th of this month *efflavit animam*. It died honorably, for the garrison marched forth *les drapeaux volants, le tambour sonnant, mèche allumée,* et *bal en bouche*;[2] there were 3000 men, 400 women besides children, in the town; all were convoyed with bag and baggage to Sluys. Such shipping as was in the haven was licensed to depart with the first wind, having a full freight of munition, artillery, and the rest of the victual that was in the town, so as the poor Spaniard might say at his entry, *in medio Romae nil repperi Romae*; and yet for old acquaintance I am sorry for the loss.[3] Sir Charles Fairfax was slain ten days before the yielding of the town by a musket shot in the head, for whom there is much moan made, both amongst his own countrymen and strangers. Now, sir, for a jig after this tragedy you shall understand that Charles Chester[4] died in London on Monday last, for whom *mendici, mimae,* balatrons, and all madcaps are very melancholy; he made Briscit his executor and left in money £400 and in jewels and toys about that value. If I should study long to furnish you with more news the stay of the messenger would make you lose this you have already, and therefore desiring to have my service recommended to Sir Michael Dormer and the lady with whom once upon a time I was so merry, I commit you to God's protection.

Yours most assured

1. James was most eager for a union of the governments of England and Scotland. Public opinion was receptive in neither country, and the negotiations ultimately came to nothing.

2. That is to say, with the honors of war.

3. Carleton had spent a good deal of time at Ostend while he was in the service of the then governor, Sir Edward Norris.

4. Charles Chester was described by John Aubrey as "a bold, impertinent fellow . . . a perpetual talker, and made a noise like a drum in a room. So one time at a tavern Sir W. R. [Raleigh] beats him and seals up his mouth, i.e., his upper and nether beard with hard wax." Dick, *Lives,* p. 318.

Sir, if your little messenger had come a day or two sooner he had come opportunely to have squired Sir William Cecil,[1] now knight of the Bath. How he sped yesterday I know not, for when I saw him on Saturday I gave him the best advice I could and since never set eye on him but once that night, when he was herded with the small game that follows the prince [Henry] and in my opinion could not be better. Our Christmas games are now at an end unless the duke of Holstein come with an after reckoning, who as they say hath somewhat in hand and broges [fishes] about for some others to bear part in the charge, which is not *bien séant à un prince*.[2] We began on Saint John's day with the marriage of Sir Philip and the Lady Susan, which was performed with as much ceremony and grace as could be done a favorite.[3] The prince [Henry] and duke of Holstein led the bride to church, the queen followed her from thence, the king gave her; and she brided and bridled it so handsomely and indeed became herself so well that the king said if he were not married he would not give her but keep her himself. There was none of our accustomed forms omitted, of bride cakes, sops in wine, giving of gloves, laces, and points, which have been ever since the livery of the court; and at night there was sewing into the sheet, casting of the bride's left hose, and twenty other petty sorceries. They were married in the chapel, feasted in the great chamber, and lodged in the council chamber, where the king gave them in the morning before they were up a *reveille-matin* in his shirt and his nightgown and spent a good hour with them in the bed or upon, choose which you will believe best. The plate and presents that were given were valued at £2000, but that which the king gave made it a good marriage, which was a book of 500 land lying in the Isle of Sheppey (whereof Sir Edward Hoby had a lease) passed and delivered that day for the lady's jointure. At night there was a mask performed by my lord of Pembroke, my lord Willoughby, Sir James Hay, Sir Robert Carey, Sir John Lee, Sir Richard Preston, Sir Thomas

Germain, and Sir Thomas Bager. Their conceit was a representation of Juno's temple at the lower end of the great hall, which was vaulted, and within it the maskers seated with store of lights about them, and it was no ill show; they were brought in by the four seasons of the year and *Hymeneus,* which for songs and speeches was as good as a play. Their apparel was rather costly than comely, but their dancing full of life and variety; only Sir Thomas Germain had lead in his heels and sometimes forgot what he was doing. The Venetian ambassador was there present and was a wedding guest all the day; but one thing he took ill, and not without cause, that being brought after dinner to the closet to retire himself, he was there forgotten and suffered to walk out his supper, which he took afterwards privately in my lord of Cranborne's chamber;[4] the Spanish ambassador was there likewise, but disguised; the French ambassador by reason of sickness hath been a stranger at court all Christmas. On Thursday last the Spaniard made a solemn dinner to the duke of Holstein and the greatest part of the court. The ladies he presented with fans and gloves and ended his entertainment with a play and a banquet. On New Year's Day there was expectation of new creations both of marquises and earls, but they are put off till the queen's lying down, which will be about three months hence at Greenwich. Yesterday in the morning the little Charles[5] was made great duke of York. The ceremony was performed in the hall, and himself with his ornaments carried by nine earls. There were 11 knights of the Bath besides Sir Charles himself and all of the king's choice, as, namely, the lords Willoughby, Chandos, Compton and Norris; William Cecil, Allen Percy, Francis Manners, Thomas Somerset, Clifford, Howard, and Harrington. They were all lodged and feasted in the court for three days, and yesterday a public dinner was made in the great chamber, where was a table for the little duke and the earls and another apart for these new knights. The mask at night requires much labor to be well described, but there is a pamphlet in press which will save me that pains; meantime you shall only know that the actors were the queen, the ladies Bedford, Suffolk, Derby, Rich, Herbert, Effingham, Susan, Ed.

Howard, Bevell, Walsingham, and Wroth. The presentation of the mask at the first drawing of the traverse was very fair and their apparel rich, but too light and courtesanlike. Their black faces and hands, which were painted and bare up the elbows, was a very loathsome sight and I am sorry that strangers should see our court so strangely disguised. The Spanish and Venetian ambassadors were both there and most of the French about the town. The confusion in getting in was so great that some ladies lie by it and complain of the fury of the white staffs. In the passages through the galleries they were shut up in several heaps betwixt doors and there stayed till all was ended; and in the coming out, a banquet which was prepared for the king in the great chamber was overturned, table and all, before it was scarce touched. It were infinite to tell you what losses there were of chains, jewels, purses, and suchlike loose ware, and one woman amongst the rest lost her honesty, for which she was carried to the porter's lodge, being surprised at her business on the top of the terrace. The court comes towards you on Wednesday next, and you will have these accidents more particularly related. Here is no news out of France since the last I showed you, the duke [of Lennox] in his passage being bound for Dieppe was driven up as high as Gravelines and there forced to land and to march with his whole troop on foot as far as Calais, from whence he is gone overland; my lord of Hertford is come up and not knowing how to put off the journey to the archduke hath this day undertaken it.[6] Our lieger into Spain [7] takes state upon him and is proud of the employment to which it was thought he would hardly have been entreated. Here have come of late many dispatches from our ambassador at Venice [Sir Henry Wotton] and his doings not over well liked. Will you not wonder if I shall tell you that Sir Walter Cope is believed not only to aspire but to be in fair forwardness to the secretaryship? I hope you have enough to entertain your thoughts withal and therefore when I have told you that your friends are well here and desired to be remembered where you are I leave further to trouble you and rest,

Yours most assured

[68]

1. Sir William Cecil, the eldest son of the earl of Salisbury, was frail and sickly.

2. Ulric, duke of Holstein, Queen Anne's brother, arrived in England in November 1604, ostensibly to raise 10,000 men for service in Hungary. The visit lasted for some time and was very expensive. See *C. S. P. Venetian, 1603–1607*, pp. 193, 245.

3. Sir Philip Herbert, later earl of Pembroke, was a handsome, extravagant, bad-tempered and licentious man who was a favorite of the king's. His wife was Lady Susan Vere, daughter of the earl of Oxford and granddaughter of Lord Burghley.

4. Robert Cecil had recently been created Viscount Cranborne. The Venetian ambassador was Nicolo Molin.

5. The future Charles I. The masque Carleton here describes, the *Masque of Blackness,* marked the first collaboration between Ben Jonson and Inigo Jones and was something of a fiasco.

6. Edward Seymour, earl of Hertford, son of the Protector Somerset and once husband of Lady Catherine Grey, had been appointed ambassador extraordinary to Brussels, to convey James's ratification of the peace treaty to the archduke.

7. Sir Charles Cornwallis. Lieger = resident ambassador.

Paris, November 4/14, 1605
S. P. 78/52 f. 336

Sir, My lord North's [1] departure is sudden and his stay on the way like to be long, so as I had not written to you at this present but that it [is] his desire to have somewhat to you. I know not how soon we shall follow him, for though my lord Norris [2] have recovered health, he hath yet no more strength than to travel betwixt bed and board; but, as soon as we are able, make no doubt that anything can stay us, for we have now no further care than to carry our bodies well home. I will not fail to bring you your satin and some toys from the palace, but you write not whether you would have boys' things or women's things and therefore am left to my conjecture that your affection is more to the female. Of the money you have received for me I would desire you to

[69]

put out £100 where you think best and for the rest to keep it by you because I know not yet what use I shall have of it. The conversion of our chaplain in Spain will prove very scandalous; I heard not of it but by your letter, yet ever suspected somewhat, since I have news he was gone to study at Salamanca.[3] I forgot to tell you in my last how the count of Villa Mediana, amongst his other baggage, transported this way a whole cartload of English and Dutch whores, which in my opinion is as needless a commodity to carry into Spain as to send trees to the wood.[4] Here is arrived a gallant ambassador from Venice, one Pietro Priuli, with a guard of Capellati and many other new fashions. The king is looked for in this town tomorrow. He hath rested himself a week at Fontainebleau after his wars and hath there framed a severe edict against duels and private quarrels, of which he found store in those remote parts, which is the special *réussite* of this summer's action. The queen is there great with child. The duke of Bouillon hath had lately a son, which is his heir, and the duke of Montpensier a daughter, which is his first and no small joy where nothing was looked for. Monsieur Plessis [Philippe du Plessis-Mornay] having but one son in the world and no more children and he a very gallant and accomplished gentleman, hath news sent him that he was slain in the Low Countries at the late enterprise upon Geldern with a shot from the walls. Colonel Dommerville was killed in the defeat you wrote of whe[paper torn] our English had so great loss.[5] They were both of the religion [Huguenots] and are much lamented of that party. Old Beza[6] died at Geneva the 23 of the last and, amongst many others in this town, two brothers, great princes, one in Prussia, the other in Transylvania, died in this time of my lord Norris's sickness and of his disease. They had all the same physicians, and we are taught *vicino incòmodo* to acknowledge God's blessing the more in this happy escape. I pray you remember my love and service to Sir Rowland Lytton. I write not to him because I hold him not ceremonious and, for news, that which I send to you is understood as well meant to him, and he hath the commodity at a second hand to be troubled with no more than he please. For our good friend in the Strand [Sir Walter Cope] since I find he makes the countenance of the great man only serve to draw dependence to himself, as to be waited on to his boat and to have intelligence (forsooth) sent him from beyond sea, I shall be hardly brought to comply with him any longer but leave him to his vanities. This enclosed to the bishop of Gloucester hath lain by me a good while, to thank him for former courtesies now I have no more to do with him. I pray you let it be delivered, with this other to my brother and hearty commendations to all our friends; and so with prayers to God for a merry meeting, I commit you to his holy protection.

Yours most assured

1. Dudley, third Baron North, was another of Carleton's connections by marriage; North's wife's sister was married to Carleton's brother George. North's chief claim to fame is his discovery in 1606 of the spring of Tunbridge Wells.

2. Francis, second Baron Norris of Rycote, whom Carleton had accompanied to Spain, and who was recovering from a serious illness.

3. Sir Charles Cornwallis's chaplain, James Waddesworth, became a Roman Catholic. See his interesting and rather ambiguous letter to Cornwallis on September 8 in P. R. O., S. P. 94/12, f. 23.

4. Villa Mediana was succeeded as Spanish ambassador in England by Don Pedro de Zuñiga in 1605.

5. The battle of Mülheim, October 9, 1605. The Dutch were badly beaten, and only a skillful rearguard action by the English contingent, led by Sir Horace Vere, prevented a much worse disaster.

6. Theodore Beza, Calvin's successor in Geneva.

Paris, November 10/20, 1605

S. P. 78/52, ff. 342–43

Sir, My last was by my lord North, who parted from hence some five days since with intention to take Cambrai in his way to Calais and to make a visit of the other frontier towns in those parts, which makes me presume this which I send by the way of Rouen will come first to your hands, and you have here enclosed one to his lordship that you may have equal weapons for the first encounter; by the other to my man I appoint him to receive certain money, about £20, which I have laid out in trinkets for my lady Lower [1] and to pay it to you. I pray you receive it for me and excuse me for troubling you these domestic *brouilleries*. I have taken up and spent £30 which I pray you repay upon my bill to Mr. [William] Willaston. Part of it is gone in books for my lord of Northumberland,[2] and for the rest I find it impossible to travel upon another man's purse without letting slip somewhat *de proprio*. Whilst I was in Spain I bestowed much in books, because they are rare of that language in England, and the like commodity of carriage happens not in an age. There are many of them *para el gusto* and amongst others a *picara* which will be a good Christmas companion for you, and I have written to Mr. Warner if you have any mind to [paper torn] you shall have your choice. I will presume my absence from thence shall not be to my prejudice, for I have leave sent me without limitation to frame my return according to my occasions and I have likewise some employment for my lord here, by which I am not altogether unserviceable to him. My lord Norris hath taken so good heart as to remove to our ambassador's, where he is lodged and settled to his contentment. You may well conceive how unfit a place that of all other is for me to rest in, so as I am left to myself and my own liberty, till either he grow weary and change garrison or that I hear the *boute-selle* for his return for England. His physicians will not allow him to venture on the way these three weeks or this month, and he apprehends the cold weather and ill ways so much that he talks himself of staying till next spring, but when he feels his own strength I hope he will have better mind to wag homewards. For the small wares you write for, if I come not myself I will not fail to send them by some fit messenger before your accustomed time of retreat into the country. Your satin I will guess you have no such haste of but that you will stay my return, to save portage, but, if you desire it against the good time, upon the first letter I will send it. Hereafter, I pray you direct your letters in a cover according to a note here enclosed. There is likewise an address to Tobie Matthew,[3] to whom I have transported your commendations by every letter. Here is little other news more than in my former. The king hath been in this town these 5 days and is gone with the queen to Saint-Germain[-en-Layé], there to remain for the space of a week, whilst the Louvre be dressed and trimmed up with hangings of the king's own handy-work, at least of his new erected *tapissiers,* for the birth of a duke of Orleans. The new Venetian ambassador is come accompanied with one to change your lieger in England. Sir George Carew's [4] stuff is come hither, and it is much marvelled that after so long expectation his person appears not, but the excuse is stranger than all the rest, that there is no money in the Exchequer to set him forward. Here is a busy piece of work about a new *règlement* in trade [paper torn] certain merchants, Mr. Bell, Willaston, and Hall have taken much pains, but the old ambassador doth so confound them with *Jus gentium* and is so muffled himself with their cloth, which he examines and sifts to a hair, that he can find no way forward but will leave it well beaten to his successor.[5] He makes report at this present of a strange piece of news, sent him as he saith from the king, and he receives it from Beaumont, who is said to be on his way hitherwards, and he from his secretary left as agent behind him in England, that the council being set and some lords besides in the chamber, a barrel of powder should be fired underneath them, and the greatest part, if not all, blown up. I have heard of men that have been undermined in their councils, but only *par manière de dire,* and cannot believe so strange and desperate a stratagem. Yet because it is so confidently reported, I may think there was some fire from whence there comes so much smoke and therefore long to know the truth of the matter. God deliver our state from that *fatale malum* which hath long reigned in Aquilone, for that I most stand in fear of is some practice against the king's person.[6] Old John Colville, that busy-brained Scot who troubled our king so much in consort with the earl Bothwell, having an ambition to be made chancellor of Scotland and ever since lived an exile, is dead in this town within few days in great want and misery.[7] My lord Sankey is here newly arrived from a pilgrimage to Notre-Dame-de-Lorette, and here is one Captain Bruce, an outworn traveller, who after 25 years' absence wends homewards for England. He takes knowledge of you and Mr. Gent for his near acquaintance. He left Sir Anthony Sherley in Fer[paper torn], who, having made a journey this summer to the emperor with [paper torn] single postillion and borrowed of him a few dollars, hath made up his company again 15 strong.[8] Sir Robert Dudley's companion at Lyons is turned to her own likeness, and [paper torn] out she hath a purpose to put herself into some religious house.[9] They are both reconciled to the Church and go lovingly to the Mass together every morning. I understand of a parley begun betwixt our earl of Arundel [10] and the duke of Mayenne's daughter, which rests a maid, but this I must pray you to make a secret. And thus having naught else for the present worth your knowledge, I commit you to God's protection, resting ever

Yours most assured

I must send general commendations to so many of our friends as I am sure the term and Parliament hath assembled with you, but I pray you offer my particular service to any that will command me.

1. Probably the wife of Sir William Lower, who on December 2, 1605, was interrogated as to those present at dinner on November 4 with Northumberland. *C. S. P. Domestic 1603–1610,* p. 266.

2. Carleton left Northumberland's employ in March 1605.

3. Tobie Matthew, son of the future archbishop of York, was a friend of both Chamberlain's and Carleton's; he had been at Christ Church with Carleton. His subsequent conversion to Catholicism brought about a considerable cooling of relations; both Carleton and Chamberlain were good Protestants.

4. Sir George Carew had recently been appointed ambassador to France, succeeding Sir Thomas Parry.

5. These negotiations followed the imposition by Henri IV of what the English government regarded as unnecessarily restrictive regulations on the importation of English cloth. Agreement was eventually reached in 1606. Parry was by no means as ineffectual as Carleton's strictures imply.

6. *Aquilone* is the Italian for "north"; the reference is undoubtedly to Scotland and the alleged turbulence of Scottish politics.

7. John Colville was a Scottish cleric who had had a notably unsavory political career and who forfeited James's confidence by his association with Francis Stewart, earl of Bothwell, whom James feared and detested because of his dabbling in witchcraft, his opposition to James's policy of reducing the Scottish aristocracy to obedience, and what James thought might be his designs on the throne—his father was an illegitimate son of James V. Bothwell, like Colville, died in poverty and exile.

8. Sir Anthony Sherley was one of a family of adventurers, whose career took him to all sorts of places, from the West Indies to Persia. At this point he was about to go to Morocco as an agent of the Holy Roman Emperor. The English government did not trust him, and he was never able to get employment from James I. He died in poverty and exile in Spain. The best account of the Sherleys is in David W. Davies, *Elizabethans Errant* (Ithaca, N.Y., 1967).

9. Sir Robert Dudley was the son of Elizabeth's favorite, Leicester, and Lady Douglas Sheffield. The legitimacy of his birth was never legally established. At this point, having failed in a lengthy and expensive attempt to prove his legitimacy and his right to the earldoms of Leicester and Warwick, he had left England, forever as it turned out, as well as his wife and seven daughters; he was accompanied by his mistress, Elizabeth Southwell, disguised as a page. They turned Catholic, were apparently married by papal dispensation, and had thirteen children. Dudley, a skillful engineer, eventually entered the service of the grand duke of Tuscany and was responsible for the draining of the marshes between Pisa and the sea.

10. Thomas Howard, earl of Arundel, was restored in title and blood by James I in 1604—his father had been convicted of treason in 1589 for allegedly praying for the success of the Armada. The rumor reported by Carleton turned out to have no foundation; in 1606 Arundel married a daughter of the earl of Shrewsbury.

London, April 17, 1606
S. P. 14/20, ff. 112–13

Sir, I have taken time enough to persuade you here should be some alteration since your departure, but all things are in state as you left them, only the Parliament hath been more busied in committees and conferences these few days past than since the

[75]

first sitting.[1] They have had four matters in question betwixt both houses: the bill of free trade into France and Spain,[2] the union, Church matters, and purveyors. The first was referred to further consideration at their meeting again after the holy days, which will be tomorrow sevennight. The second point was resolved in this sort, to have the former act continued by a small bill till the next sessions, which otherwise would now expire because it extended but to this meeting.[3] For Church matters there were four points very curiously and learnedly handled by four Apostles of the lower house: deprivation, citation, excommunication, and the authority of the high commisions, by Sir Francis Bacon, the attorney of the wards, the recorder and the solicitor,[4] in which the bishops took time this day for answer, and as there was then a general fast and prayers amongst the brethren in this town for good success in their affairs, so do they now hasten Good Friday a day sooner and are all at their devotions. The bill of purveyors [5] was the main matter which bred trouble on all sides; for first it was arraigned by the attorney at a conference and 10 charges laid to it as impossibilities to have it pass, which was reported to the lower house; and Sir John Saville made a collection out of the 10 objections, reducing them to 4: hanging the innocent, damning the ignorant, raising rebellion, and starving the king; whereupon Yelverton,[6] the old tribune of the house, took upon him the answering of the attorney, as desirous to nurse and foster a babe which had been bred with so much pain and travail, and as he used this metaphor in the house so was it his flourish at the second conference, which he stood somewhat too much upon, and the lords looking for it were well provided of an answer, saying that his love to a babe of so small hope was rather fondness than true affection and that it were better be crushed in the cradle than nursed up and prove a monster; whereupon Ned Wymark,[7] who seldom speaks at a conference, could not contain himself from expressing his sorrow in an audible voice to see their babe so betrayed in so good company. For material points they were handled well and substantially, but the judges overruled all on the prerogative side and gave it out for law that the king had both prising and pre-emption and that he was not bound to payment but upon

[76]

these terms *quand bonnement il peut* and delivered one judgment in all men's opinions of dangerous consequence, that the prerogative was not subject to law but that it was a transcendent above the reach of Parliament. In the end the lords closed up the matter with the king's favorable intentions that in kindness he would do much but upon constraint nothing, and that of himself he would see that reformation in this disorder which Parliament could not provide for. It was then only observed how Nick Fuller,[8] not well marking what was said but conceiving that the lords did promise a passage of the bill, desired to be heard and prayed their lordships there might be a proviso put in for the city of London; which made merry end of a sharp bickering. Here is much preparing for Saint George's solemnities, wherein they say we shall have two new knights, Salisbury and Montgomery for Cumberland and Devonshire. The earl of Montgomery hath upon persuasion given over his suit for Portsmouth, which is thought to be reserved for one of the Veres. Sir Horatio sets forward tomorrow towards the Low Countries. My lord of Devonshire's funeral will be performed in Westminster about three weeks hence. There is much dispute amongst the heralds whether his lady's arms shall be impaled with his, which brings in question the lawfulness of the marriage, and that is said to depend upon the manner of the divorce, which though it run in these terms that she was to be separated from her late husband *a thoro et mensa, propter varia et diversa adulteria, confessata et commissa tam in suburbiis quam intra muros civitatis* [of] London, yet are they tied in the conclusion not to marry any other. Her estate is much threatened with the king's account, but it is thought she will find good friends, for she is visited daily by the greatest, who profess much love to her for her earl's sake; meantime amongst the meaner sort you may guess in what credit she is when Mrs. Bluenson complains that she [the countess] hath made her cousin of Devonshire shame her and the whole kindred.[9] Since the search [10] at Montague House it is remembered by some country people that they saw a man cross the marketplace with a cloak only over his shirt and slip shoes. Old Yelverton the pensioner, for challenging a cloak and a rapier which was found in the house and proved to be none of his but suspected to be Gerard's, though he denies it, and for answering impertinently to the Lords, was sent to the Tower four days since. The marquis of Saint Germain is on this side of Paris on his way hitherwards. It is guessed he comes not by Brussels, to have some excuse of prolongation of the delivery of Owen as not able to resolve without speech with the archduke.[11] The Hollanders have made great spoil of late in the East Indies, both by sea and land, and have sent home two ships of twelve they have upon the coast, well-laden with the pillage of two carricks they burnt before Goa. It is said their army will be first in the field and that they will attempt the recovery of Lingen. Spinola is not yet returned.[12] The king of France is gone back to Fontainebleau, and it is said the duke of Bouillon with him. The king of Denmark's coming is much hearkened after, yet no more certainly than that Somerset House is making ready and for him, as they say.[13] The sickness is well abated to twelve this last week. My friend you left sick in Chancery Lane is recovered and gone out of town. I think not to stir from hence till next term, being for a time the French doctor's prisoner; meantime I shall be glad to hear of your health and the good company where you are. So praying you to remember my service to Sir Henry [Fanshawe] and my lady with my best wishes and commendations to yourself I commit you to God's protection.

Yours most assuredly

I must not fold up my letter without adding
an especial postscript of commendations from
our Cripplegate family.[14]

1. Carleton was M. P. for Saint Mawes in this Parliament, but on account of his alleged connection with the Gunpowder Plot he was not allowed to sit in this session, which ended in May. On November 16, 1606, two days before the next session was to begin, he wrote to Salisbury asking to be allowed to resume his seat (*C. S. P. Domestic 1603–1610*, p. 335). Salisbury granted his request. (*Journals of the House of Commons* I, 324.)
2. A bill to allow any of the king's subjects to trade with France, Spain, and Portugal. It eventually passed (3 Jac. I, c. 6).

3. The "former act" was the Act of 1604 (1 Jac. I, c. 2), which empowered commissioners to meet with their Scottish counterparts to discuss the possibility of union. Their commission extended only to the next session of Parliament; it was now renewed (3 Jac. 1, c. 3).

4. The grievances mentioned here were the deprivation of ministers who did not comply with the Canons of 1604; that there should be only two high commissions, one in London, one in York; that a man cited before one or the other should know the charges against him and the identity of his accuser; and that excommunication should not be imposed for trifles. Sir John Doddridge was solicitor general; Sir Henry Hobart, attorney of the Court of Wards; Sir Henry Montague, recorder of the city of London.

5. Purveyance was the king's prescriptive right to be transported and supplied at less than the market price. By this time it had evolved into a tax collected in each county by a group of undertakers, often the leading Justices of the Peace, based on the difference between the "king's price" and the market price. For a discussion see G. E. Aylmer, "The Last Years of Purveyance," *Economic History Review,* Second Series, X (1957–58), 81–94. James did not want the question discussed in Parliament at all; the fact that it was, was a considerable victory for the opposition, led by Sir Edwin Sandys. Commons eventually passed the bill, but it was lost in the Lords. The debates can be followed in Willson, *Bowyer.*

6. Sir Henry Yelverton, a politician of rather inconsistent views, who in 1617 was to succeed Francis Bacon as attorney general.

7. Edward Wymark, who, like Chamberlain, was a man-about-town of some wealth, was a close friend of both Chamberlain's and Carleton's. The references in the letters suggest that he had a witty and salacious turn of mind, which at one point almost got him into trouble. See *L. J. C.* II, 178, n. 6.

8. For Fuller see below, letter of August 27, 1607.

9. Charles Blount, Lord Mountjoy, became earl of Devonshire in 1604. In 1605 he married Penelope, Lady Rich, Essex's sister, who had been his mistress for years and had been recently divorced by her husband in the ecclesiastical courts. The marriage was of doubtful legality. Blount died on April 13.

10. For Catholic priests.

11. Hugh Owen was suspected by the English government of complicity in the Gunpowder Plot. It tried vainly to obtain his extradition from the archduke. The marquis of San Germano was an ambassador sent to England by Philip III to congratulate James on his escape from the plotters.

12. Ambrogio Spinola, the commander of the Spanish armies in Flanders, had been in Spain. He returned to Flanders in May.

13. Christian IV, James's brother-in-law, visited England in the summer of 1606. See below, letter of August 20, 1606.

14. Carleton's brother-in-law Alexander Williams and his family lived near Cripplegate.

London, May 2, 1606

S. P. 14/21, #4

Sir, I returned no answer by your messenger that come from Ware Park because I imagined you would then be gone to Knebworth.[1] Ever since I have been a houseling and scarce stirred out of doors, so as I can send you little news, unless you will be content with such as my sister Williams hath gathered together in her visits; and first you may understand that Mrs. Doctor of Aldermary Church is brought to bed of a goodly daughter, which her husband took almost as a miracle; for in open audience of his gossips he made it a great wonder it should be so great since he had taken so small pains for it. Sir Thomas Stukely[2] came to town about a week since and upon a tobacco sickness sent up for his wife in post, who brought up her great belly behind one of her men in a day and a half; upon sight of her he recovered, and here they are for a fortnight at least, not a little busied in borrowing and broking for money to pay for a purchase they have made of a manor of my lord Lisle's in Hampshire, which cost them £4000. It was looked yesterday that Garnett should have come a-maying to the gallows which was set up for him in Paul's churchyard on Wednesday, but upon better advice his execution is put off till tomorrow, for fear of disorder amongst prentices and others in a day of such misrule.[3] The news of his death was sent him upon Monday last by Doctor Abbot, which he would hardly be persuaded to believe, having conceived great hope of grace by some good words and promises he said were made him and by the Spanish ambassador's mediation, who he thought would have spoken to the king for him. He hath been since often visited and examined by the attorney, who find him shifting and faltering in

[80]

all his answers, and it is looked he will equivocate at the gallows, but he will be hanged without equivocation, though some do yet think he shall have favor, upon a petitionary letter he hath written to the king. The Spanish ambassador [the marquis of San Germano] had quick dispatch: he came to the town on Thursday, had audience on Saturday, was feasted on Sunday and took his leave next day; he was met at seaside by Sir Lewis Lewknor,[4] at Canterbury by the sheriff of Kent, at Rochester by the earl of Perth, and was welcomed to the town from the king by the earl of Pembroke; he was conducted to the court by the earls of Southampton, Shrewsbury, and Northampton. At his parting he had a present of 4000 ounces in gilt plate, and one Vlasco d'Arragon (who in Spain had the charge of accommodating my lord admiral) had to the value of £500. I hear not of any great matter he had to treat more than to congratulate the failing of this late treason: he said nothing concerning Garnett, and in requital there was as little said to him touching Owen, about whom here is a final answer come from the archduke that he shall not be delivered and upon these reasons: that being a banished man from hence he is naturalized in that country, that claiming his privilege they could not deny it him, that there is no precedent for delivering of such as fly from one state to another for protection unless it be betwixt such allies as agree *de restituendis et reddendis utrumque fugitivis,* which is not in our treaty; but if the king did require any such matter in courtesy and would begin on his part by sending back such as they would ask (as Caron, Levinus and some others) they would hearken better unto him.[5] There was appointed to have come from thence one Norcarmes upon the same errand as the Spanish ambassador, but he is stayed upon a quarrel the archduke hath picked that the king, not inviting his ambassador or the Venetians for fear of discontenting either in regard of priority, hath brought them to terms of equality.[6] Sir Henry Carey's ransom was set down £2500, of which there is £300 abated by the Spanish ambassador at the king's resquest.[7] My lord of Devonshire's funerals will be performed on Wednesday next, in which my lord of Southampton is chief mourner, my lord of Suffolk and Northampton assistants, and 3 other earls. It is determined his arms shall be set up single without his wife's. His places remain as when I wrote last. Portsmouth is hardly laid to by divers, but they say it is kept for Sir Francis Vere, who is sent for, and upon his coming home it is looked he will be made a baron and advanced to be our chief conductor when we have need of a soldier.[8] The king hath a purpose to give some new honors upon the queen's delivery, and because the Parliament house is sufficiently fil [paper torn] they begin to think of making knights banner [paper torn], which have place above all others but were wont to be made upon service in the field. It is thought my lord Knowles shall be created E[paper torn]. The lord of Buccleuch, who is come hither out of the Low Countries, shall have the first honor of being created a Scottish viscount, and he shall have Sir John Ramsay for companion and be both sent to the Parliament in Scotland.[9] It is thought our Parliament will break up tomorrow sevennight. I hear of nothing worth note done lately in the House save only of a speech of Johnson's touching the proclamation about purveyors that it cost him 3ᵈ and was not worth 1ᵈ ob.[10] I am come to small money with you; and therefore my stock being even spent it is time to desire you to bestow commendations for me where you are; and from hence I send you many with many wishes for your return, so I commit you to God's protection.

Yours most assured

My physician hath let me twice blood, by which I find myself lightened but not much eased, which will make me forever abjure such horse leeches.

1. Knebworth was the house of Carleton's cousin, Sir Rowland Lytton.
2. Sir Thomas Stukely was Chamberlain's nephew and had been married to Carleton's aunt; this was his second wife.
3. Henry Garnett, the Jesuit, was executed on May 3 for complicity in the Gunpowder Plot. May Day was a day on which apprentices frequently got overboisterous. George Abbot was the future archbishop of Canterbury.
4. Sir Lewis Lewknor was master of ceremonies, the equivalent of a present-day chief of protocol.
5. Sir Noel Caron was the agent of the United Provinces in London. Levinus

Munck was Robert Cecil's secretary; he was born in Ghent and was naturalized by 1601.

6. The dispute over precedence between the representatives of the archduke and the Venetian Republic went on for years.

7. Sir Henry Carey, master of the king's jewels, was a prisoner in the hands of the archduke. There was considerable haggling over the size of his ransom, which was eventually paid. See March 8, 1606, Salisbury to Sir Thomas Edmondes, M. S. Giuseppi *et al.,* eds., *Report on the Manuscripts of the Marquess of Salisbury,* XVIII (London, 1940), 73–74, and July 16, Chamberlain to Carleton, *L. J. C.* I, 231.

8. Vere obtained Portsmouth but not the barony; he became constable of Portsmouth Castle on June 15. *C. S. P. Domestic 1603–1610,* p. 321.

9. Walter Scott, laird of Buccleuch, is best known for his daring rescue of "Kinmont Willie" Armstrong from Carlisle Castle in 1596. Since 1604 he had commanded with distinction a regiment of borderers in the Low Countries under Count Maurice. He was raised to the peerage as Baron Scott of Buccleuch in 1606. John Ramsay, James's favorite, became Viscount Haddington in the same year.

10. Sir Robert Johnson, an officer of the ordinance, on May 3 introduced a bill to prevent purveyors from exceeding the limits of their commissions. Willson, *Bowyer,* p. 144. *Ob.* presumably is the abbreviation for *obolus:* i.e., ½d.

London, May 11, 1606

S. P. 14/21, #22

Sir, I had no sooner written to you the last day but was recalling my letter, having even then received a summons from my lord Norris to meet my cousin Pawlett at Rycote about Saturday next, which, because I cannot answer but by appearance, I must pray you to hold me excused to Sir Henry [Fanshawe] and my lady with assurance that wheresoever I am my heart and good wishes will be with them. I pray you look to the growth of the apricots for I am not in despair of my part, though to tell you true I cannot now brag of much hope. Tomorrow I mean to see in what forwardness the peaches be at Syon and by the way will take my dinner at Cope Castle, where my lady Norris remains as an exile, being at this present strangely and suddenly cast off by her melancholy lord and upon terms of separation.¹ Sir Francis Bacon was married yesterday to his young wench in Maribone Chapel. He was clad from top to toe in purple and hath made himself and his wife such store of fine raiments of cloth of silver and gold that it draws deep into her portion. The dinner was kept at his father-in-law Sir John Packington's lodging over against the Savoy, where his chief guests were the three knights Cope, Hicks, and Beeston; and upon this conceit (as he said himself) that, since he could not have my lord of Salisbury in person, which he wished, he would have him at least in his representative body.² We hear out of France that the king of there hath made as fair an escape of water as ours of fire, having had his coach with the queen, Caesar, Monsieur and the princess of Conti overturned in a ferry betwixt Saint-Germain and Paris; and all, especially the queen, on whose side the coach fell, in danger, but all saved. Sir W. Godolphin is sent to congratulate the escape. There were lately two notable insolencies committed, one in the court at Fontainebleau, where 10 mad *fripons* took so many of the Scotch guards' coats and forcing a Spaniard's lodging as if it were by authority, who was there with his young wife, took them both into the woods and abused her in his sight, for which 4 of them which were taken were fairly broken on the wheel; the other at Paris, where the chevalier du Guet's wife was stabbed in her bed by her own brother, she being great with child and he half drunk, but he was hanged for it when he was sober. There have been two surprises failed in the Low Countries upon Sluys and Wesel, at both which the assailers had great loss; though at Sluys they were in the way of much gain, having won a port which they broke by petards; and if they had been well seconded, which the waters hindered, there had been no recovery. I send you a letter which I met with in Paul's from Mr. Winwood. I made so bold with you to look for my name in it and have borrowed your Venetian proclamation, because you have seen it already and it will serve me for news where I go. In place of it I send you Don Quixote's challenge, which is translated into all languages and sent into the wide world. I have a letter from Mr. Matthew wherein you have commendations and no more news than that we shall not see him in haste. All Cripplegate ward salutes you. The doctor, for his Chaucer's rhyme in his sermon and somewhat else he said in favor of the silenced ministers, is committed to his lodging by the bishop of London and so rests.[3] And thus I rest.

Yours most assured

1. Lord Norris's brooding disposition, which led to his bizarre suicide, came upon him early. His wife was a daughter of Edward de Vere, earl of Oxford, and thus a granddaughter of Lord Burghley.

2. Francis Bacon's young wench was Alice Barnham, whose mother had married Sir John Packington *en secondes noces.* The three knights, Sir Walter Cope, Sir Baptist Hicks, and Sir Hugh Beeston, were all associates of Salisbury's.

3. The silenced ministers were those who had been deprived for refusal to accept the Canons of 1604. The bishop of London, Richard Vaughan, was comparatively restrained in his handling of the Puritan opposition.

London, August 20, 1606
S. P. 14/21, ff. 18–21

Good Mr. Chamberlain, I am so used to the Spanish march in my progresses that I shall not see you so soon again as I promised, for as I was long a-coming to town, so is my stay here longer than I meant, and I doubt my return will be *muy de espacio,* for some friends, whom I found sick by the way, I left in worse state and since I hear they are little amended, and good company, they say, is their best physic. Here I am entertained with the like treaty by my lord of Northumberland as I was at Ascot by my lord Norris, and I am willed to stay a while in town to know his resolution what he will do for me, and somewhat I am promised and do believe will come if it be worth laying hold on; but I doubt it be rather to engage my service than for any good is really meant; and having once so fairly escaped shipwreck I would be loath to embark my fortunes in the same vessel again unless it were upon a good adventure.[1] My uncle Hickling is dead since I saw you,

[85]

which should go amongst my losses, if I may account that lost I never had. Corbet, the Gloucestershire knight betwixt whom and Sir H. Wallop[2] there hath been so much stickling, is lately dead, and the heralds are sent for to his funerals, which shall be performed with solemnity. My lord of Northampton is recovered of his sickness, which was terrible for the time, and it was not looked his age could have withstood such a fever; but his greatest grief was that lying at Greenwich during the whole time of his sickness he was not once visited by the king, whereas my lord of Salisbury, keeping his house but one day here in town for a distemper upon a heat strucken betwixt him and the Spanish ambassador about the late suspected traitors, was not only visited by his grace but kindly comforted with these words, that he was very sensible of his sickness and must have care of his well doing, for if he should once fail there were no more safe hunting for the king of England. The two kings[3] parted on Monday was sevennight as well pleased one with the other as kings commonly are upon interviews. The gifts were great on our king's side and tolerable on the other. *Imprimis* a girdle and hangers with rapier and dagger set with stones, which I heard valued by a goldsmith at 15000. Item, the old cup of state, which was the chief piece of Queen Elizabeth's rich cupboard of £5000 price. Item, a George as rich as could be made in proportion. Item, a saddle embroidered with rich pearl, 4 horses with their furnitures, 2 ambling geldings and 2 nags. To the king of Denmark's 6 counsellors was given 2000 pounds' worth of plate and each of them a chain of 100 and to 22 gentlemen chains of £50 apiece, and £1000 in money amongst the servants, the guard, and sailors in the ship the king went. The king of Denmark gave nothing, as I heard, to the king but made an offer of his second ship in hope to have it requited with the *White Bear,* but that match was broken by my lord of Salisbury, and he had his own given back with thanks. To the king's children he gave presents to the value of £6000 and as much to the king's household, which was divided amongst those only which attended him and came to round sums, the number of them being but small. At the installment at Windsor[4] he gave the heralds but 20 marks, and the whole ceremony was suitable to that liberality, bare and penurious.

They stayed there but one night and the progress thither and back again was hasty but well laid; by Richmond and Oatlands going, and by Hampton Court, Nonesuch, and Sir George Carew's by Croydon as they returned, but the king of Denmark was not observed much to admire anything he saw, though he was curious to see much (as here in town nothing escaped him, neither Paul's, Westminster, nor the exchange) nor was he much transported with our hunting but found fault with it as a sport wherein were more horses killed in jest than the Low Country wars consumed in earnest, and yet was the chase so royal at Theobalds and all things fell out so luckily for the credit of stag hunting that our king said upon news of the small pleasure his brother of Denmark took in it that he knew not what God could do but mortality could show no better. There was one solemn tilting day at which the king of Denmark would needs make one, and in an old black armor without plume or bases or any rest for his staff, played his prizes so well that Ogerio [5] himself never did better. At a match betwixt our king and him in running at the ring it was his good hap never almost to miss it, and ours had the ill luck scarce ever to come near it, which put him into no small impatiences. The feasting was plentiful but not riotous at court, but at the ships they played the seamen for good fellowship. First off Chatham, where 22 of the king's ships were set out in their best equipage and 2, especially the *Elisabeth Jonas* and the *Bear,* trimmed up to feast in, betwixt which there was a large railed bridge built upon masts and in the midst, betwixt both, butteries and kitchens built upon lighters and flat boats. All things there were performed with that order and sumptuousness that the king of Denmark confessed he could not have believed such a thing could have been done unless he had seen it. At his ships, where was the last farewell, what was wanting in meat and other ceremony was helped out in drink and gunshot; for at every health, of which there was twenty, the ship the kings were in made 9 shot, and every one of the other (there being 8 in all) 3, and the two blockhouses at Gravesend, where the fleet lay, each of them six (at which I must tell you by the way our king was little pleased, and took such order at his own ships not to be annoyed with smell of powder), but good store of healths made

[87]

him so hearty that he bid them at last shoot and spare not and very resolutely commanded the trumpets to sound him a point of war. Sir Francis Vere of all the company had the honor to be the soundest drunk; and your good friend Sir Hugh Beeston, who came in his company, was as well wet both without and within but of another liquor: for, standing on the edge of a small boat with Sir John Lucen to get up into the ship, they toppled it over and went both down together to the bottom of the water, to search, belike, whether there was no gunpowder treason practicing against the two kings. Sir John Lucen was first ketched up and being pulled by the breeches, which were but taffeta and old linings, had them clean torn off, and the first things which appeared (as Ned Wymark relates, from whom you have this story with especial recommendation) was his cue and his cullions, which as the Danes confessed could be no discredit to Kent or Christendom. Old Hugh, all this while, had his head under the water and, like a crafty knave (as saith mine author), held his breath and having hold with one of his hands on the edge of a boat was spied by a waterman when he was giving over himself and all else had given him for gone. In this interim Sir Francis Darcy with 2 other Darcies in his company had his boat split with the wind of a piece and down went they to look [for] Sir Hugh, but came up again before him. The good knight by this accident hath changed his name and is called about this town Sir Water Beeston, and because Damon shall suffer somewhat with Pythias in his fortunes, though it be but in the name, yet he must be content that he is styled Sir Hugh Cope. I met this latter as I came into the town, with Sir Edward Michelborne plotting and devising how to rob the king of Spain of his Indies.[6] Here is speech of some preferment towards him, as if in all haste he should be vice-chamberlain to the queen, Sir George Carew being to be made president of Wales in place of my lord Zouche, who, for his indisposition (as they say), hath a disposition to give it over.[7] Upon fear of some new revolts in Ireland here is a project to send a president and council to Ulster as is in Munster, which, coming to Tyrone's ear, he hath written to the king rather to banish him that realm than to subject him to any such (as he terms it) tyrannical government.[8] The king hath been marvelously well pleased of late at the news of a great point he hath gained in the Parliament at Scotland, where all the acts which were made in former Parliaments in favor of the Presbytery are generally revoked; which piece of service is said to be done by my lord of Dunbar's golden eloquence but thought rather by those who understand more to be effected by the lord of Fyvie, who made himself head of that party to play them this *faux* bound.[9] We hear out of France the duchess of Mantua is come thither and received with as much and more solemnity than the king of Denmark was with us. The cause of her coming is her passage into Lorraine, there to marry one of her daughters to the duke of Bar, as in her return she shall do the other to one of the princes of Savoy, who is sent into Spain, and the opinion is she shall do a Christian deed by the way and make the dauphin *Christianus,* lest he stay till he be *Christianissimus.* The war betwixt the Pope and the Venetians is still threatened and thus far like to go forward that the king of Spain hath offered the Pope his assistance with his person and all his power. The Romans give a million to the charge of the war, the duke of Urbino doth furnish 2000 foot paid, and he of Savoy 3000 foot and 600 horse, with his own person for general of the army. The Venetians continue still peremptory but make no great preparatives. I send you the copy of a pasquil upon this occasion, with the king of Spain's letter.[10] I hear nothing out of the Low Countries, which makes me think there is no great matter done. The three armies, both offensive and defensive, do front one another in Friesland, at Bergen, and at Sluys, but those in Freisland make the greatest head. There is much complaint of the hard usage of soldiers on both sides. To the States many French are lately gone and not by connivance as they were wont but allowed by passport. Our ambassador in Spain hath lately sent over a very grievous complaint of many hard usages but especially of neglect of his person, being suffered to dance attendance three hours sometimes at the duke of Lerma's [11] door when in 3 weeks he cannot obtain an audience, and to the king's presence he cannot be admitted once sometimes in 3 months. The Spanish ambassador here hath lately dealt with the [lords of the council] and disputed the matter very earnestly either to have some proceeding against Ball (who is delivered out of the Tower) or some solemn act and publication of his innocency.[12] My lord Montague crept out of the Tower two days since to his father-in-law's house upon composition of £200 with the lieutenant [of the Tower] which is all his fine and ransom. There is warrant for the remove of Mordaunt and Stourton to the Fleet, but it is stayed till extents be out upon their lands for their fines, which comes likewise upon my lord of Northumberland, but his liberty is not like so soon to follow.[13] The king of Denmark was dealt with to speak to the king about him, as likewise about my lord Grey and Sir Walter Raleigh, but his answer was he had promised the king to be no man's solicitor and because he would do no good; it is somewhat ill-taken at his hands that he did some hurt, which was to complain since his departure by a letter to the queen upon my lady of Nottingham for a letter of defiance she sent after him upon a scorn or disgrace she conceived to be offered her husband in the king's ship at the last feast which touched her in honor. The matter was no more than that our king, asking what o'clock it was and desirous to be gone, my lord admiral as willing to hasten him answered four; the king of Denmark seeking all means to stay them said it was but two and for doubt of not being understood made a sign with his two fingers to my lord admiral, which the good man took no worse than it seemed to be meant, but she being now with child and jealous of her credit would not so put it up, but thought to revenge herself with a railing letter, for which she is banished both the king's and the prince's courts.[14] My lady of Bedford [15] had the grace to be sent for one day to the court; and she had not the grace but to come, where she was openly laughed at by the queen as she began to dance, and all she said to her (not having seen her since her discourting) was that her brother of Denmark was as handsome a man as the duke of Holstein. The archbishop of York was installed at Lambeth on Monday last, who complains much of my lord treasurer for hard measure showed him in the payment of his first fruits and of waste and spoil which hath been made in his archbishopric during the vacancy, besides £500 a year loss he hath by the exchange.[16] Dr. James, the new bishop of Durham, contents himself as little, having Durham House taken from him and given to the duke of Lennox. Newton, the prince's schoolmaster, succeeds him in the deanery.[17] There were three Latin sermons whilst the king of Denmark was here, whereof the first was at Theobalds by Dr. Playford, who played the reading clerk and more than half shamed himself; the second was on the day of the king's delivery by the bishop of Chichester, who in all men's opinions exceeded himself at any other time; the last at Rochester by Dr. Parry who stepped so far out of divinity into philosophy treating of *anima separata* and was so obscure in it that he lost himself in the separation.[18] I came on Sunday to town to the sermon at Paul's Cross, where the preacher fell very foul upon the mayor and aldermen, noting some of them in particular by way of rebuke of the sins of the city. Our parson here hath a prebendary of Windsor newly added to his late good fortunes. The sickness is hot in our parish but yet far enough from our doors. And now you may bid me welcome home, having walked you weary I am sure, as I have done myself. But you are at good leisure and so am I and therefore if I had anything to add further would rather write still and so entertain myself than walk the empty and solitary streets, which are at a dead low ebb after a spring tide, and Bartholomew Fair [19] is like to be little better than a market. I met with Will Fanshawe here in town, by whom I have sent your commendations to Ware Park, where your friends are all well. My mother removes this week to my brother Doctor's, my sister Williams to Barnet and then you know who keeps house here who cannot be persuaded to change garrison. I must not forget their commendations to you nor Tobie Matthew's, from whom I met with a letter very luckily the first day I came hither; and so I commit you to God's protection.

Yours most assured

1. This is a reference to Carleton's narrow escape from serious difficulty with the government in the aftermath of the Gunpowder Plot, because of his association with Northumberland. Carleton had written Northumberland on August 14 asking for a job (*C. S. P. Domestic 1603–1610,* p. 329); so he was either having second thoughts or being disingenuous.

2. Sir Henry Wallop was a good friend of Chamberlain's and a connection of Carleton's: his wife was the stepdaughter of Carleton's cousin, Sir Rowland Lytton. Wallop's daughter Winifred is often referred to by Chamberlain as his "wife." Wallop's wife was a Corbet; the reference is doubtless to a family dispute over property.

3. Christian IV of Denmark had been visiting England, a visit steeped in an aura of alcohol. He had been in England about a month.

4. Christian formally took his place as a knight of the Garter.

5. This is probably a reference to the hero of the medieval French romance, *Ogier le Danois*.

6. Sir Edward Michelborne had just returned from his famous plundering voyage in the Indies, which did so much damage to the local reputation of the East India Company.

7. This rumor turned out to be false. Edward, Lord Zouche, a prominent official who held many different offices during his career, remained president of the council of Wales until 1615. Sir George Carew was ambassador in France.

8. Tyrone was becoming more and more discontented at the government's effort to break the territorial influence of the Irish aristocracy by bringing the lesser landholders into direct dependence on the crown. The government suspected that he was planning a new rebellion; his flight in 1607 upon receipt of a summons to London would suggest that the suspicions were justified.

9. Carleton was anticipating a bit; this Parliament did not overturn presbyteries directly, but it did accept James's "supreme authority, princely power, royal prerogative, and privilege of his crown over all estates, persons and causes whatsoever," and it repealed the Act of 1587, which annexed the temporalities of episcopal benefices to the crown. Sir George Home of Spott, earl of Dunbar, was lord treasurer of Scotland and until his death in 1611 the chief of those instruments which enabled James to govern Scotland with his pen. After his death Alexander Seton, Lord Fyvie, the chancellor, succeeded to his influence.

10. Pope Paul V had laid Venice under interdict in April 1606, climaxing a long series of disputes between the papacy and the Republic. James's government encouraged Venice to resist the papal demands. The quarrel was eventually mediated by France.

11. Francisco de Sandoval y Rojas, duke of Lerma, was Philip III's favorite, the dominant figure in the Spanish government.

12. John Ball, an Irishman, and a servant of the Spanish ambassador, was accused of a plot against the king's life. July 19, 1606, Salisbury to Winwood, Sawyer, *Memorials* II, 246–47.

13. Anthony Brown, Viscount Montague, Henry, Lord Mordaunt, Edward,

Lord Stourton, and Northumberland were all in prison on account of their alleged complicity in the Gunpowder Plot.

14. The lord admiral, Charles Howard, earl of Nottingham, the commander of the fleet which had conquered the Armada, was seventy years old and had recently married, as his second wife, Elizabeth Stewart, the granddaughter of the regent Moray, who was more than forty years younger than her husband. Hence her sensitivity to Christian's gesture.

15. Lucy, wife of Edward Russell, third earl of Bedford. She is best known as a patroness of poets, including John Donne.

16. The new archbishop was Tobie Matthew, translated from the richer bishopric of Durham. His son, Carleton's friend, embarrassed his father in this year by becoming a Catholic convert.

17. Sir Adam Newton was tutor to Prince Henry and Prince Charles successively, and, among other things, translated the king's attack on the theologian Conrad Vorstius into Latin.

18. "Dr. Playford" was probably Thomas Playfere, one of the king's chaplains. Lancelot Andrewes was bishop of Chichester. Henry Parry was the future bishop of Gloucester and Worcester.

19. Bartholomew Fair was held annually in August, around Saint Bartholomew's Day, in West Smithfield.

Cripplegate, December 18, 1606

S. P. 14/24, #23

Good Mr. Chamberlain, I was in hope the end of the Parliament would have afforded somewhat worth your knowledge, which made me defer writing till this present, but we are broken up this day on a sudden, referring the report of all that is yet done till the next meeting, which is appointed the 10th of February, and meantime we have liberty to bethink ourselves what to allow or disprove of such things as have been agreed on by the committees at the conferences, which have been many and long and sometimes morning as well as afternoon, and little or nothing done in the House, only some idle fellows, having speeches in store, picked small quarrels to disburden themselves of them, as Sir H[enry] Poole for one, who slipped out of a private bill for the naturalizing of a French doctor into a large discourse of the union, wherein he styled the act done by the commissioners with the title of the Blessed Instrument. Sir W[illiam] Morrice pressed hotly upon the motion to have the king's title of Great Britain confirmed by act of Parliament, but he was answered by one James, who concluded a long declamation with this description of the Britons, that they were first an idolatrous nation and worshippers of devils. In the beginning of Christianity they were thrust out into the mountains, where they lived long like thieves and robbers and are to this day the most base, pesantly perfidious people of the world. Mr. Hare [1] came soon after with a bitter word against our neighbors, calling them the beggarly Scots, for which he is in danger to be shrewdly hunted; and thus you may see what extravagancies we have had both pro and contra. The Lords at the beginning of our conferences were very mild but ended, like the month of March, in storm and tempest, which lighted heavily on the city of London as not thought a place of that moment as that the consideration of the subsistence of it should be put *in equilibrio* of the due regard we ought to have of the general safety purchased to the kingdom by this happy union, which came out upon occasion of our standing much upon the honor of our trade, wherein honest Nick Fuller was somewhat too forward, saying that the Scots in other countries were more like peddlers than merchants, for which he was shrewdly chidden; and the merchants, having upon commandment set down in writing their reasons against community of trade with the Scots, for concluding with a petition that all might remain as it did without further uniting, which in their affairs could breed nothing but confusion, were roundly shaken up by my lord chancellor, wherein they hold their pains which they took upon commandment ill repaid. There were given us at the two last conferences certain mementos against we meet next, as one that perforce we must yield to many conditions though we foresee we shall be losers, then that there is nothing required in the instrument of the union which the king cannot do of himself, and lastly that Scots in state as they are are no aliens. The matter of escuage, which you left so hot in dispute, was concluded by the chief justices in one word, that, though the service ceaseth, the king's profit must continue.[2] And thus have you all I can readily bethink myself of, referring you to Sir Rowland Lytton for more ample relation, who hath stayed it out to the last and goeth down tomorrow. When you meet, forget not to call for a story of Augustus and Cinna which is worth your hearing. I have done nothing in my private affairs since you went, which will find me work here in town now you have all leave to play; so as I doubt I shall not stir from hence all this Christmas. Tomorrow I go to the lords to get leave to speak with my lord in the Tower,[3] which the lieutenant hath refused me. There is no speech of any to fetch home Mr. Winwood, but of him you were told of when he went;[4] and he, upon the same hope belike, hath of late put on *mascara de grave* and banished all the good wits from his house to have the greater freedom for his studies, which he employs, as I hear, in conning of French and gathering up old shreds and remnants of negotiations to suit himself for the purpose; notwithstanding all these preparatives I would wish no more fortune that way than he is like to fail of. You shall hear from me again shortly and meantime wishing you a mery Christmas with my due remembrance to Sir Henry [Fanshawe] and my lady I commit you to God's protection.

Yours most assured

From Cripplegate, where all rest in state as you left us, and send you many commendations. My brother is gone through with Sir Owen Oglethorpe for the whole purchase of Hocum, for which he pays £2700.

1. John Hare, who had previously behaved so intemperately over purveyance that the Speaker of the House labelled him an "unconsiderate firebrand." *C. S. P. Domestic 1603–1610*, p. 289.

2. Escuage was the obligation of a feudal vassal to military service. The question arose in connection with the debate over the union with Scotland; it was argued in Parliament that such tenures should now cease, *"cessante causa, cessat effectus.* Shewing how escuage was founded upon the service to the king in Scotland and Wales as against enimyes, which now they noe more be . . ."

Willson, *Dowyer*, p. 201. This was, in effect, an attack on the system of wardship.

3. The earl of Northumberland, who had been condemned to life imprisonment after the Gunpowder Plot. He was released in 1621.

4. Rumors of reshuffles in diplomatic appointments were frequent in this period and were eagerly seized upon by people who, like Carleton, were hopeful of getting one, or, if possessing one, hoped for a better.

London, August 27, 1607

S. P. 14/28, #37

Sir, I was in haste when I wrote last, and I perceive by yours, which I found here last night at my lodging, that you were not half well satisfied with so bare a narration of the stay of our journey.[1] To acquaint you with all particulars were a discourse *de trop longue haleine* to be run over in a letter; and yet for your better understanding you shall know that the tide being turned upon my coming up for going with the commissioners and our purpose to go by the way of Calais made known to my lord of Salisbury, a passport was accordingly sent us signed by the lords of the council and mentioning the especial affairs of Sir Walter Cope knight, gentleman of his Majesty's privy chamber, together with Mr. D. C. and Mr. John Pory;[2] Sir Hugh Beeston (you must understand) had drawn his stake out of the game or rather was shut out for a wrangler. The provisions were all in readiness, my lady Cope's jumbles and biscuit-bread ready baked; besides she had well passed over her crying and Betty had new put up her pipes; Mr. Pory had provided his double case for one mould, besides jerkin, hose, cloak, hood, and bases all of a piece, and a new male and malegirths for his own wearing, a new pair of tables besides his old ones, out of which he had not yet scoured his Parliament notes and had taken a solemn leave of the prince [Henry], lords and ladies, and all the ambassadors and charged himself with large packets of letters as well for France as the Low Countries. I for my part had the grace not to be at one penny cost nor

[96]

to charge myself with any commissions, which I must ascribe rather to my good fortune than any special foresight, for I misdoubted nothing less than the stay of our journey. Monday in the afternoon was the time of our departure and our rendezvous appointed at the Strand, where accordingly we met in all equipage and, looking still for the *boute-selle,* at last out came a letter from my lord of Salisbury mentioning many important considerations for the stay of the journey, as hasty posting to and fro being now so straitened in time, a winter passage by sea at our return, and danger of losing more by absence than were like to be gained by this short experience. These careful respects were accompanied with a kind invitation to come in all haste to Salisbury and to make an end with his old friends of a merry progress. The first part of this letter took place, in which master was willingly overmastered, but for the latter (though he was once resolved to post thither in all diligence) he better bethought himself and, being somewhat out of countenance with himself for playing the mock journey, sent his mind to my lord of Salisbury in paper, which could not blush, and in these very words. "Long have I lived and much have I longed for a general peace when with Diogenes I might creep out of my tub and view the face of the world, and now Janus' temple being shut, which hath not been this 27 year before, etc." I have sent you a pattern by which you may guess at the whole piece, but whether he be as lucky at prose as at rhyme judge you. I hope you will not doubt but that this was a child of his own mother wit. He now stays till the court come to Windsor, and for my comfort he tells me that he will take care my lord of Salisbury shall repair by some good benefit the displeasure he hath done us by the stay of our journey. I am like to stay in these parts till I see how mindful he will be of his promise, and then if you remove not in the meantime I will not fail to see you at Ascot. Sir Henry Fanshawe I hear is much troubled with a cold and is fallen again in love with tobacco. Ned Wymark goeth this day towards Sir Anthony Mildmay's.[3] He hath held me in hand he would rid my hands of my horses, and we were at a price; but he hath now bestowed more money and bejaded himself in Smithfield. Tobie Matthew hath had leave to go as often as he will with his keeper to Sir Francis Bacon and is put in good hope of further liberty. Nick Fuller hath been pitifully trounced by the High Commission and cannot yet wind himself out of the briars, but the more he struggles the more he is entangled.[4] Many, and most of our Puritan Parliament men, are put out of the commission of the peace, as Sir Francis Barrington, Sir Jerome Horsey, Dunkum and others; and if Sir Anthony Cope hold in he hath good luck, for he was the foreman in my lord chancellor's list to be put out. There are many unruly borderers confined in the same manner as Sir Henry Widdrington[5] and all to several places, amongst others Lancelot Carleton, who was a good freebooter in the queen's time but an honest man ever since. Here are commissions going out into the several counties to enquire of enclosure,[6] and the men employed are most lawyers and taken out of Kent, Surrey, Sussex, and such places as are least interested in that business. From foreign parts I know not whether there be any news or not, but here comes little without Cripplegate and I go little into the town for fear of the sickness, which was thought by the bells the last week would have been risen, but by the bills the number is lessened. You have many commendations from all this company, and I pray you do mine in all hearty manner to Sir Michael [Dormer] and my lady, and so I commit you to God's protection.

Yours most assured,

1. This was a trip to France and the Low Countries, projected by Cope, Beeston, John Pory, and Carleton. Carleton was clearly hoping that some sort of employment might result from it. Salisbury may have changed his mind about permitting the journey because Cope at the last moment changed his plans; instead of going to the United Provinces with the commissioners (one of whom was Winwood) appointed to participate in the Spanish-Dutch peace negotiations, Cope decided to go first to Brussels, August 15, 1607, Levinus Munck to Salisbury, *Salisbury Mss.* XIX (1607), p. 218.

2. John Pory was a traveller and geographer, a former assistant of Richard Hakluyt's. He went on the journey anyway. He was an acquaintance of Carleton's, the "D.C." referred to in the letter, and subsequently tried to interest him in a scheme to introduce the weaving of silk-loom stockings into

England. (*C. S. P. Domestic 1611–18,* p. 54.) Chamberlain did not think much of him. While Carleton was in Venice he wrote, "You had not need meet with many such moths as Master Pory, who must have both meat and money, for drink he will find out for himself if it be above ground or no deeper than the cellar." *L. J. C.* I, 472.

3. Chamberlain commented at the time of Mildmay's death in 1617 that "Ned Wimarke for all the auncient acquaintance between them hath not so much as a rush-ring for a remembrance." *L. J. C.* II, 99.

4. Nicholas Fuller was a barrister, an M. P., and a Puritan. He was in the process of defending two clients who had been imprisoned for refusing to take the oath to answer all questions truthfully before the court of High Commission. Fuller's argument that the High Commission had no right to fine or imprison was put in so zealous a way that he was himself imprisoned. It was Fuller's case which led to the famous confrontation between Archbishop Bancroft and Sir Edward Coke before King James on the nature of the law. For a good brief account see Gardiner, *History,* II, 36–42.

5. For Sir Henry Widdrington see below, letter of September 16, 1607, n. 3.

6. The spring of 1607 witnessed several riots against enclosure, especially in Northamptonshire. On June 28 James issued a proclamation ordering an inquiry by the judges into the abuses of enclosures. Steele, *Proclamations* I, 121.

London, September 16, 1607

S. P. 14/29, #51

Good Mr. Chamberlain, I am sure you have looked for your friends or their letters before this time, but I was ever as indifferently betwixt writing and going as your Montaigne's man was *entre le jambon et la bouteille,*[1] so as I could resolve to do neither, and now, for the one, for many good causes I am settled here for a time; for the other I have little to supply me, the town being empty and no news stirring. The king in his crossing from Windsor to Waltham touched at Whitehall for no greater business than to see his new building,[2] which, when he came into it, he could scarce see by reason of certain pillars which are set up before the windows, and he is nothing pleased with his lord architect for that device. He was likewise with the archbishop at Lambeth to hearten him in his conflict with Nick Fuller, who had procured an inhibition from the judges to the High Commission to proceed no further in that cause; but upon better advice they have sent (as I hear) a retractation of their inhibition, and poor Nick is nicked as before. Sir Herbert Crofts and Sir Roger Owen are put out of the commission of the Council of Wales,[3] which was a matter of much consultation at the council table and went not so current but had some contradiction, though at last it was so determined. Sir Henry Widdrington's brother was sent for out of the north (at such time as the rest were confined) and committed to the Fleet.[4] His quarter was first appointed at Saint Albans, but upon consideration of his recusancy he was more straitened than his fellows. They all complain of hard measure, not so much for being banished their countries and forced to live elsewhere as for penury and want, their own means being sufficient to maintain them amongst their own provisions, where things were at a good rate, but the small rents they make of their livings coming far short of other country-reckonings. Young Sir Thomas Sherley is committed to the Tower, but if you ask me why, I can tell you no more than my sister Williams tells me, for being turned Turk.[5] There was a French captain, one Fierebras, taken the last week at the French ordinary by two which prosecuted him out of France; he hath been long since and in many places hanged in effigy for notable murders and villainies committed by him, but now the original is like to follow the copy. There was help given by our officers here for his ketching and conveying over, which shews that our amity with France as well as our union with Scotland will hang well together. The Parliament is ended in Scotland; but what they have concluded I hear not, only in general that they are no more fond of the union than we here; yet they please the king better than we by their quick dispatch. Our Parliament will be put off (as I hear) till Candlemas, and there is speech of putting off the term. I send you the bill of last week's sickness. There is better hope this week, but it is not good to prognosticate, for since I have been here both our hopes and fears have been still deceived. We are here in good health, I thank God, but a full family, my cousin Elms and his wife with one of his daughters being come up with my brother Williams, all the little children here, and the plague as near as the little lane which joins to the tavern; but we think to withstand it by multitude. Sir William Stone of Cheapside died on Monday last at his house in Leighton of a fever coming little short of the plague; he took the infection of a quart of sack which he drunk of to the king's health the week before. We hear nothing from the States and less than nothing out of France, from whence here is come the duke of Luxembourg's son with two coachfuls of *lolleroes,* who make a great bustle in this poor empty town. I pray you let me hear how your Jesse lie after your remove from Ascot. At Ware Park I shall be ready to meet you. Meantime with a general salutation from us all here and mine more particularly to Sir Michael [Dormer], my lady, and yourself I commit you to God's protection.

Yours most assured

You may look I should write you some news from Kensington.[6] The *monts* and *merveilles* which were promised do turn into mole-hills of counsel and advice, to patience and long suffering. But I have learnt the *picaro*'s cry, *da me dineros y no consejo,* else I shall hardly hold myself well paid.

1. "If we were placed between the bottle and the ham," wrote Montaigne, "with an equal desire to eat and drink, there would doubtless be no help for it, but we must die of thirst and hunger." E. J. Trechmann, trans., *The Essays of Montaigne* (London, 1935) II, 60.

2. This was the banqueting hall, which James ordered built in 1606. It was destroyed by fire in 1619, and James thought of rebuilding the whole palace. All that was done was to rebuild the banqueting hall itself; the result, designed by Inigo Jones and embellished by its magnificent Rubens ceiling, still stands. The "lord architect" mentioned here was the surveyor of works, Simon Basil. It is possible that Jones had a hand in it too. See John Charlton, *The Banqueting House, Whitehall* (London, 1964), pp. 15–16.

3. For what one surmises were very different reasons. Croft had Catholic leanings and ultimately retired to Douai. Owen was a member of the opposition in Parliament.

4. The Widdringtons (also spelled Withrington and Woodrington) are a good example of the sort of border family which James's government was

anxious to suppress. Sir Henry "has in all times past had the following of . . . the most notable thieves and broken men in the Border"; his wife was a Catholic and his brother "the most dangerous recusant in that county [Northumberland]." See *Salisbury Mss.* XIX (1607), pp. 4, 487.

5. Sir Thomas Sherley was the brother of Sir Anthony (see above, letter of November 10/20, 1605, n. 8). He had served in the Low Countries, and in the 1590s turned privateer to help get himself and his father out of debt. He had recently spent two years as a prisoner of the Turks; the offence for which he was imprisoned, however, was not for having turned Turk, but rather for interference in the operations of the Levant Company.

6. Sir Walter Cope built a house there in 1606–1607, called Cope Castle.

Huntercombe, July 14, 1608

S. P. 14/35, #17

Sir, though I am prevented by Mr. Gent, who hath sent you the act, questions, and Oxford news, yet I cannot forbear my relation likewise, because you may be the better informed of our university proceedings, which were chiefly memorable at this time for a deluge of doctors, there being 21 of all professions, and a great concourse of strangers, but none almost of note or appearance. I had the good fortune to meet with Sir John Bennet,[1] with whom I spent the small time that I was there, which was Monday and Tuesday. Sir William Paddy[2] was no small grace to the town, who made a solemn entry in a coach with four white mares and six men in liveries well mounted. The Saturday exercise was not much spoken of; only the music lecture, which was read in the morning by one Shepherd, sounded long after, who took upon him a Cambridge quarrel, first remembering a ballet that was made there in disgrace of the king's entertainment at Oxford, and then answering one Cecil the proctor of Cambridge, who this last commencement inveighed against a book set out by the orator of Oxford touching the exercise that was there performed before the king, and for the first part he said it was neither *cantus,* nor *cantio, cantilula,* not *cantilena,* nor any thing in Latin but, *Anglice,* a ballet and those that made it might properly be called *balatrones*. The ditty he turned into Latin *Isti vani Oppidani qui dicuntur Aldermani*; the tune he put to it was *T'o the Parliament the Queen is gone,* and because being in a narrow pew he said it was not *locus ad agendum amplissimus,* he came out into the school and there played it upon a viol, but (said he) since now *sicelides musae* do *paulo majora canere* he would deal with Cecil, and reciting all the invectives made by Tully in his oration against Cecillium [3] he said they were prophecies of this man and went on with more than an hour's speech, all in this mad merry tune, and had great audience as well of Cambridge men as others. In the Monday exercise there were likewise many invectives, as the philosophers in the question *an terra sit naturae magneticae,* against Dr. Gilbert and all his secretaries, which they called Gilbertinos, wherein *il y va de votre* interest,[4] the physicians against the civilians, and the civilians against poor women. The divines descanted one upon another, as Dr. Thornton [5] had his name divided into *Spina* and could not *perfecte implere legem* when *dolium* might be so easily both filled and emptied, and many such young conceits not so well befitting their gravities and professions. At supper in Christchurch it was my hap to light in a mess with Dr. White, Dr. Perin, and Sir Edward Ratliff, whose wits and fooleries did so well encounter that it made good amends for our long sitting up, which was fully past midnight before we rose from the table. I am now here again at good leisure, as by my scribbling unto you you may well conjecture, and purpose to spend a month if not more betwixt this place, the Grange, and Ascot. Sir Michael [Donmer] and my lady go on Saturday next to Hampton Poyle [near Oxford], and I defer my going to them till their return from thence because I would not so soon part from them. Sir Henry Savile [6] and my lady come about a fortnight hence to Oxford, there to stay for a month. My lord Norris was gone to the [town of] Bath before I came into this country and doth there purpose to stay as yet five weeks. Sir Michael Dormer doth threaten a journey to go see him and I have half passed a promise to accompany him, which I shall the better perform with my wife's leave if you come into the country in good time, that you may moderate matters between such disputants as I doubt the women will prove at Ascot about their little faiths. We persuade ourselves you will hasten your coming for our sakes; as I assure you it is for yours that we do the more linger, in hope to see you before we return, and thus with all kind remembrances to yourself and the two good societies of Kneb-worth and Ware Park I commit you to God's protection.

Yours most assuredly

1. Sir John Bennet, a civil lawyer who was a judge of the prerogative court of Canterbury and chancellor to Queen Anne, was well thought of at Oxford. He was ultimately impeached for maladministration of the estates of intestates and fined £20,000.
   2. For Sir William Paddy see below, letter of October 4, 1609.
   3. This was the famous *De divinatione,* a cutting attack on Q. Caecillius Niger, a creature of Verres, the awful governor of Sicily.
   4. Chamberlain was a close friend of William Gilbert's and shared his house for a time in the 1590s. Hence he would be interested in this controversy.
   5. Possibly Thomas Thornton, canon of Christ Church.
   6. Carleton's father-in-law.

Eton, September 20, 1608
S. P. 14/36, #23

Good Mr. Chamberlain, you will marvel much at my peregrina-tions since I parted from Ascot, for no sooner I came to the Priory but finding myself within a day's journey of the Bath, thither I went, and from thence to Bristol; since, have I been at London and Hanworth and am now retired to my winter garrison here at Eton, from whence I am not like to stir much. I thought the meeting my lord Norris at his coming to Rycote would have drawn me again into that country, but my seeing him at the Bath did sufficiently discharge that complement. I told him of Sir Michael's [1] purpose to have seen him there or at leastwise to have fetched him home, which, if leisure serve and no great impedi-ments, were a journey well bestowed; for in very truth I know none at this present to whom that lord stands better affected, whereof whilst I was there he made many demonstrations and one amongst others to very good purpose, for Judge Williams [2] being with him he fell in talk of the next sheriff that should be and the judge named Sir Michael as a man already set down and a place affected of Sir Michael himself, in which my lord assured him of the contrary and said enough that upon any signification of Sir Michael's desire to the judge he may, if he will, be excused, so as the matter as it seems rests in his own hands, and thus much I pray you inform him of, that he may make use of it as he please. I found my sister Williams well at London and mistress alone, as busy as a bee (I would you should know it) about fending and proving with the casters of the town ditch, who are now at work in her quarters, and (forsooth), being advised by her learned counsel the marshall, in an instant up went all her woodwork and she laid her garden open towards the ditch, in opinion that the city would build it up again and more substantially, but the fear is she must make it as it was before or have all the dirt flung into her garden. I stayed there but one night and left the town the sooner for this dirty business; my good fortune was in this short time there to meet all my court friends and principally to have a sight and some speech with my lord treasurer,[3] which was enough to live upon a good while after; when I hear of your return (which I may if you please by this bearer) I will waylay you at Sir William Borlase's and you shall have a large account of my courtship. I was at Swallowfield [4] *cum impedimentis,* where you were often and kindly remembered; the master of that house is not a little perplexed in that the ill carriage of a matter you wot of, *sine intentione,* hath put all out of square betwixt that house and Billingbear: the gentlewoman that was in speech that way is to be married to Sir Richard Brooke.[5] The king was there lately and solemnly entertained, but was not so busy with the young wenches as the time before, having his head much troubled about an answer of his book, which is lately come over and done, as is thought, the most part by Parsons, though some of it by others, as may be seen by the difference of the style.[6] The earl of Dunbar is re-

[105]

turned out of Scotland with a new legion of Scots worse than the former. Sir William Godolphin hath been lately there employed by the king to survey the mines,[7] of which he speaks so great wonders and gives the country such large commendations that we may well know what to believe of both. The treaty of peace in the Low Countries is broken off, and the breach of· it signed in a solemn instrument with more than a hundred hands of the States, but there is a new proposal of truce, which is well entertained.[8] The Parliament is put off till February next in regard of the sickness, which doth still increase though there be very good order taken, more than usual. Sir Thomas Lowe hath buried one of his daughters of it, and Sir Thomas Smith was in great danger to have lost his young son, not of the sickness, but of a sudden convulsion that took all his body. Now all the news I have for you is that Captain Whitlock in this miserable time *morari inter homines desist,* who is so lamented by all bon [*sic*] companions as if the world had not been worthy of him: his death was sudden, as were all the actions of his life, and as he lived amongst lords so was he buried in a vault amongst my lord of Sussex's ancestors, at whose house he died. You will now have somewhat to do to say enough to Sir Michael and my lady in my behalf and my wife's for our long, good entertainment, which we can pay only with hearty thanks for want of better acknowledgment; and so with our due remembrance to them and kind commendations to yourself and Mr. Gent, if he be with you, I commit you to God.

Yours most assuredly

1. Dormer. Chamberlain was his guest at Ascot.
2. Sir David Williams, justice of the King's Bench, who made a fortune as a lawyer.
3. Salisbury, who succeeded to the office on the death of the earl of Dorset earlier in the year.
4. Swallowfield was the home of Chamberlain's good friend Samuel Backhouse. Sir William Borlase was another of his friends.
5. The "gentlewoman" was Catherine Neville, daughter of the diplomatist Sir Henry Neville, who lived at Billingbear.
6. The book in question was the *Apology,* written to defend the oath of

allegiance imposed on Catholics in the wake of the Gunpowder Plot. Robert Parsons (or Persons), the Jesuit, was a particular *bête noire* of James's.

7. The silver mines at Milderstone, near Linlithgow, of which high hopes were entertained. Lythe, *Economy,* pp. 55–56. Sir William Godolphin was receiver-general of Devon and Cornwall.

8. In July the Spanish government had decided against a permanent peace and had declared for a truce of some years instead. July 5/15, 1608, Philip III to Archduke Albert, in M. Lonchay, J. Cuvelier, and J. Lefèvre, eds., *Correspondence de la cour d'Espagne sur les affaires des Pays-Bas au XVIIe siècle,* I (Brussels, 1923), 284–86.

Eton, December 11, 1608

S. P. 14/38, #22

Good Mr. Chamberlain, you do with that true affection embrace my poor affairs that I perceive both the prosecuting and success of them turn more to your trouble than I could wish. An old tired jade will not mend his pace for any spurring; and if you think a lock of hay will draw him faster forward I will not spare to try that skill, though it must be of a short crop, you know, and very fine for such choice creatures, and therefore I must take time for provision.[1] At this time I am too dull for such a purpose, having been these two days together plodding with my father Savile amongst his Greek letters, and in time I may grow serviceable to a printer; but I am not like to stick by the occupation, being growing as you hear (though it was long before I could well believe it) towards the world and therefore must think of setting up for myself in another trade. If it please God to make my wife a mother she purposeth to make herself a nurse, to which she is as well led by my lady Smith's example as her own desire, and therefore I am thinking of going to that the sooner which I must needs come to at last, which is to housekeeping; and to this purpose do make all the enquiry I can after a house in Westminster, which place is in many respects the fittest for me, and if you hear of any within my compass of £30 a year rent and such a one as you shall like I pray you bespeak it. Mr. Clarentius[2] can tell you if there be any in the college and hath good intelligence in the town, and by our Lady Day next, which is the time of my remove from hence, I would fain be provided. In hope hereof my *spòsa novella,* with her mother, is not a little busied to furnish herself with *masserizia,* and a New Year's gift I must provide for the lady[3] to win more favor. I have sent you by this bearer a Bible in folio unbound which I had at Norton's when I came last from London. I would desire you to get it changed for one of ruled paper in the same volume, allowing what he shall demand for exchange, and to get it bound at the place in Fetter Lane where you were with me when my Spanish books were made up for my lord of Salisbury. I would bestow a mark or 15 shillings on the binding besides the ruling; you are used to commissions from your friends and therefore I make as bold with you as others, and one thing more: if you can put out £100 for me which lies in the deck [*sic*] at my sister Williams, you will do me a pleasure.[4] The money I left with my uncle Carew I hear is gone, but I know not yet whether I have Mr. Elmes's bond or Sir Henry Wallop's. When you see Sir Rowland Lytton and Sir William Borlase I pray you let me be remembered to them. I am sorry their travellers perform their parts no better.[5] My wife commends her often and often to you, and I pray you do the like for us both without Cripplegate. So I commit you to God's protection.

Yours most assured

1. The reference is to Chamberlain's efforts to prod Sir Walter Cope into speaking to Salisbury on Carleton's behalf.
2. William Camden, the historian, Clarenceux King-of-Arms, a good friend of Chamberlain's.
3. Carleton's mother-in-law.
4. Chamberlain, wisely or cautiously, declined to do so. *L. J. C.* I, 276.
5. The "travellers" were the sons of Lytton and Borlase, who were in France and out of funds.

Sir, I was out of the way when your messenger was last in town, and I received your letter late last night by Mr. Duckett, and the old man is returning early this morning, so as you must not expect much in so huddling haste, and much here hath not happened since your departure more than you have already: for in the news of the Low Countries and the articles of the treaty [1] (which I purposed to have sent you) I perceive I am prevented. Our commissioners are sent for home by express letters from the king, wherein he styles them his ambassadors and gives large and liberal approbation of their doings. Some difference there is in judgment betwixt them and our great statesmen here touching the treaty, they making no doubt but that it will be ratified in Spain without further dispute or difficulty and the opinion being here that it will be utterly rejected, whereupon are built many new projects and designs; but methinks the commissioners are on the surer ground, the articles being set down with that indifferency on both sides, and the matters offensive of the Indies, of religion, [2] and some others, so covertly included or cunningly blanched, which would not have been if there had been any secret purpose to have left the king of Spain an *échappatoire* or starting hole to have flown out at; and I see no reason but he might have better crossed it [the treaty] in the beginning, or in the progress, or at least before it came to conclusion than now, that the kings who have been mediators may justly make themselves parties for maintainance of their own act. There is no sudden resolution like to be taken whom to send in place of Sir Ralph Winwood, and it is in doubt whether to send one qualified as agent or ambassador, wherein we are like to be led by example of the French, and I think Sir Ralph Winwood himself at his return may strike a great stroke in the appointment of his successor; wherein you advise me *omnem movere lapidem,* I do *movere,* I assure you, as much as I can, but *promovere* as little as ever you knew, for those I rely upon stir like stones, and the chief stone of all is hardly moved; and though I have small comfort given me I will not be in despair till I see more likely pretenders than any yet appear.[3] I was this last week with my wife at a solemn dinner at Kensington, where we encountered much good company and besides good cheer and the fair show of the house newly tricked and trimmed for the purpose, we had a morris dance and the king's cormorant to entertain us. The holidays have been spent at court with some little variety. On Easter day the dean of the chapel to the household and the bishop of Chichester [4] before the king befitted the solemnity of the time with as good sermons as ever I heard from either of them, and the king was as well pleased with the bishop, whom he entertained all his dinner while in discourse about his sermon. The Tuesday, which was for bear and bull baiting, was as well fitted with a preacher, one Dr. Smith,[5] head of a house in Cambridge, who so well baited the great courtiers, whom he termed *suffragatores aulicos* for bribery and corruption and so schooled the king himself for being led by other men rather than by his own judgment and that so particularly and plainly that I know not how he hath escaped baiting himself; the rest of his sermon was a plain invective against the course of law and lawyers for prohibitions.[6] Yesterday was the funeral of my lady of Exeter at Westminster, where my lady of Northumberland was chief mourner; of earls there was only Worcester and Montgomery, two countesses, five barons and as many barons' wives; of others of all sorts, not above 100; the sermon was made by Dr. Layfield, who gave the dead lady her due and held us two hours.[7] My lord Lumley [8] died the last week at Nonesuch and is likely to be buried *in tenebris.* Sir Adolphus Carey shall have a solemnity of funeral kept the next week at Barkhamsted, which is discharged by his brother Philip, to whom he left all he had. The College of Physicians called a council about his death and had Doctor Antonie before them, whom they charged directly, by his unknown medicines, to have killed him and acquitted his other physician Sir William Paddy by solemn act. I am very sorry for the news you write from Lechworth.[9] My lady Wallop is well, for aught I hear to the contrary, and her husband in physic in the same place you left him, for so I was told the last day by Dudley Norton, with whom I lighted in a boat coming from court and Hugh Beeston in company, who (by the way) stole an arresting the last day in Chancery Lane for £40, but this must be in council. Would you think that young Sir Henry Neville should, upon a mistaking of Neville for a Knevitt,[10] be arrested for a pirate by a French merchant? but so it was on Good Friday last and with that violence that he hardly escaped the encounter. My brother hath had a sudden and shrewd fit of sickness in the country, about which he is gone to Oxford to take physic. There died fewer by 7 of the plague this week than the last. All our friends here are well, I thank God, and we much miss your company; you have recommendations from all, which I desire you remember from me to Sir Henry [Fanshawe] and my good lady. I wish my self heartily with you but am too good a husband. I stay your messenger too long, wherefore, adieu without more ceremony . . .

Yours ever most assured

1. The Twelve Years' Truce between Spain and the United Provinces. Sir Ralph Winwood and Sir Richard Spencer were the English commissioners; their efforts had much to do with successful conclusion of the negotiations.

2. The Dutch demanded the right to trade in the Indies; the Spanish, freedom for Catholics in the United Provinces to practice their religion. Neither side was successful.

3. Chamberlain had written in December 1608 that a major reshuffle of diplomatic appointments was expected in the summer of 1609 and that Carleton "must *omnem movere lapidem* to step in upon these removes." *L. J. C.* I, 275. The "chief stone" was, of course, Salisbury.

4. Lancelot Andrewes, whom Carleton came greatly to admire.

5. William Smith, master of Clare and later provost of Kings.

6. Prohibitions were writs issued by the royal courts to stop proceedings in an ecclesiastical court until the king's court could determine whether the case in question properly belonged there. Sir Edward Coke, while chief justice of the court of Common Pleas, issued the writ liberally and became involved in a serious controversy with Archbishop Bancroft, which resulted ultimately in his transfer to the court of King's Bench.

7. Dorothy, countess of Exeter, was the wife of Lord Salisbury's elder

brother Thomas. John Layfield, rector of St. Clement Danes, was one of those who worked on the King James version.

8. John Lumley, Baron Lumley. His library, said to be one of the best in England, was bought up by the king.

9. Chamberlain had written that Sir Rowland Lytton was having eye trouble and that his son had smallpox. *L. J. C.* I, 289.

10. Knevitt: the pun is obscure; the most prominent Knyvet was Thomas, just raised to the peerage as Lord Knyvet of Escrick. It was he who discovered Guy Fawkes and the gunpowder under the houses of Parliament on November 4, 1605.

The Priory, October 4, 1609

S. P. 14/48, #81

Sir, I have made since I saw you a journey amongst my friends at Eton, Hanworth, Fulham, Kensington, and London, where, hearing that all was not well at Ilford, I went thither likewise, and found my brother in great weakness by reason of a double tertian which had held him a fortnight; my sister Alice had been likewise in an ague, but her thin sides could afford substance but for three fits; little Tom was newly crept out of a dangerous disease which they call the disease of the country and ended with a great bile on his back, which is cousin-german to the disease of the city. Our aunt Sproxton continues sick still and is in a fair way to a consumption; my poor boy [1] I left very ill of a cough and a cold, which draws us the sooner out of these parts, my wife being one of the fondlings and not to be held longer from him, so as tomorrow, God willing, we go to Eton; the next day I am again to return to London, where I am like to hear my lord treasurer's doom touching my employment, which unless it be into Ireland I see nothing now left for me. [2] Our ambassador at Venice shall continue there, as is said, for 3 years longer; Sir Stephen Lesieur is set down for Florence; for Spain and the arch-duke either they will think of ambassadors, and for those places they look after men which are some way qualified, or otherwise the secretaries of the ambassadors which they have left behind them will be continued. I have seen Sir Thomas Edmondes at London and since at Hampton Court, and he is the same man he was wont to be. In the difference betwixt him and our good friend [3] he is somewhat warmer than the other, but losers may be allowed to speak. Sir Thomas Smith continues sick of his old disease but is somewhat better than he was. Sir Henry Maynard was even at death's door of the same sickness and was given over by the physicians but is recovered by the means of one Owen, a professor of certain secrets though no professed physician, who now doth take Sir Thomas Smith in hand. Joseph Earth went into his mother earth at Wanstead two days before the king came last thither. Sir Robert Wingfield hath left both court and country and is gone to God. Ned Jones was going the same way, of an extreme swelling over all his body but is, as I hear, recovered. You have heard I am sure of a great danger Sir William Paddy lately escaped at Barn Elms, where the house was assaulted by Sir John Kennedy by night with a band of furious Scots, who besides their warlike weapons came furnished, as Ned Wimarke said, with certain snippers and searing irons, purposing to have used him worse than a Jew, with much more ceremony than circumcision. Sir William, having the alarm given him, fled like a valiant knight out at a back door, leaving his breeches behind him, and the lady by his sweet side went tripping over the plains in her smock with her petticoat in her hand till they recovered the next castle, and now he walks London streets with three or four men in defense of his dimissaries. The matter betwixt Sir John and his lady is in hearing before the Lords, which is so carried that Sir William is not so much as mentioned.[4] There is one Coe, a poor pelting lawyer, who, for a petition presented to the king in ill terms against my lord chancellor, is committed to the gatehouse by the Lords, and upon his censure he gave himself a light hurt in the breast with his knife as if he would have stabbed himself but obtained no more by it than to be kept close prisoner. The court is full of Dutchmen, who come to treat about the several pretensions to the duchy of Cleves, which is thought in the end will come to *partage,* though as yet there is arming on all hands.[5] The duke of Florence [Cosimo II, grand duke of Tuscany] hath lately put to sea 5 small ships and in them a great man, one who gives himself out to be elder brother to the great Turk [Sultan Ahmed I] and with that probability that the Italians are at facile cr [paper torn] Sir Robert Sherley[6] was lately at Florence, betwixt whom and this new Turk was a solemn interview with as much ceremony as if the meeting had been betwixt the great Turk and the Persian. His brother, in the meantime, Sir Anthony, hath received a sound box of the ear in the court of Spain by a nobleman of that country, which they say he is content to packet up with some verbal satisfaction. Young Haydon that belongs to the prince hath unfortunately lost one of his hands in a brabble on the way betwixt him and Ramsay, my lord Haddington's brother. You have all, and of all sort of news I know for the present; from London you shall hear from me again and more particularly touching myself. I shall be glad to meet with a letter from you, which I pray you direct to my father's lodging by Salisbury court. Thus with a general salutation of all this company to Sir Michael, my lady, and yourself, and my wife's and my kind commendations to Mr. Gent I commit you to God's protection,

Your assured loving friend

1. Carleton's infant son, who died shortly thereafter.
2. In February Carleton had decided to refuse the second secretaryship for Ireland because it paid so little. That he was now resigned to an Irish position indicates how desperate he was.
3. Sir Ralph Winwood. Edmondes, who was ambassador in Brussels, was about to receive the appointment to Paris, which hardly made him a "loser."
4. Sir William Paddy, named physician to King James in 1603, was several times president of the College of Physicians. Sir John Kennedy came south with James in 1603 and married Elizabeth Brydges, the daughter of the third Lord Chandos. The legality of the marriage was in question; Kennedy was alleged to have left a wife behind him in Scotland.
5. William, duke of Cleves, died in the spring of 1609, leaving no male heir. This was the beginning of the tangled question of the Cleves-Julich succession, which was to plague English diplomats, Carleton among them, for years.

6. The third of the three adventurer-brothers. In 1608 he left Persia as the shah's agent, accredited to the princess of Europe, James I among them, to improve commercial relations and promote a coalition against the Turks. Rudolf II had just created him a count palatine of the empire. At the time of Carleton's letter he had gone from Florence to Rome; by the end of the year he was in Spain.

II
THE VENETIAN EMBASSY
1610–1615

Venice, February 7, 1611/12

S. P. 99/9, ff. 65–66

Good Mr. Chamberlain, my sorrow for our late heavy news out of England [1] made me in ill tune to set pen to paper more then necessity required. So as I am now in some arrearages with you and am straitened in time to come out of your debt. So as I must pay you some now and take day for the rest. My lady Cope hath just cause to except against her drinking glasses, for they were not worthy of her but for ordinary use, and I remember for the commodity of sending by a good ship we took such as we could then find, but I will undertake to furnish her better. [2] I pray you prevent by all means her sending anything hither, for they have many better occasions of pleasuring me than by presents. The senate here hath the news of the likelihood of Fabritio's [3] employment, and they say it is a whipping with his own rod; but I do not think he will have that sense of it. Your news at Oxford from Padua is too good to be true. The truth is there is no such matter, and at Rome there are some cardinals, both young and old, dead of late, but no new creation. [4] Our friend Candido [5] hath tasted (as is thought) of a fig from thence, for he is dead in a strange manner, and his physicians, which opened him in presence of some senators and many gentlemen, his scholars, conclude there was some such cause and have signed a writing to that purpose, which I think by the next I shall send you in print. You may guess what a loss I have of him, and though I complained of him to you in one letter, when he saw I was sensible of his neglect he quickly made double amends. He died on Monday last and was buried in the Church of the Servi on Wednesday, which you know was not his parish, but he was carried thither by his friends for fear lest some violence should have been offered his body if he had been interred anywhere else because he stood excommunicate. During his sickness he sent me my lord of Ely's letter, which you conveyed hither, as likewise that in answer, which he had formerly sent me open and had ever since lain by him, which, because it is the last my lord can have from him, I send it you here enclosed in form as I received it, and I pray you accompany the delivery of it with the recommendation of my service to his lordship. That which I sent you in my last was the last that ever he wrote and the last time I think that he set pen to paper, for the next morning he was taken with his disease, first in his head and the most part of his body like an apoplexy. After, he came somewhat to himself again, but his right arm and side continued still dead till all went after it, and hereupon many wise discourses are framed that he was taken in this sort at such time as he was writing against our new miraculous maid. You may satisfy them out of your letter, which (as I said) in all probability was his last writing, whether there was any such matter. But the miracle hath found greater adversaries of the *Capucine,* into whose convent the maid is cloistered, for they, being jealous forsooth that a begging nun should so far outstrip them in sanctity, look so narrowly to her and so watch her fingers that she can make no more blood come, and she hath a trick for them by saying that as long as she is thus locked up she hath it by revelation that her *vertu* ceaseth. Would you wish more exact *Mariolatria?* and yet here want not which have put their handerchiefs stained with her blood into silver boxes for relics. Our carnival is let loose, and the Spanish ambassador [6] hath taken up his place at San Stèfano, where he wallows after his wonted manner in his gondola and hath seen himself once played already. He was lately feasted in the Arsenal, where his followers committed such disorders that Don Antonio Mesquit (paper torn) with a man of Count Collalto's were banished thereupon by sentence of Pregadi [the Senate] which upon his suit was since released for the Don, but the other was fain to be packing.[7] The French ambassador [8] hath taken the opportunity to show the sobriety of his nation, being feasted there yesterday after the same manner without any disorder. Our Neapolitan traveller [9] is come well to us, and if he hold on as he hath begun in this journey he will spend as fast as his father will save, but I dare send no such discomfortable news where there is already so much heaviness; wherefore this is only to your self. We are all well and salute you kindly and I rest . . .

Yours most assuredly

1. Carleton's mother, who lived with his brother George, had just died.

2. Carleton had sent four dozen glasses to Lady Cope; four were broken en route. She was "nothing pleased," wrote Chamberlain on December 31, 1611, "for she says they were all bare glasses and without covers, and her humor is altogether for fantastical fashions." *L. J. C.* I, 324–25.

3. In January Sir Henry Wotton, now frequently called *Fabritio,* had been named ambassador to Savoy. January 10/20, 1611/12, Antonio Foscarini to the doge and senate of Venice, *C. S. P. Venetian 1610–1613,* p. 277. Foscarini was the Venetian ambassador in England.

4. The report at Oxford was that the old quarrel between the Pope and Venice was about to flare up again and that the Pope had created eleven new cardinals at Christmas. January 15, 1611/12, Chamberlain to Carleton, *L. J. C.* I, 330.

5. Chamberlain and Carleton gave the label *Candido* (perhaps to contrast with *Fabritio*) to Giovanni Marsilio, a Neapolitan theologian who had just died in Venice. He had been in correspondence with Lancelot Andrewes, now bishop of Ely. King James knew his writing and had recently praised him to the Venetian ambassador. *C. S. P. Venetian 1610–1613,* p. 305.

6. Alfonso de Cueva, marquis of Bedmar, who was involved in 1618, after Carleton's transfer to The Hague, in a "conspiracy" to betray the city to Spain. The details of this business are not at all clear, and it may have existed only in the imagination of the Venetian government. Bouwsma, *Venice,* p. 509. For the view that a conspiracy was contemplated, see H. R. Trevor-Roper, "Spain and Europe 1598–1621," in J. P. Cooper, ed., *The New Cambridge Modern History,* vol. IV: *The Decline of Spain and the Thirty Years War* (Cambridge, 1970), pp. 275–76.

7. The Arsenal was a famous showplace which visitors to Venice wanted to see. The government often honored distinguished tourists, as well as ambassadors, by entertaining them there. Rambaldo Collalto was an Italian aristocrat in the Habsburgs' service.

8. Charles Brulart de Genlis, prior of Léon in Brittany.
9. Carleton's nephew John, the eldest son of his brother George.

Venice, March 20, 1611/12

S. P. 99/9, ff. 141–42

Sir, since my last of the 28th of February I have received yours of the 12th, with the enclosed, which was a meter fit for the Mitre and a perfect piece of poetry *in suo genere,* only the author was somewhat bold to bring so many great folk amongst those great fools, and I marvel how Johnson was missing amongst the good fellows.[1] The things you sent by sea to Mr. Horne and my sister [2] are delivered here in so good order as if they had been removed only out of one chamber into another. Some house provisions at several times are come to me with like success, and they here make a miracle at our ships that come hither with such speed and safety, the sea being so much molested with pirates, and indeed these Venetians have had the ill luck of late that they can no sooner peep out of the gulf but they are had by the backs. Here is newly come into Malamocco [3] a Low Country ship richly laden, which was set upon by three Tunis-men and fought withal three whole days, but held it out stoutly though the master was slain in the fight, in exchange of whom they brought away a desperate Turk, who, as they were grappled together, ran up into the cradle of the Dutch ship with purpose to have cut all the tackle, whilst in the meantime the ships were again parted, and he caught like a bird in a cage. Here is a great convoy of Dutchmen newly set out towards Amsterdam, by whom I have sent Sir Ralph Winwood's glasses. I have received the king's protestations against Vorstius [4] from him, so as you need not send it; but hereafter I will pray you in respect of the portage not to forbear pleasuring me with anything of moment which is of no greater bulk, for I shall willingly bear it, especially if you have any thing of my lord of Ely's, and if it be too big for one packet you may divide it into two or three and so convey it at several times. Doctor Marta [5] is, as you have heard, at Padua, where I head him well knocked down by the unruly scholars at his first lecture, when commonly they have more patience, and the *podestà* and captain, who were there to grace him, could not help the disorder. The reason hereof I understood afterwards to be because he stole the most part of his oration *ipsissimis verbis* out of a printed book, wherein his auditors were better read than he imagined. He is a man of good appearance and fair conversation, and, in the questions wherein he formerly declared himself so superstitiously papal, he hath the wit to be silent. The great man whom our Candido did so much depend on was the means of his preferment. I promised you the judgment of physicians upon Candido's death, which I send you here enclosed. We have had many good resolutions here taken of late in our litigious questions with the Pope and his partisans upon occasion of a tax the Ferrarese exact upon such boats of merchandise as come down the Po near the port of Goro. The general of the gulf hath commandment to draw thither with his galleys and make prise of such as molest that passage. [6] Three of the confessors of Treviso who, as you may remember, had made a certain *casella della penitènza* upon such monies as they wrung from the collectors of church subsidies under confession, are banished for life, and the 6 of this present the *bando* against the Jesuits was renewed and openly proclaimed at Saint Mark's and Rialto upon discovery of their enticing away many young gentlemen from Brescia and Verona to be trained up in their discipline by means of a college they have built in the confines at Castiglione only for this purpose. [7] Now, to requite your Mall Cutpurse, one of our famous courtesans, Isabella, who dwells in Canale Grande had this last week both her water gate and back door set on fire in one night (I mean honestly, not as Ned Wimarke will take it when you tell him the story) and another had all her windows broken down by a troop that came disguised like the Scuola di San Fantino. [8] An ancient man and a rich in Canale Reggio, as he was landing at his door out of his gondola, was slain about the same time by two fellows that lay there in wait for him with pistols, and no greater cause is spoken of but that some loss was like to be to his next heirs if he lived to make a will. There hath been some bickering of late at Zara betwixt the Venetian horse, which lie there in garrison, and the bordering Turks, wherein the captain of our horse was hurt and 40 Turks slain, and the consequence hereof would be somewhat fearful but that we have certain news that the wars are renewed betwixt the Grand Signor [9] and the Persian without further speech of peace. Our travellers, which went with Mr. Pindar [10] to Constantinople (Mr. Pawlett and Lakes only excepted), mean to make one step further to see the Persian army before their return. Mr. St. Johns,[11] who went the last week towards France, through Germany, hath promised me to see Phil Lytton in his way at Sedan. We have had here a long and an uncomfortable winter, but now the old sunshine appears, and we are already sensible of the warm nights, which bring out our old acquaintances, the lizards and nightingales. Besides [paper torn] Lent began, we have the singing nuns and preaching friars who beat down the pulpits after the old manner, but none is this year so happy in his followers as your old friend Fra Felice. You may have a piece of a ser [paper torn] in a letter I have sent by my nephew to Sir Walter Cope, which is the choicest matter I can pick out for him, not having patience *lambicarsi il cervello* for curious conceits. I have been very negligent in writing to Sir Rowland Lytton, for which I pray you make my excuse and let him have his part always in your letters. The like I wish Sir Henry Fanshawe, when there is anything worth his knowledge.

Thus far I was gone by way of provision, when I received yours of the 26 of the last with the enclosed from Mr. Clarenceux, for which I pray you give him many thanks in my name until upon the first occasion I may thank him myself, and when Mr. Roger Manwood,[12] whom he commends unto me, shall come hither he shall find the fruit (in what I am able) both of his recommendation and my respect to his father. I shall much long for your next letters in hope to hear of the continuance of my lord treasurer's amendment, as well for public respects as my private interest. Since you say that others are in the same case as I am for slack payments I must have the more patience, though I suffer much, not having yet helped myself by any extraordinary means since your departure, finding the service to be somewhat prejudiced by too common traffic in that kind; but I have the better contentment in all public business by how much more I spare of my private benefit. I shall be glad to hear in particular who they were that put out their heads in my lord treasurer's danger;[13] and thus with all good wishes, I commit you to God.

Yours as ever

1. Chamberlain had sent a copy of John Hoskyns' *Convivium philosophicum,* a poem describing a (real or imaginary) gathering of literati and wits at the Mitre in Oxford. Johnson is Ben Jonson. For Hoskyns see L. B. Osborn, *The Life, Letters, and Writings of John Hoskyns* (New Haven, 1937). The text of the *Convivium* is on pp. 196–99.

2. Thomas Horne was Carleton's chaplain and subsequently canon of Windsor. Carleton's unmarried sister Alice accompanied him to Venice.

3. Malamocco was the port of Venice.

4. Conrad Vorstius, a German theologian of radical persuasion, had been offered a chair in theology at the University of Leyden. King James found Vorstius' views abhorrent and was putting pressure on the Dutch government to withdraw the offer. Among other measures he had recently published a pamphlet, *His Majesty's Declaration against Vorstius.* See F. Shriver, "Orthodoxy and diplomacy: James I and the Vorstius Affair," *English Historical Review* LXXXV (1970), 449–74.

5. Dr. Jacopo Antonio Marta became professor of canon law at Padua in 1611. Carleton regarded him with distaste as a supporter of papal supremacy.

6. Ferrara was a papal town. The Venetians were about to send an expedition to put an end to the Ferrarese attempt to tax their ships going to Goro. Carleton described the raid in a letter of March 27 to Winwood; Winwood, *Memorials* III, 351.

7. The Jesuits had been expelled from Venice in 1606, at the height of the quarrel between the papacy and the Republic. They were not readmitted until 1657.

8. Moll Cutpurse, a "notorious baggage," had done penance at Paul's Cross; "she wept bitterly and seemed very penitent," wrote Chamberlain, "but it is since doubted she was maudlin drunk, being discovered to have tippled of three quarts of sack before she came to her penance." *L. J. C.* I, 334. The Scuola di San Fantino was a fraternity located in the Campo di San Fantino. It called itself the society of Santa Maria della Giustizia, or della Buona Morte,

since it took upon itself the job of accompanying criminals to the gallows and then to the grave; the local wits called it the Scuola dei Piccai (hanged). I owe this information to Mrs. Marina Stern.

9. "Grand Signor" was the customary way of referring to the sultan of Turkey.

10. Paul Pindar was a successful merchant who had made money in Italy, served as consul for the English merchants in Aleppo from 1609 to 1611, and in 1611 was named ambassador in Constantinople.

11. One branch of this family was related to Chamberlain. I have not positively identified this individual. Philip Lytton was Carleton's nephew.

12. The eldest son of the antiquary Sir Peter Manwood, an acquaintance of both Chamberlain's and Carleton's.

13. Salisbury had been seriously ill; after a brief recovery he was to die in May.

Venice, April 3, 1612
S. P. 99/9, f. 166

Good Mr. Chamberlain, I will rather give you a short salutation than that you should hear from none of us this week, having received yours of the 11th of the last, and I thank you very much for your confirmation of my lord treasurer's recovery, as well as for the benefit the world enjoys by him as for prevention of such as were so ready to divide his spoils. Those two you named to me are indeed *suggetti papabili,* but I would be glad to know the rest that were no less in their own conceits, and for that you write of Fabritio, *Dii talem nobis avertite pestem.*[1] As light as he makes of Candido, he is much lamented and missed, as one of whom there was principal use; Tully said of one, *et potest et audet.* He hath left those behind him that can do as well and perhaps better, but they want his courage, and now is a time when there were use for such a spirit. The Jesuits have their rage inflamed through all Italy upon the *bando* that was here lately published against them, and they rail against the Venetians both in pulpit and in all places else where they have audience as if they were worse than heretics. I know not whether I wrote to you how at Castiglione they had begun an order of Jesuited nuns, which makes good the saying *Jesuita omnis homo* because by this new invention they are *utriusque sexus*. Here hath been an apothecary lately imprisoned by the inquisitors of state, with two others, whereof one is a priest, for holding intelligence (as is thought) with those of that society at Parma. A *sotto-canonico* of Saint Mark's, whom you may remember to be in hold for libelling, was sent a week since *sotto l'acqua,* without any more noise. There is a good revenge taken in the confines of Ferrara for the violence used by the Ferrarese upon certain wood-grounds in question betwixt the Church and this state, where they having felled and squared out a good quantity of timber whereof some was laden into carts, the Venetians have set both the wood and carts on fire, at which the nuncio here doth kindle a little and the Cardinal [Orazio] Spinola (who is legate at Ferrara) much more, threatening that this fire shall not be so soon quenched, but for all their brags it is likely enough to go *en fumée*. This course notwithstanding, which was taken by order of this state and performed by the general of the galleys, is a plain act of hostility, such a one as hath not been heard of these many days in Italy and will therefore cause much rumor, and I desire for some respects you should rather hear it from others than any from you. In my last of the 20 of March I have answered you touching Doctor Marta, who is at Padua, but neither of much name nor fame, save that the books which come both out of France and England in question of jurisdiction bring him anew upon the stage, who otherwise would be buried alive. I have sent Mr. Finet a letter from Signor Tintoret.[2] We have had here Sir Charles Somerset and my lord Arundel's son, who are gone this week towards England.[3] Here enclosed I send you a letter from one who by this time is arrived with you and at Paris I hear hath spit as much malice, and in hearing of my best friends as at Lyons you may see he used good words. What should a man judge of this world? I see there is no other way, but *fare il callo,* and to strive no longer with slander. Wherefore if you will forgive the curiosity of my last letters and the trouble

[126]

of these, you are likely to have no more of this subject; and so with all our kindest remembrances, I commit you to God.

Yours most assuredly

Being about to seal, I received the enclosed from Mr. Rooke, wherein you may find your name. I pray you send or deliver it to Sir Richard Smith, with return of those many kind remembrances I have received in yours, and commend us to all our old friends, for I grow out of love with new ones.[4]

1. Chamberlain had written that the two most frequently mentioned candidates to succeed Salisbury were Sir Thomas Lake and Sir Henry Neville, but that people who knew Salisbury best feared that he would recommend Wotton. *L. J. C.* I, 338.

2. John Finet, the future master of ceremonies, was in the service of the earl of Salisbury at this stage of his career and had visited Venice in the entourage of Salisbury's son in the winter of 1610–1611. He is best known as the author of *Finetti philoxenis,* published in 1656, a tract on the treatment of ambassadors in England. *Tintoret* is Domenico Tintoretto, the son of the great painter and himself a painter. A letter of Carleton's to Chamberlain on July 30, 1613, not here reproduced, suggests that Domenico had done a portrait of Chamberlain. P. R. O., S. P. 99/13, ff. 149–50.

3. Charles Somerset was a younger son of the fourth earl of Worcester. The reference to lord Arundel's son is puzzling. Thomas Howard, Lord Arundel, the famous art collector, was the only son of his father, was at this time 26 years of age, had been married only six years, and was in England. Later in the year he was to visit Padua for his health—the first of his many visits to Italy.

4. Sir Richard Smith, receiver-general of the duchy of Cornwall, had two sons in Venice and frequently thanked Carleton—via Chamberlain—for his kindness to them. George Rooke had been in the embassy in Venice during Wotton's tenure; he was now in Padua, acting as tutor to Smith's sons. See November 13, 1611, Chamberlain to Carleton, *L. J. C.* I, 314–15. There is a brief account of Rooke in Stoye, *Travellers,* pp. 151–53.

Sir, I have received your last of the 23 of March, and by your postscript you have put me in some longing for your next, as I shall be glad to hear you have received my two former of the 5th of March and the 3rd of this present, the subject of both which is fit for no man's view but your own.[1] You cannot do me a greater pleasure than to continue me in my lord of Ely's remembrance, to whom I should most gladly perform all possible service. The panegyric apology you write of,[2] to tell you truly my conceit, I always took to be rather in the author's brain than in paper, for, as he would not spare sometimes to feed his friends with such fancies, so was he no niggard to show what he had extant, but I will enquire better after it, all of his papers being in the hands of Nicolò Contarini, to whom he bequeathed them. You must think he had his memory about him at the last cast when he sent me my lord bishop's letter, and if there had been any thing else fit for me he would not have forgotten it, as he did not amongst other legacies omit to bestow a certain *pelliccia de' conigli* (which you know who promised him) upon one of his friends, but the 100 crowns from Lyons he took no care to bestow. I stole to him when he was in his deathbed, but he was then no more himself. As I remember, I wrote to you of a certain *Somaschi*[3] who was tampering with him to make him recant from what he had published against the papacy in the time of the late variance, for which he was fain to show a fair pair of heels. Since that time there hath been a more vigilant eye over all that company, and their chief means being an hospital of orphans some of them have been found vicious in that which is not to be named, for which the charge is taken from them and they forced to depart the city for need. Our Lenten sermons ended with as little noise as they began, and one of the parish of Santi Apostoli was overheard by our little French doctor[4] to complain of their friar that he did *predicar l'Evangelio troppo chiaro*. We had here yesterday a new miracle springing at San Jeronimo's, where the fellow to the *pizzòchera,* who troubled the town so lately, found in a little corner of a cloister a crucifix bleeding, whereupon the patriarch was sent for in all post, but when he saw it and the world began to run, he caused the doors to be shut up for fear of a new chiding. Our musician's house over the way is turned to a convent of *Capucine,* so as now we shall not want miracles. The Pope takes the doings of this state towards Ferrara very patiently and is not stirred at other matters which at another time would make his Bulls bellow very loud, and I think we should not lose the advantage of the time, but that even now we have cross news of a peace betwixt the Turk and the Persian, with some harsh usage of our *bailo* [5] at Constantinople, which doth somewhat startle us. The States' ambassador is there arrived and received, and notwithstanding much labor both in the French ambassador and the *bailo* to hinder him. Our new ambassador doth well acquit himself, and the old makes no haste away. [6] Mr. Hare and the other travellers that were going to the Persian army have changed their course to Jerusalem. I am sorry I can so well requite your news of pirates, there being taken, within these three months by those of Tunis and Algiers, two Venetians, two French, and two Flemish ships, and one of the Flemings a ship of great force, having 24 pieces of ordinance, and was empty and fought long and was taken at last by strong hand, with which they are so strengthened that no ships dare pass without strong convoy. We have an English ship in this port which hath endured two fights in one year in these seas without any great loss, and all the rest of our nation have been yet very fortunate. After the apothecary, of whose retention (as I remember) I wrote to you in my last, the inquisitors of state have laid hold on the Spanish ambassador's physician. The *cavaliere* Badoer [7] is in the meantime fled, he that was imprisoned about four years since for meeting the nuncio at a friar's cell in the Frari and excluded ever since from all counsels, except the *gran consiglio* only, where (you may remember) you had a sight of him, and there is a very rigorous *bando* published against him for being an intelligencer to divers princes (without specifying any) against this state. Our good old duke [8] hath been lately sick of a pleurisy, of which he was cured by letting of blood and voiding some at the mouth, whereupon you will conclude he was in danger, and though commonwealths cannot die, a great part of the honor of this had gone with him. He got his sickness by a cold taken in visiting his new buildings. I thank you for your good news of my lord treasurer's amendment, which keeps us here alive. We are well (I thank God) and I this day at the end of a short course of physic, which I took, I must confess, more for commodity of the season and fear of what may come than any present necessity. Thus wishing you health and contentment and remembering very kindly all your good friends as you are saluted by all, I rest as ever

Yours most assuredly

1. A reference to his remarks on those who were ready to divide the spoils if Salisbury died.

2. Giovanni Marsilio, or Candido, whose death Carleton had recently reported (see above, letter of February 7, 1611/12) was supposed to have written a "panegyric apology" for King James, who was anxious to see it. *L. J. C.* I, 343.

3. An order of friars, localized at Venice. Carleton elsewhere describes them as "not much differing from the Jesuits." Winwood, *Memorials* III, 342.

4. Jacques Asselinau, a Huguenot physician, who was a friend of Paolo Sarpi's. Bouwsma, *Venice,* pp. 360–61.

5. *I.e.,* the Venetian representative, Simone Contarini.

6. Paul Pindar had recently replaced Sir Thomas Glover as ambassador in Turkey.

7. Anzolo Badoer, accused of selling state secrets to Spain. See May 11, 1612, Carleton to Sir John Digby, English ambassador in Spain, P. R. O., S. P. 99/9, ff. 245–50.

8. Leonardo Donato, who died shortly thereafter.

Venice, June 26, 1612
S. P. 99/10, f. 60

Good Mr. Chamberlain, I have thought it high time to bestir myself, finding besides your kind advertisement some effects of such ill offices as have been done me which do not much trouble me, for I am not obnoxious, and malicious slanders will quickly vanish.[1] I have enclosed this packet in your letter, wherein I have borrowed an occasion to write to the prince, and having now broken the ice I shall use it oftener hereafter; if you have a walk to Saint James's it may be in delivery of my letter to Mr. Newton.[2] He will say somewhat to you, but you may do herein as you please, so you send it, with charge to the messenger not to tattle, and yet I guess there will not be cause of so much jealousy as heretofore. We have no news here save only of two French gentlemen at 'Padua, who have fought a *duèllo* without doublets in one of the bulwarks. One of them is dead in the place, the other run through the body. The Italians laugh at such folly and allow much more of a priest, who slew the day before a young gentleman with a pistol at a courtesan's door, where they were rivals. One of our *notre-dames* here at the turning of a lane having some water dashed upon it by accident, a poor woman finding it cried out our Lady wept, whereupon followed such a tumult and concourse of people that the image was forced to be cut out of the wall and carried to the Church of Santa Maria Formosa, which proves likewise too little to receive the throng of the halt and lame, but chiefly of the blind that flock thither. I pray you excuse this haste after a wearisome day's writing and receive all their salutations here with mine, who ever rest,

Yours most assuredly

1. On May 27, 1612, Chamberlain wrote to Carleton that Salisbury was dead and reported the various rumors as to who would succeed him in his various offices. He passed on Cope's advice to Carleton to write occasionally to the earl of Northampton and to the king's favorite, Rochester, and, as his own suggestion, urged writing to Prince Henry, with whom Wotton was said to be familiar. Hence Carleton's bestirring himself. *L. J. C.* I, 350–53.

2. Adam Newton, dean of Durham, tutor and then secretary to Prince Henry.

Good Mr. Chamberlain, you have kept me alive with your weekly letters, which, in a sharp and dangerous sickness I have lately suffered, were my best comfort and entertainment. Your last was of the 23rd of July, with the Carmelitans' packet enclosed, and I do not marvel if, passing through such hands as it did, it had the same fortune before it came to yours or mine as if it had been in the Lazaretto.[1] For your care in conveying mine, which I made bold to direct unto you, I very heartily thank you and promise not often to put you to the like trouble, for I shall not often put myself to that labor of courtship, which I find very contrary to my genius. I only now attend with great devotion to see what star I am to follow, according to which I shall constantly and without alteration direct my course, and if good wishes could make one shoot back again it should not be long undone. Sir R. W. hath advertised me of his arrival in Holland and expectation of his return into England again before long, though he doth not much build upon it, and in case that fall out he hath written to me to the same effect as I understood by you in your former letters concerning my particular, with this addition that both he and Sir H. N. had treated with some principal persons at home to the same purpose.[2] So as the matter is advanced further than I thought and I am no whit sorry for it if it take effect, for I think no place can agree with me for health worse than this, and you know there is nothing more considerable. I am now upon the point of taking a house at Padua, both for the benefit of that air and opportunity of exercise, and even change of place will be some help, at least yield entertainment. My wife and my sister hold up their heads well, and all the rest, now they know what belongs to good order, find nothing amiss. We have at this present a great confluence of English from all parts: my lord Roos and one Mr. Cansfield in his company by the way of Augusta, Tobie Matthew (who is so broken with travail that Gregorio, not knowing his name, terms him *il vècchio*) and one Gage, a sworn brother of the same pro-

[132]

fession.[3] They are going to Naples, there to winter if a journey to Jerusalem do not divert them, of which they are treating upon the good success of Mr. Willoughby and Mr. Bowes (whom you knew here), who are both safely returned, though the latter have an ague on his back. Of seven Dutch gentlemen, which made the journey with them and came back as far as Cyprus, three they buried in that island and flung other three overboard betwixt that place and this. The weakest of all, and he that was longest sick and seemed in most danger, made a scambling shift to get hither and is well recovered. Mr. Hare left them at Cyprus and took a course towards Naples by Malta. I look here daily for Sir Thomas Glover,[4] who is come as far on his way as Patras and there stays to recover some goods which were stolen from our English merchants by some barbarous Jews, who first rid them by poison and after made themselves masters of all they had. We had here lately a tragical accident near us at Mestre (whither we have found the way to wear out some idle time), an abbess of a convent in a monastery of nuns being found dead in her bed, having her throat cut and the knife sticking in it. Upon examination of the fact, three of the young nuns at least were found with great bellies (for so many are publicly spoken of), for which a prior and a priest are laid fast at Treviso upon suspicion, but as yet it is not known how the murder was committed. Here are brought prisoners to this town a bishop of Lesina in Dalmatia, and a captain of a place subject to the patriarch of Aquileia, for hindering the accustomed obsequies which should have been performed for the late duke, saying that he was *principe herètico,* and was not therefore to have Christian burial.[5] The *Uscocchi* [6] have lighted upon one of our Venetians who was going with his wife and family to a regiment in Dalmatia. They have here a great hope of the rebellion of Nasuk Pasha, as they now rest assured the peace will no further proceed betwixt the Turk and the Persian.[7] You see I seek far to return you somewhat in exchange of so much plenty and variety I have from you. If you could conceive how much difference there is betwixt the heats of this year and the last, or at least how much I am less able to support them, you would think I had done well for once, who have not wrote so much since

I fell sick, and thus with all our kindest commendations to yourself and such of our good friends as may be present wherever this
letter may find you, I commit you to God's holy protection.

Yours most assuredly

1. The Lazaretto was the famous Venetian pesthouse. For the Carmelites see
below, letter of February 25, 1613/14.

2. As yet the king had made no decision on Salisbury's successor as secretary.
Sir Ralph Winwood was hopeful of receiving one of the two secretaryships,
and Sir Henry Neville was a strong candidate for the other. Winwood had
told Chamberlain he would urge Carleton on the king as his successor at The
Hague if he became secretary. See Chamberlain's letter of July 2, *L. J. C.* I,
363–66.

3. William Cecil, Lord Roos, was a great-grandson of Lord Burghley and
was to be a principal in a scandalous series of charges and countercharges,
notably that he had committed incest with his step-grandmother, after his
marriage to Sir Thomas Lake's daughter. Gardiner gives a properly Victorian
synopsis of the matter in *History,* III, 189–94. For Tobie Matthew see above,
letter of November 10/20, 1605. George Gage was Matthew's close friend,
occasionally referred to by Chamberlain as his *fidus Achates*. Both were Roman
Catholics. Augsburg (Augusta), at the other end of the Brenner, was a
common stopping-place on the way to or from Venice. Gregorio was Gregorio
de'Monti, Italian secretary at the embassy. See below, letter of March
29/April 8, 1616.

4. Glover was returning to England after being replaced as ambassador in
Constantinople.

5. Lesina, an island off the Dalmation coast, was a Venetian possession. The
patriarch of Aquileia had jurisdiction over a large part of the mainland possessions of Venice. The charge of heresy against the late doge, Leonardo
Donato, is one more reflection of the bitterness which still lingered in the aftermath of the quarrel between the Republic and the papacy. Donato had been
doge during the quarrel.

6. The *Uscocchi,* or Uskoks, were Slavonian pirates who preyed on shipping
in the Adriatic. They were especially obnoxious to Venice and somewhat less
so to the Turks. They were under the protection of the Austrian Habsburgs
and were occasionally subsidized by the papacy on account of their anti-Turkish
activities. They were thus a source of friction between Venice and both the Pope
and the Austrians.

7. They were wrong on both counts. Nasuk Pasha, the grand vizier, ar-

ranged a peace with the Persians and received as reward, among other things, the hand of the sultan's three-year-old daughter. Nasuk was not a reliable sort —he engaged in various intrigues, though not in rebellion—and the sultan disposed of him in November 1614. I owe this information to Professor Sabra Meservey.

Venice, December 14, 1612

S. P. 99/11, ff. 174–75

Good Mr. Chamberlain, I had laid by all thought of writing to you this week, having saluted you by both the last ordinaries, but am called to it again by your two letters of the 4th and 12th of the last, which came to my hands both together yesterday, and though they contain in them matter of much heaviness, yet, in that which cannot be avoided and must be known, it is some contentment to understand all particulars, but you may imagine in what affliction I rest at this present, for having now these fourteen days entertained myself with my own thoughts upon the grief of our great and untimely loss,[1] now I have your surcharge with other friends' relations out of England and at the very same time receive the lamentations of many gentlemen now in Italy at Florence and in other parts, who were all our late prince's servants and fastened all their hopes upon this sun-rising. Most of them are gone to Naples hereupon, to outride their sorrow if it be possible; at least some of them pretend that to be the motive of their remove from thence, but as we cannot here start from it, where I dare undertake is as much and as general heaviness, so I think they will find that *post equitem sedet atra cura*. Sir Thomas Glover, who was come thither [Florence] on his way towards England and had appeared one day like a comet, all in crimson velvet and beaten gold, and expected as much feasting and entertainment, *cum multis aliis,* as he found by the Spanish viceroys in Sicily and Naples, had all his mirth marred on a sudden and retired himself to Leghorn to ship himself for Marseilles. Sir Robert Dudley[2] entertained no small hopes of returning into

[135]

England by means of the prince's favor and to be employed in some special charge about the king's navy. There was a royal present now prepared by the grand duke [of Tuscany] to be sent the prince, which was the 12 labors of Hercules in statues of brass set upon so many pillars of ebony and three goodly coursers of Naples, which would have so well suited with the greatness of his spirit and exercises wherein he took most delight that it seems they were not to seek what would be most acceptable. We begin to wind out by degrees of this intricate business betwixt the Archduke Ferdinand and this state,[3] and we are at this present at so dead a calm that here is no news nor hath not been a good while of their old pastimes of *stilettatas* and *arquebusatas* but in place thereof many strict and severe sentences of imprisonment and confinings for old crimes, which is the cause (we may think) of this new good order. If what I have written to you in my two last letters touching my own particular, being upon the first heat of an unexpected news, be not necessary to be participated to other friends (which you will judge as you see occasion) I shall be content all may rest with yourself, for such cross interpretations are made of my poor affairs by some which can but vent out any part of them that I willingly betake myself to an old Italian rule, *riga tu diritto et lascia dire* (and I will add) *far chi vuole*. Touching Fabritio, the devil owed him a shame and now he hath paid him; but he hath had the fortune to overcome greater matters and so I believe he will do this.[4] For other matters, I refer them to one that hath more leisure, and with my own and my wife's kindest remembrances I rest

Yours as ever most assuredly

P.S. I write not to Mr. Wake[5] because I conceive he is by this time returning, though (I perceive) he hath been long in going. I perceive by a kind letter I had from Sir W. Cope this week that Signore Foscarini's kindness (whereof I wrote to you in my last) proceeded of the old score of his entertainment at Kensington, at which house Sir W. Cope devised how to do me the most honor that ever I received, and it seems he continues his care to make the place upon all apt occasions lucky unto me. I pray you acknowledge thus much in my behalf, which I will do myself before long when I have some matter to send him besides compliment, which is ill payment for such real courtesies; and favor me with the remembrance of my service to both the ladies.[6]

1. The death of Prince Henry in November 1612. Carleton's sorrow was genuine enough; like all those government officials who regarded the Catholic menace as serious, he had had great hopes of the prince. He consoled himself, as he wrote Chamberlain on December 1 (in a letter not reproduced here), with "the hopeful expectation of the prince that is left and the present happiness of him that is gone, and God knows best who is fittest for heaven and whom he designs to this world as instruments of his glory." P. R. O., S. P. 99/11, f. 147.

2. For Sir Robert Dudley see above, letter of November 10/20, 1605.

3. The Venetian government was hostile to Archduke Ferdinand of Styria, the future Ferdinand II, on account of his support of the Uskoks. There had been a real possibility of an outbreak of hostilities between the two earlier in the year.

4. This comment was elicited by Chamberlain's report of James's anger at his learning of Wotton's famous quip on the character of an ambassador: *Legatus est vir bonus peregre missus ad mentiendum Reipublicae causa.* James was angry because a Catholic controversialist used it to deplore the character of a king who sent out ambassadors to lie to his fellow sovereigns. Wotton was "down the wind, and his business begins to quail," wrote Chamberlain. *L. J. C.* I, 385.

5. Isaac Wake was Carleton's secretary; Carleton had recently sent him to England via The Hague, in order to discover what Carleton's hopes of advancement might be in the reshuffle which was bound to follow Salisbury's death. See *L. J. C.* I, 386.

6. Cope's wife and daughter.

Venice, April 16, 1613

S. P. 99/12, ff. 202–203

Good Mr. Chamberlain, though I am straitened in time and was half resolved to have put off writing unto you until the next, yet

I cannot but thank you for your last of the 25 of March howsoever it brings not so good news as I expected of your perfect recovery. But I hold it a good sign when the patient gives over the physician and not *a convèrso* and the good time drawing on with you, in which we are here well entered, will (I assure myself) quickly restore you, whereof I shall be glad to hear, for I suffer with you and so do some other of this company. Mr. Wake doth droop after his long journey and is indeed so much the sicker in that neither he nor his doctor knows what he ails. I have been these three days past single at Padua, save only that I had with me one of my old Ostend comrades, who brought me a letter from Sir Ralph Winwood and is gone in company of Mr. Manwood [1] and an old Cambridge traveller Mr. Boys, first into Hungary and after through Germany into France. Little lame Torderby [2] hath found his legs to come hither the last night, having had the news of the death of his father and how he is bound to his good behavior for his inheritance, which he takes somewhat unkindly, especially seeing in a letter which I gave him when I was now last at Padua from his father he was charged with some particular offences, whereof I dare answer he is no way guilty. He came recommended to me from the bishop of London and Mr. Chancellor of the Exchequer, [3] which hath made me overlook him the more narrowly; and the most I can condemn him of is rather doing nothing than doing ill, which in a place of so much temptation to vice deserves a charitable construction, and I pray you so persuade Sir Richard Smith and set Mr. Rooke [4] a work to do this poor gentleman a friendly office. For it were pity to see idleness so sharply punished in a time when great villainies escape so free, and even now he had settled himself to a new course. He is in doubt whether he shall presently go for England in company of Sir Francis Harris and Sir Thomas Skinner, who set forward tomorrow, or stay here until he can give some better proof of himself. You may see by an epitaph I send you here enclosed that we have here likewise some angry fathers, but upon greater cause, for these brothers (whom the advocate would not vouchsafe to name his children) are famous in this town for their disobediences. We have had here this fortnight past many embassages from the several cities subject to this state, which recompense their long stay from saluting the election of this prince [5] by the extraordinary cost in their equipage. The duke of Savoy, whilst he was treating with the duke of Mantua of a match for his daughter, hath played with a petard against one of his towns in Montferrat, which is a new love trick.[6] We have here no news of the Bull you write of,[7] and I take the voice to be spread rather *in terrorem* than that there is any such thing *in esse*. But whether it be so, or *in potentia,* it is not now so terrible a beast (thanks be to God) as in the old blind world. You will be entreated by my brother Williams to assist him in adjusting an account for me with Signore Burlamac-chi,[8] which, if you find troublesome, I pray you intreat Mr. Rooke to take the pains for me, who is perfect in such businesses. And so wish [paper torn] health and strength with as mu[paper torn] and as hearty affection as any [paper torn] to myself. I rest

Your assured loving [paper torn]

1. Probably Roger Manwood. See above, letter of March 20, 1611/12, n. 12.

2. Chamberlain had written on March 25 (*L. J. C.* I, 439–40) of the death of Torderby's (more properly, Tollerby's) father, who left his son £100 a year. If the executors of the will found that the young man stopped misbehaving, he could have £400 a year; hence Carleton's comments on his way of life.

3. The bishop of London was John King, a distinguished preacher; the chancellor of the exchequer was Sir Julius Caesar, an undistinguished careerist.

4. For Sir Richard Smith and George Rooke see above, letter of April 3, 1612, n. 5. Sir Richard was one of the executors of Tollerby's father's will. Chamberlain passed Carleton's remarks concerning young Tollerby on to him, which, said Smith, "shall stand him in great stead." *L. J. C.* I, 452.

5. The new doge was Marc Antonio Memmo, elected in the late summer of 1612.

6. For Savoy and Mantua see below, letter of May 28, 1613, n. 3.

7. Chamberlain had written on March 25 of a rumor that "there is a Bull come from Rome against the King and clapt upon the court gate" and that the Pope was organizing armies to invade Ireland. *L. J. C.* I, 440.

8. For Burlamacchi see below, letter of May 28, 1613.

Venice, May 28, 1613
S. P. 99/12, ff. 359–60

Good Mr. Chamberlain, I never received a more welcome letter from you than your last of the 29 of April, both for the assurance it brought of your good recovery as likewise for the great likelihoods of the good fortune of some of our best friends, and I heartily wish continuance of the one and accomplishment of the other.[1] Mr. Gent, who was then going and since, I hear, is departed, would have made me the more sorry but that his years were so many and his indisposition such that he could not last long. But he showed towards you *in articulo mortis* how kind and officious he was to his friends in his whole life; as others, whom he hath followed, made the last act answerable to the whole play. I have recommended unto you a troublesome business betwixt me and Signore Burlamacchi, which being once made even I will then think how to take that course in my exchanges which you write of and I shall thereby save a great deal which I now lose.[2] If you go not abroad or remove into the country (as I guess you will do as soon as your strength serves you) I have desired Mr. Rooke to assist my brother Williams; and by a letter I have had from him this week of the 4th of this present, he writes that he purposed that day to visit you. I pray you let him know of the receipt of his letter and of two to be sent to Padua, which I shall tell him myself by the next opportunity. By the last I sent you in my brother Williams' packet the duke of Savoy's manifest postiled in this town by the resident of Mantua according to a publication made by the duke of Mantua to the same effect; and thereby you may judge of the justice of this quarrel betwixt those princes, which continues still very hot, the duke of Savoy having taken two other places in Montferrat, though from Nizza della Paglia he rose upon the Spaniards marching that way. The emperor's commissary and the Pope's nuncio post often betwixt Savoy and Mantua to take up the matter, but it seems they are far from any terms of agreement, Savoy protesting that he will rather be buried in Montferrat than relinquish all he hath taken and Mantua

[140]

refusing so much as to treat until he have full restitution made with reparation of damages.³ The Venetian ambassador at Turin ⁴ is returned hither and was conducted into the College ⁵ with more than ordinary solemnity to show that his licensing by the duke of Savoy was not here held as any disgrace unto him. He found a tragical accident in his house, his sister (being married to one of the best families) having broken her neck out of a window in an hypochondriacal humor and without any help (as is verily thought), though such desperate pranks be very rare in these parts, where life is so much set by. For an intermedium to these tragical accidents you shall understand that a poor *contadina*, sister to the substantial miller whom (as you may remember) you saw near the count Collaltos' tower at Mosestre [Mestre?] is made a countess this last week by the lottery. Her chance was first to draw one lot (having put in for no more), wherein she had a grace of ten others, and nine of those being blanks the tenth was a county in Friuli to the value of 14,000 crowns. Not long before a greater in value was drawn by a young fellow of Ragusa, who coming hither scarce with a cloak is gone home with 16,000 crowns, and now all is ended. The *Uscocchi* do still molest us, having, since the taking of the galley which I wrote of in my last, ransacked and spoiled a fair which was held in an open island near Sebenico and cut in pieces both men, women, and children. The worst is the state is so much distracted by these troubles by land that they cannot prosecute these Robin-hoods so roundly as at other times, and indeed the wars are so fair betwixt the Spaniard and the duke of Savoy that no man knows what to judge of them; but it appears they are here much affrighted when as they fall to their devotions *per la pace d'Italia,* for which there was a public procession and the *quaranta hore* in Saint Mark's Church this week with preparations and ceremonies the like whereunto hath not ben used, as their records do testify, since Pope Alessandro's coming hither for refuge in his flight from Frederick Barbarossa.⁶ Many do marvel at this action in regard that these signori have the reputation of doing nothing *a caso,* but upon good ground; yet to tell you my private opinion, I think these are but *terrores panici* and that they will quickly vanish.

Thus with all our kindest remembrances and congratulations for your good recovery, which comes (I assure you) most unfeignedly from all hands, I rest

Yours as ever most affectionately

1. Chamberlain predicted very confidently that Sir Ralph Winwood would become secretary, along with Sir Henry Neville. *L. J. C.* I, 445.

2. Philip Burlamacchi, a naturalized English citizen, is described by Robert Ashton, *Money Market,* p. 20, as "the greatest financier of the age." The 1620s was the decade of his most extensive operation; then, as in 1613, he transmitted money for use abroad, for ambassadors and others. Chamberlain's advice to Carleton was to employ an expert in matters of exchange rates; he calculated that Carleton could save £100 a year. *L. J. C.* I, 442.

3. Duke Francesco of Mantua had recently died, leaving only a daughter, whose mother was the daughter of the duke of Savoy. Mantua was a male fief, and passed to the late duke's brother. Montferrat, however, had come to the dukes of Mantua through a female, and the duke of Savoy claimed it on behalf of his granddaughter. A small war broke out, in which Savoy was aided at first by the Spanish governor of Milan, Don Juan de Mendoza, marquis of Inoiosa. The policy of the Spanish government soon changed, however. The ducal family of Mantua had French connections, and Casale, the major fortress in Montferrat, was being defended by the duke of Nevers, a cousin of the duke of Mantua; neither France nor Spain wanted an Italian war at this time. Spain was able to force a truce, mentioned by Carleton in his letter of July 9, 1613; see below.

4. Vicenzo Gussoni, who had been recalled by the Venetian government to forestall his enforced departure. The duke of Savoy was resentful of Venetian support of Mantua in the present crisis.

5. The College was the official executive body of the Republic, though real power lay with the Council of Ten.

6. In 1177 Pope Alexander III came to Venice and there negotiated a settlement with Frederick Barbarossa, whose army had been beaten the year before at Legnano. Legend had it that the Pope came to Venice in disguise and remained concealed for some months in a monastery.

Good Mr. Chamberlain, I could not sooner answer your last of
the 10th of June, which I received by the former ordinary, and
now our wars of Montferrat being at an end we are of a sudden
in a dead calm, and nothing is offered worth the writing, all that
rests now being the expectation of disarming, to which, though
they seem willing on all sides in respect of charge, yet they strain
courtesy who should begin, and the governor of Milan, as he was
suspected to have protracted the troubles longer than was needful,
so now it is likewise laid to his charge that he doth willingly up-
hold these arms, whereof to have a strength on foot for the
countenance of the designs of the House of Austria in the imperial
diet now at hand.[1] I hear from Constantinople that the Grand
Signor's return thither proves but *à reculer pour mieux sauter* and
that he is like to be quickly heard of again in Transylvania. There
was a fire lately which burnt 2000 shops and houses, and great
spoil was committed by the Janissaries in places which the fire left
untouched. The States' ambassador with the Grand Signor finds
many difficulties in his admission, and is like to be fetched over
at his first entrance by the craft of his dragoman for 20,000 sequins as money, which he pretends to be disbursed for him to
procure his reception. I send you here enclosed the list of his
presents. I am certainly informed out of those parts how that,
within four hours after the departure of the grand duke's[2] galleys
from the fortress they surprised in Caramania (whereof I am sure
you have the relation in print), there came treasure of the Grand
Signor to the self-same place, slenderly guarded to the value of
40,000 sequins. The duke of Epernon's oldest son, who was one
in that enterprise (and is scarce specified in the printed pamphlets
which are spread abroad), they say here was the man who with
his own hands planted the petard against the gate, and so do some
Frenchmen here maintain who were in his company and take it in
great snuff he hath not his due. Others here are of the same nation, newly come from Casale, where they have remained with

the duke of Nevers and mutiny not a little against the duke of Mantua's brother Don Vicenzo for suffering them to appear in the army of Italians and Spaniards, who were all in good equipage, and they poor snakes without arms and upon hired horses. Here in this town they take care to be better mounted, and if Don Vicenzo and his train (who are expected here shortly) will be content to ride in their saddles, they need no better reevnge. Don Luiggi d'Este, the second son to the duke of Modena, who was lately in England, hath presented himself to this state as a *personaggio* with provision of 6000 crowns a year and hath been here for the space of 3 weeks with a good retinue of Modenese and behaved himself without exception, only his mistress complains of him that for the first night's lodging he gave her but 15 light hungers, which she sent back again with a message like that you know, *Quamquam ego digna hac contumelia,* etc. On Sunday last there was a regatta performed unto him which I cannot describe better unto you than in this unproper term, a horse-race of boats, and truly, considering the circumstances of the windows, well furnished through the whole Canale Grande, the multitude of gondolas on both sides, with certain large boats of ten oars, which were gilded and painted and the rowers all in liveries, which carried gentlemen in them who had the marshalling of the sport, it was the best entertainment I saw since I came to Venice. The French ambassador and myself were placed in the two ambassadors' houses, who are designed into our quarters, where we were feasted and treated *à l'envie,* and in the voice of the town who examine the *spesa,* ours had the pre-eminence. The Spanish ambassador stood at his own house with the whole *facciata* thereof fairly furnished with Persian carpets, but the company that filled the rooms were most of them Levant Jews and others of the ghetto, which was a pitiful spectacle; only with himself in a window apart he had the two residents of Florence and Urbino. We had here Sir Thomas Puckering, who came opportunely from Naples, and two gentlemen, whereof one is a Scottishman and a pensioner, who were of the lady Elizabeth's train. They tell us my lord of Arundel and his lady, whom they left with the duke of Lennox at Strasburg, will return through France home without passing any further, but I rather believe they were so told to be rid of their companies, and the more because I hear my lord had taken Inigo Jones into his train, who will be of best use to him (by reason of his language and experience) in these parts.[3] Master Pory [4] is come to Turin with purpose to see these parts but wants *primum necessarium* and hath therefore conjured me with these words (by the kind and constant intelligence which passeth betwixt you and my best friends in England) to send him 14 doubloons wherewith to disengage him where he lies in pawn, not knowing how to go forward or backward. I have done more in respect of his friends than himself, for I hear he is fallen too much love with the pot to be much esteemed of any and have sent him what he wrote for by Mathew the post. I am glad to understand that my nephew Anthony Williams found his taste so well as to choose a pear before a mellow apple, which was rotten at the core. I wish my nephew John Carleton speed no worse pro rata, if all be as well as I hear.[5] I pray you let me hear somewhat from you of him and his father, for from them I have no letters, and by the first traveller you light on or the next ship I will desire you to send me Sir Francis Bacon's last essays,[6] with whatsoever else is new in Paul's churchyard, not omitting so much as English almanacs, whereof we have a great miss. I shall send you a second part of *Ragguagli* [7] very shortly if they be not forbidden at Rome, as we hear they shall be, for which the author (whom we have here amongst us) hath uttered this charitable censure openly upon the piazza, that in the court of Rome they do busy themselves with nothing else than in forbidding *libri* and *libretti* and following *putti* and *puttane*. In these troubles of Lombardy, he had this conceit, that Savoy and Spain did make betwixt them *una tela*, whereof *l'ordimento* (the woof) was *di Savoya*, and *la trama* (the web) *di Spagna*.[8] I have some writings of his touching priests and Spaniards which will not abide the press, with which I hope to make you laugh one day; meantime I have no better counsel to give you but that which I wish I could follow, *salutem tuam cura*, and so God keep you.

Yours most assuredly

[145]

1. These designs were variously reported as an effort to elect either Philip III or Archduke Albert king of the Romans and hence the successor to Emperor Matthias, who was old and childless.

2. Cosimo II of Tuscany. Caramania was an area on the southern coast of Anatolia.

3. Princess Elizabeth, James's daughter, had recently married the elector of the Palatinate. Lennox and Arundel were among those who formally escorted her to her new home at Heidelberg. Sir Thomas Puckering was the son of Sir Henry Puckering, lord keeper of the great seal under Elizabeth; he had been in the household of Prince Henry. Carleton, when he went from England to Venice, took Puckering with him as far as Paris, where he studied for a time. Inigo Jones was the famous architect.

4. For John Pory see above, letter of August 27, 1607, n. 2.

5. Chamberlain reported on August 1 that John Carleton, with whom he spoke at Anthony Williams' wedding, promised "large relations" for his uncle. John was one of the king's equerries; Chamberlain doubted that he would hold the job long, since he was not diligent enough in attendance. *L. J. C.* I, 471.

6. A new edition of Bacon's *Essays* had recently appeared, a collection which included *On Deformity,* a venomous posthumous assault on Salisbury.

7. Trajano Boccalini's *Ragguagli di Parnasso;* Chamberlain had thanked Carleton in his letter of June 10 for the first part. *L. J. C..* I, 457.

8. This sentence illustrates the shakiness of Carleton's Italian. *Ordito* (not *ordimento*) means *warp,* and *trama* means *woof.*

Padua, September 30, 1613

S. P. 99/13, ff. 309–10

Good Mr. Chamberlain, we have been here as sparing in troubling the good time you have given yourself in the country this vacation by forcing you to read letters as you have been in writing; and indeed we have taken the *buon tèmpo* these few weeks past more than in all the time since we came into these parts. Now I conjecture this letter may find you not only returned but settled at London and that you can be content to know how the world wags abroad, which is after that manner as if it were every day blown with a several wind. One while we speak of peace, another while of war; whilst in the meantime we have in these parts the name of the one and the effect of the other. The Spaniard hath caused the wars to cease betwixt Savoy and Mantua and now lately betwixt Modena and Lucca,[1] but made no agreement betwixt the parties, so as all continue in arms, and the forces of the state of Milan quarter upon their countries as peacemaker but eat and consume them worse than enemies. This state, keeping pace always with their neighbors, hath a great charge lying continually upon it both in respect of their own forces as likewise of the assistance they give to Mantua. That prince continues sick both in mind and in body, in which respect I defer my journey to him.[2] The galleys of Sicily have taken a great prize of 7 Turkish galleys, the manner whereof is diversely reported, some saying it was by fight at sea, others that they surprised them in port whilst most of the men were at land. In their return they touched at Zante,[3] and there made some stay, which it is doubted will fall heavy upon the Venetians, against whom the Turks do usually wreak themselves of the blows they receive from others. The Grand Signor is come out of Constantinople with purpose at first to come to Adrianople, but hearing of the plague in that place he takes another course, and it is thought he will come to Belgrade to be nearer Transylvania, where he intends to make war if he be not admitted to peaceable possession. I have a large letter from the Persian court of the reception of the Turkish ambassador, which was with much show and ceremony but a general commandment given (which was strictly observed) that during his abode there neither prince nor peer nor any other should speak one word unto him but give him as many audiences as he would require, which they say was done in regard the Persian ambassador was so used at Constantinople; yet saith my advertiser the peace is like to follow in those parts, which may seem very strange that so great a bargain should be driven with so few words. The news of the Diet of Ratisbon [4] finds a nearer way unto you. Our extraordinary Venetian ambassadors are there arrived and make ample relations of their good reception, which in regard of the troublesome difference with the archduke Ferdinand was somewhat suspected.

The Spanish ambassador whom you left at Venice is fallen into a new contestation with the state for one of his servants who was taken in his livery accused for an assassin by one of the same profession who was setting forward towards Saint Mark's pillars,[5] and matters prove so foul against him that he is in danger to go the same way. The French ambassador, being at a villa near Zonkeys towards Treviso and returning back with his two secretaries in coach with him, made the coachman drive *alla Françoise* until they were overturned *alla Tedesca* and were all so well bruised, with some broken heads, that they appeared not in many days after. My lord Arundel is gone privately to Florence, having left his lady at a villa hereby towards Cataio.[6] Their entertainments at Venice were concluded by a *festa di gentildonne* made by Signore Barbarigo, where were about 20 of the most principal women, some of them very fair, all rich, in pearl and chains; and they took more liberty than ordinary in dancing to show what they can do when they are suffered; wherein they became themselves very well. The feast ended with a banquet, and all without disorder, which was strange in respect maskers were admitted to the dancing. Only it fell out that at the going into an inner room to the banquet where none were suffered to enter but English and the husbands of the gentlewomen, the door being kept by six Venetian gentlemen, a masker, who pressed to enter and was repulsed by one of the gentlemen, challenged him that gave him the repulse to one of our Tramontan [northern] duels and desired him to go home to his house, where he would presently find him and discover himself unto him. The gentleman accepted the challenge publicly and went immediately to his house, where the masker appeared not, and so the fray ended. Before I end I will tell you that I have taken order with a merchant at Zante to send two vessels, one of wine of the best in those islands, the other of oil of Corfu, which I design to Sir Ralph Winwood, if they come whilst he is in England as I hope they will; and you shall be sure to have your part. If he be by any accident returned I leave them to your disposal; and thus with all our kind remembrances I rest

Yours as ever most assuredly

1. The conflict between Modena and Lucca was over the Garfagnana district; it was on a small scale but relatively destructive.

2. Carleton had been instructed to pay a courtesy visit to the new duke of Mantua, Ferdinando Gonzaga; the visit had just been postponed, ostensibly because the duke had not yet ceased to be a cardinal. It became clear that the duke did not want the visit to be made, and it never was.

3. Zante, one of the Ionian Islands, was a major Venetian entrepôt, the headquarters of the important trade in currants.

4. At this Diet the emperor Matthias vainly attempted to search out a common ground between the quarrelling Catholic and Protestant factions in the empire; it was impossible to reach agreement on anything.

5. Criminals were often executed between the pillars of the Piazza San Marco.

6. It was Arundel's habit to travel ahead of his wife, and, when he reached a place where he wished to stay for a time, send for her to join him.

Padua, November 4, 1613

S. P. 99/14, ff. 104–105

Sir, I wrote to you since I heard from you, and this place is very barren of occurrents, yet you shall know what we do here, as within few days I shall tell you how we find Venice. Since my lady of Arundel's departure with her train (who went from hence towards Florence about a fortnight since) [1] we have been more sensible of solitariness than heretofore and therefore have made a starting journey to Arquà, [2] where Petrarch is buried, and had his house at commandment but made no stay in regard of the foul weather which threatened us and since our return hath made such an inundation that for the space of ten days it hath been impossible to pass that way either by coach or boat. The tempest was so great at sea that two Venetian ships laden with moscadins [3] were cast away in the port of Malamocco and 50 men drowned. An English ship coming lately out of the Levant lost by a calanture[?] 10 of 22 men she had in her in the space of 12 days, and half of the rest so sick that they could not work, yet they got to Venice, where some fraud they used to cozen the Signori della

[149]

Sanità [4] brought them into that danger, that I had much ado to save them from the galleys. The ways are made very troublesome to travellers by reason of the *contumacia* [quarantine], which all Englishmen are generally put to, which way soever they come, unless they return out of Italy, and yet as I am informed London is clear of sickness. Here are newly come three young gentlemen by the way of Germany, who have been forced to do twice *contumacia* betwixt Trent and this place. Others I hear have lain a good while at Verona, amongst which, unless Phil Lytton be one, I shall not expect him this winter, and if he were there, methinks I should hear from him. We were never since our coming into these parts so barren of English as at this present. Mr. Pory, I think, is settled here for this winter and, if he behave himself no otherwise than he hath done hitherto, he might surely have challenged of his friends at Paris a better report *for I find him no ways disordered.*[5] I should say stet, but yet the poor man cannot stand, being (even whilst this letter was writing) brought home reeling by your cousin Lottrel. The lectures are begun here with great emulation of concurrents, but the number of scholars is very small in respect of the difficulty of passing out of Germany. We have here a podestà,[6] son to that famous Foscarini who laid the foundation of his fortune in London, a man very ambitious of the honor to have reformed the disorders of this place, which he began the last winter with the scholars and, by imprisoning two or three which he fetched out of their chambers for walking with forbidden weapons in the night, hath ever since kept them in good rule. This summer he clapped up one Boromeo, a gentlemen of good account, with 12 others of this town for defrauding the poor of the use of such moneys as are in the *montes,* which hath been a practice continued for many years, and other governors, being either idle or obnoxious, did not look into it; and now this week he hath caused a Zaratine scholar to be fetched from the altar of a church where he took sanctuary and by his means discovered 6 *còrsi* who had lately broken up a merchant's house in this town whilst he was in villa and stole to the value of 5,000 crowns in money and plate, and the next week it is expected they shall be all executed. I write you these particularities in regard of the effect they work, which is of a most dissolute and disordered town (as you have known it) to be more quiet and secure than Venice itself, and hereafter it will not be thought a matter so impossible *rifare il mondo*. At Venice the noise of the Turks' arming to sea puts them to their wonted preparations. They are not yet free from their mistrusts at land as long as they see an army continued in the state of Milan and the duke of Savoy makes no haste to license his soldiers. The young count Rambaldo Collalto (at whose old castle we were upon the Sile) is the emperor's ambassador at Rome to demand aid of the Pope for the wars of Transylvania, where he hath hitherto obtained nothing but crosses and blessings. The grand duchess hath been at Loreto and there bestowed in presents upon that Lady to the value of 10,000 crowns. The *pizzòchera* at Venice, who about two years since was shut up for counterfeiting the stigmata of Santa Catharina di Siena, is newly dead in the convent of the Capuchins over against my door, and for the brags those poor nuns make of her religious life since she came amongst them is in danger to be made a saint, she being the first that is buried in that convent. You see what poor stuff I am fain to entertain you with, and if here were anything worthy of Sir Ralph Winwood I should pray you to make him partake. The token I mentioned in my last letter I have caused to be addressed to your brother Richard. Here is a speech that old Mr. Willoughby [7] hath a purpose to go into England with my lord of Arundel. It was written to me about 6 weeks since out of England that the bishop of Ely was dead, which I hope is not true because I see his name amongst the commissioners of the divorce.[8] Thus with all our kindest remembrances I commit you to God's holy protection.

Yours most affectionately

1. Arundel had decided to stay briefly at Siena, in part because it would be a less conspicuous point of departure for his projected journey to Rome, where he had arrived by January. See M. F. S. Hervey, *The Life, Correspondence, and Collections of Thomas Howard, Earl of Arundel* (Cambridge, 1921), pp. 80–83.

2. Arquà Petrarca is a small town in the hills near Padua. Carleton was by

no means the last English visitor to Petrarch's grave. Byron came two centuries later and acquired material for a passage in *Childe Harold's Pilgrimage*.

3. Presumably muscadine grapes, from which muscatel is made.

4. The Signori della Sanità, the board of health, was established in the later fifteenth century; one of its major responsibilities was to prevent the importation of goods from any area where plague existed.

5. The seven italicized words were scored through by Carleton. The next sentence was then added in the margin of the letter.

6. Giovanbattista Foscarini. Carleton got on well with him; at Carleton's request he had recently obtained the release of some silk which the earl of Arundel had brought into Venice illegally. Carleton spoke well of him in a speech thanking the Venetian government for its courtesies to Arundel. See *C. S. P. Venetian 1613–1615,* pp. 52, 56, 68.

7. Richard Willoughby, described by Wotton as "an infectious Papist, of a still and dangerous temper." He decided to remain in Padua and died there in 1617. Smith, *Wotton,* II, 114.

8. The divorce was that of Frances Howard from the earl of Essex, so that she might marry her lover, Lord Rochester, King James's favorite.

Venice, December 10/20, 1613
S. P. 99/14, ff. 214–15

Good Mr. Chamberlain, I am so much scanted in time that I should not now answer your letter of the 11th of November received by this last ordinary, save only to give you knowledge of my cousin Phil Lytton's safe arrival here, who came from Lyons in company of an English merchant, one Davis, and hath had a sharp journey but bears it well and is so perfect a monsieur that if we can make him as good an Italian he will be a complete traveller. Yesterday was the first time I saw him, and this night he enters commons with us both at bed and at board, which will hinder him of much good fellowship abroad, there being a strange Dutch humor crept into our English gallants to drink themselves friends in place of all other caresses. Two of them (whereof one hath been formerly named unto you) finding better wine abroad than in my house tumbled lately into one bed in a house where they never lay before, and one of them had all his clothes taken away or hooked out of the window with a good stock of doubloons in his pocket before he wakened; if his bedfellow's clothes had been fastened upon he had been in danger to have lost *corpus cum causa,* for he lay in them all night. I hear you cry out, *o tempora, o mores*; but to our former purpose. I write not to Sir Rowland Lytton until I can advertise him of all particulars concerning his son, we being yet but mere strangers. Our friend[1] (I perceive) is like to be brought upon the stage again, which I pray God may be with a plaudite. These troubles of Italy are like to end comically in a marriage, the king of Spain having declared to the duke of Mantua that if he will not render the daughter he must take and marry the mother, his brother's widow, because they two cannot be divided, and he weary of striving against the stream hath given his consent. There is in the meantime treaty[2] of disarming, but as yet little done, only this state draws some men from the frontiers towards Milan to furnish their garrisons upon the gulf for fear of the Turkish preparations by sea. The late *bailo* at Constantinople is newly elected ambassador to Rome, and the last duke's brother is to go proveditor general into Dalmatia. Signore Barbarigo,[3] ambassador to his majesty, winters in a cold and uncomfortable climate, being entertained with business for his masters amongst the Grisons and Swiss. We shall have this year a short carnival, but good company, here being many English gentlemen arrived from all regions. My lord Roos will be here this next week; my lord of Arundel hath not his health, which hinders his coming during this cold weather, which is sharper than ever I felt it since my coming into these parts, or else I am grown more tender. The great storm and inundation you write of[4] happened much about the time of tempest in the Mediterranean, wherein they write that Genoa in shipping and goods was lost to the value of 2 million of ducats, and at Villafranca [Ville-franche] (as I wrote you) our pirates lost their whole fleet. I write not to Sir Ralph Winwood as long as you can acquaint him with that little these parts afford or until I hear of his absolute stay or return, but I must pray you to remember my service both to himself and his lady, and so wishing you from us all the *buone feste con molti e molti anni,* I rest

Yours as ever most assuredly

1. Winwood, who was in England on private business. He had asked if the king wanted him to return to the Netherlands and was told that James would let him know after returning from Royston. *L. J. C.* I, 484–85.

2. Between Savoy and the Spanish governor of Milan.

3. Gregorio Barbarigo, who had been ambassador in Savoy; his departure for England was delayed by the negotiations with the Grisons, with whom Venice was anxious to renew her former alliance. The importance of the Grisons lay in their control of the Valtellina pass, an essential link between the Habsburg possessions in Milan and the Tyrol.

4. Chamberlain had written of a fierce storm which produced severe flooding and property damage along the southeast coast from Norfolk to Kent. *L. J. C.* I, 485–86.

Venice, December 24, 1613/January 3, 1614

S. P. 99/18, ff. 153–54

Good Mr. Chamberlain, hitherto our post is not come (and it is now Thursday night late) so as I know not whether I shall hear from you this week, yet I am loath to suffer too much time to run on without saluting you, though otherwise it runs on without much alteration, for you know how the entertainments as well as the affairs of this place have their course and come about in their seasons like our children's sports in schools. The carnival is already begun without inhibition this year by reason of the shortness thereof and this day my house furnished out a sufficient band of maskers, wherein Phil Lytton, in my sister's wild company, made his first entrance and already prefers Venice much before Paris, though somewhat short of Sedan. My lord Roos made haste from Florence to be present with us at our Communion on Christmas day, at which he was accompanied with his Spanish servant Diego, a man of good sufficiency, both learned and intelligent and much esteemed for his honesty and fidelity to his master. You will imagine how welcome this news will be to Rome, where they have long had this young lord in their catalogue as one of their converts, and I think this is the first Spaniard that did ever so good a work on this side the mountains. How our friends at Siena [Arundel and his entourage] do, I hear not, by reason that the freezing of the rivers doth hinder the passage of the posts. The affairs of Savoy and Mantua rest at a stay in expectation of the proceeding of the match betwixt the duke of Mantua and his brother's widow, which as it is made by the authority of Spain so the finishing of it depends upon their slow resolutions. But for the perfecting of a comedy this is set down for the last act, the first whereof was the duke of Savoy's assaulting and taking the towns in Montferrat; the second, the rendering them back again; the third, the *allées* and *venues* betwixt the deputies and commissioners to and fro and treating at Milan; and the fourth, the demanding of the *Principina*. Now for the actors, we have the Spanish Captain played by the prince of Ascoli [the Spanish commander in Milan]; the Doctor by the nuncio, or the writers in the law point touching the *tutèla*; the Tedesco, which was the emperor's commissary; the Monsieur, whereof there were enough at Casale, and the Magnifico which is the Venetian secretary at Mantua; and thus you see how the descant runs of all our great stirs, and for the laying of the plot of this play and carrying it along with so many intricate varieties we are beholden jointly to the duke of Savoy and the governor of Milan. There is yet no haste made to rid the stage, so as the world is in expectation of some tragedy or other before all be ended, but not to be played in these parts, and therefore our friends on the other side of the mountains have cause to look about them unless the coming down of the Turk upon Hungary divert the storm. This state continues their strength on foot though they be persuaded by the governor of Milan to disarm and save unnecessary charges; and, though our letters from Constantinople advertise generally of the Turk's preparations to sea, with much speech of invading of Candia, it appears they are not here apprehensive of any such danger in that a proposition being made in Senate by the *savii grandi* for the changing their *sopra comiti* into *provveditori* (a course always used in such perils) it passed not by some few balls.[1] I have now received your letter of the 25 of November with the enclosed from Sir R. Winwood. There hath been some negligence used or pretense of too much care in the token I intended to him, the providing whereof I referred to one Hales, an English merchant at Zante, who had been sometimes a scholar in Merton College in Oxford.[2] And at such time as I thought it had been with you or near you at least in England, having had some of the same kind from thence here sent me to Venice, I understand that he hath written hither to have some vessels sent him, there being none good for long carriage at Zante, so as Robin Hassal[3] hath about a month since furnished him with vessels, and his direction is to send them to your brother Richard with a letter of advice to you. Here is nothing to add to what I formerly wrote before the arrival of our post, whose stay hath been by reason of our frosts, which kept him in a gondola betwixt two cakes of ice betwixt this and Mestre from three hours before day until 23 at night. Thus we all wish you a good and merry new year with many more, and I ever rest

Yours most affectionately

I am heartily sorry for the wants of the two poor strangers,[4] though I am neither guilty of their going from hence nor suffering there, but as it was their own desires and the consents of others. Signore Biondi writes me that Sir Henry Wotton is absolutely appointed for France and that he hath obtained the king's leave to go with him; besides that Mr. Morton is to be speedily dispatched for Savoy, so as all that company (if all be true) is provided for, and I must conclude of Sir Thomas Edmondes' revocation, which I should be sorry to hear were to leave him to uncertainties, unless he be better furnished with patience than he was wont.[5]

1. This refers to a method of secret voting by dropping different colored balls into an urn, from which the expression "to blackball" derives.

2. Anthony Hales was the merchant in question. The "token" for Winwood, a "vessel of muscadine," was almost given to Carleton's mother-in-law by mistake; see Chamberlain's letter of January 20, 1614, *L. J. C.* I, 501. Merton College men played a large part in Carleton's life: his father-in-law was warden of Merton; his secretary, Isaac Wake, and his chaplain, Thomas Horne, were fellows of Merton. Stoye, *Travellers,* p. 140.

3. A Robert Hassall is listed by T. K. Rabb, *Enterprise and Empire* (Cambridge, Mass., 1967), p. 309, as a member of the Levant Company.

4. For the "poor strangers" see below, letter of February 25, 1613/1614, n. 2.

5. Giovanni Francesco Biondi was an associate of Wotton's whom the latter had sent to England on mission in 1609. He and Carleton corresponded occasionally. There is a biographical sketch of Biondi in Smith, *Wotton,* II, 463–64. As it turned out, Wotton was sent, not to France, but to the Netherlands in connection with a renewed outbreak of fighting over the vexed question of the Cleves-Julich succession; he was then appointed to succeed Carleton in Venice. So Sir Thomas Edmondes' temper was not tested after all.

Venice, February 25, 1613/14

S. P. 99/15, ff. 127–28

Good Mr. Chamberlain, my business the last week and the charge which others took to write unto you was the cause that I have now your two letters of the 20th of the last and 3rd of this present, both to answer at one time, and first, concerning our friend's advancement and my own subsisting,[1] there is no more to say but to refer all to God and good fortune. The Neapolitan's arrival in England and the Carmelitans' reconversion fall out unluckily together,[2] if things be judged by the events, yet I know not the success of the former but have little better conceit of him than you have. Such, notwithstanding, hath been the course and carriage of both those businesses that if the like occasions should present themselves to me tomorrow next I could do no otherwise, neither should I think of other proceeding than hath passed in both these. I must confess to have been ever jealous of the Carmelitans since I heard of their base and beggerly courses when

[157]

they had so little need but cannot believe they parted from hence upon that lewd resolution which they now pretend, for besides many demonstrations of their affection to be received into our Church and kingdom, they showed sufficient grounds of learning and observation for their departure from their former profession in religion. It is very likely they have been practiced withal and regained by great promises, since their conversion was held no small disgrace to their monastical orders. You will have heard of a friar, whose mountebank tricks you saw at Santi Apostoli, how he could not suffer our late queen of happy memory to sleep quietly in her grave after so many years' rest, for which, upon complaint to the prince, he hath been called before the council of ten and so well schooled and lessoned that he finds this no place to vent any more of his lying miracles. I remembered your doctor's caveat of pulpit hornets but could not suffer this poisonous-tongued fellow to sting the memory of so great a queen.[3] But shall I tell you in sport, betwixt you and me, what had like to have happened? The very day and time when he was before the council of ten, a bear being chased by dogs toward the ghetto broke loose and came into the square court behind my house, from thence climbed up by the vine which joins to my back door to the top of the gondolier's house next to mine, and so was coming into the window of my dining room, which it might very well have done. If this had happened, and any hurt followed, Jesu Maria, what a miracle? in what danger was the poor Capuchin, by breaking loose of a bear from the stake, to be made a saint? but let no body laugh at this but yourself, lest they laugh at me for telling such an idle story. This Lent hath ministered nothing else to write. The late duke's brother Donato, a man for his sufficiency commonly voiced to succeed this duke [Marc Antonio Memmo] (who cannot last long), is newly dead general in Dalmatia. Priuli,[4] our other general *in terra firma,* gives some alarms to this state upon the removing of the Spanish army out of Montferrat towards the confines of this state, but they are not very hotly taken, upon good advertisement that they are not of strength for any great enterprise, and all our towns are well provided against surprise. We have here the marquis of Coeuvre,[5] privately, whose coming doth little help or hinder the affairs of Savoy and Mantua, though that be his errand, because they receive their form out of Spain, and are protracted according to the accustomed delays of that court and more irresolution than that nation is commonly noted withal. I am sorry the error in the wine proved no better. True it is, that which you lighted upon was my wife's provision for my father Savile; the other, for Sir Ralph Winwood, is to be directed to your brother Richard. It is strange that that which I have from the same place is so perfect good and that which we send so ill.[6] I assure you we wish it of the best. Touching my brother Williams I am neither ill satisfied in the means nor in the effect of his soliciting for me, and the course I was thinking of was out of opinion that my business might be a hindrance to his own; but if he do not so find it, I shall think myself both in charge and in care much eased by his means, for any other course would be more costly, and as the world now goes, few hands are to be trusted with any great sums; therefore I desire only that he will continue as well satisfied of me as I am of him, and then for that point my greatest care is taken.[7] You will have heard happily how our great merchants of these parts and in other chief cities have been blown up lately and bankrupted like a train of powder, which began at Lucca with the Cenami and Spada for 300,000 crowns, so to Lyons with the Cenami and Bernardi for the like sum, from thence to Florence with the Gondi and Giacomini for 350,000 crowns. So hither to this piazza with the Albertini and Cambii for 250,000 crowns, in which sum is comprised 15,000 which was the greatest part of the stock of our old Florentine resident. We hear likewise at the same time of the *buon tempi,* both at Bologna and Antwerp, which are gone in *mala ora* for 250,000 crowns and of one Cobaut of Amsterdam for 80,000; and now our English travellers begin to suspect Tom Stone and his correspondent Philip Come at Florence, by whom they make most of their exchanges. Thus you may see how that wants like the late tempests and floods are universal and rain over all the world, and it seems masters of ships and mariners have no better luck than merchants, for we have some here at present in our port (little for the credit of our nation) without either money, credit, or victuals. I pray you remember my service to Sir Thomas Edmondes and Sir Ralph Winwood as often as you see them and so with all our best wishes to yourself I rest

Yours most affectionately

1. The promotion of Sir Ralph Winwood to the secretaryship and Carleton's possible transfer to The Hague as Winwood's successor.

2. In 1612 Carleton had recommended two ex-Carmelite friars to the archbishop of Canterbury. They came to England and professed their conversion. In January 1613 Chamberlain remarked on their discontent with their treatment. Now, Chamberlain wrote, they "are returned to their vomit and prove notable knaves, professing now that they were never other than Romish Catholickes wherein they will live and die, and that their coming hither and their dissembling was only for *quadagnare et fornicare.*" *L. J. C.* I, 504–505.

3. Archbishop Abbot on March 30 conveyed to Carleton the king's approval of his action in silencing the friar, which must have taken some of the sting out of the unfortunate result of the business of the Carmelites. Abbot's letter is misdated 1613 in *C. S. P. Domestic 1611–1618,* p. 178. Carleton wrote an account of the sermon to James on February 11/21; it is given in *C. S. P. Venetian 1613–1615,* p. 94.

4. Antonio Priuli, who later became doge.

5. François Hannibal d'Estrée, marquis of Coeuvres, was sent to Rome and Milan by the French government in an effort to settle matters between Savoy and Mantua. He accomplished nothing.

6. Chamberlain had written that, when the wine Carleton sent was tasted, there was debate as to whether it was opened too soon, or spoiled in transit, or simply bad to begin with. *L. J. C.* I, 501.

7. Carleton's brother-in-law, Alexander Williams, was acting as his London agent in money matters.

Venice, March 11, 1613/14

S. P. 99/15, ff. 164–65

Good Mr. Chamberlain, you guess not amiss in your last by the former ordinary of the 10th of February at my longing desire to hear of the good success of our friend's expectations, which, if they rest upon service to be done in Parliament and that there (as you say) he must win his spurs, he is like to meet with so skittish a jade of the mutineers' corner that, instead of winning the spurs, he must take heed of losing the saddle.[1] For I have heard this judgment given of that place, that it is very fit and proper for an obscure and unknown person to win credit and for one that hath credit before to lose it, so hard a matter it is and almost impossible in a multitude to satisfy expectation. If France be the only hindrance to the Low Countries, the troubles now risen in that quarter will soon withdraw the occasion,[2] but in a matter of this nature methinks presence and absence should not sway it, for there are others present and always near hand whose hopes and pretensions are as great as the best and, though their labor hath been hitherto chiefly for the exclusive, yet when it comes to dealing they look for a share. But greater wheels must assuredly have motion before these lesser shall stir, and howsoever it succeed with our friend for the main matter I make no doubt but he will fasten upon some suit of that good value that will salve all sores of private profit and contentment, if not of public reputation. Yet who can justly except against those successes which depend upon others? I am sorry to hear of the escape of that fellow who with his companion hath filled me with much grief and shame,[3] but I make no question of his punishment wherever he goes, especially if he appear at Rome, where other examples do show what he must look after. My lord of Ely's opinion touching new and sudden converts [4] is not to be gainsaid, but every man is to have a beginning, and these men (especially the elder) could give at their first conference with Mr. Horne so good an account of themselves, both for their reasons grounded upon good learning of their relinquishing the Church of Rome as likewise for their resolution, accompanied with show of much modesty and humility of entering and perservering in ours, that I must confess I presumed more of them than of many others who have offered themselves to me in the same kind, and I was willing enough to stop our adversaries' mouths, who make so great boasts and brags of every poor convert but *abeant in malam crucem,* which I make no doubt will be their end. You make me marvel you are such a stranger

[161]

with my lord of Ely, seeing his kindness towards you. If you had been penned up for so many years together, as now I have been, from changing almost a word with any man of merit unless it be with a public minister (whose conversation consists only of compliments) or a straggling traveller (who hath no more for you than he gathers upon the highway), you would know what it were to lose so good an opportunity. He is much reverenced by such learned men in these parts as dare read his books, and in that point here are many give themselves more liberty than in times past, which appears by some of these *nòbili* who have been heard this Lent using his arguments and disputing with their preachers in their church doors. Our Capuchin at Santi Apostoli proves a byword amongst them that *per spasso* they will go hear him tell his *belli miracoli.* To magnify our Lady's power above our Savior's, he said this last Saturday that she was the fountain of grace, He of justice, and her office was that, when Christ said *ite maledicti in infernum,* to catch them one after another by the hand and pull them into paradise, which, to express more effectually, he stooped down many times amongst his audience as if he would have pulled them one by one into the pulpit, and though the women (who are his especial *dévotes*) were so far transported with the love of our Lady that they parted with their rings and bracelets for alms; there were divers gentlemen who were as liberal in another kind, charging their preacher with open blasphemy. We have many more of this kind, but you will say this is too much, yet you know Venice so well that you can expect little else at this time. All our thoughts are bent towards the Turk's preparations in the Levant and the troubles rising in France, but the former is so much greater in fame than effect that here is small preparations; the other not so certain to proceed that any courses can be changed in that regard, though some hang in suspense. It is here generally concluded that the trouble of those parts will be the quiet of these, and the news is daily expected when the duke of Savoy shall march towards his county of Bresse,[5] which you may remember the captains of horse we met with at Lunenburg liked much better than Saluzzo. The Pope is chiefly busied at the present in traffic about new cardinals and canonization of saints, the former men of so mean account that the grand duke's brother [Carlo de' Medici] makes suit to be created alone, the latter (according to the legends we have of them) will confirm the saying of Bessarion that the abuse in making these new saints did make him *dubitare de antiquis.* I pray you remember my service in both the Saint Bartholemews if both our friends be still with you, and so with all our best wishes and commendations to yourself I rest

Yours as ever most affectionately

Stone of Cheapside is fallen so heavy upon Philip Come at Florence that he is *sospeso* if not broken for 74,000 crowns, and Henry Purvis [6] here is in danger of no small loss by Come, which he can hardly spare; he is 11,000 crowns deep yet holds up his head.

1. Chamberlain had written that Winwood was on tenterhooks, in daily expectation of being appointed secretary of state. *L. J. C.* I, 506. Carleton's forbodings about the difficulty of managing Parliament were justified by the disastrous session of 1614.

2. Chamberlain had written in his letter of February 10 (*L. J. C.* I, 506) that the coming to London of Sir Thomas Edmondes, who was then ambassador in France, had been used as a reason to delay Winwood's appointment. Carleton believed that Edmondes would be urgently needed at his post, and, indeed, the troubles in France were serious. The feeble government of Marie de' Medici was faced by a serious crisis provoked by the prince of Condé and his allies among the upper aristocracy. Their major objective was power and pelf for themselves and for the aristocracy as a caste; their ostensible objection to the policy of the government was to the Spanish marriage treaties. In May 1614 they forced the government to go a long way toward meeting their wishes and to agree to a meeting of the Estates-General.

3. The two ex-Carmelites; see above, letter of February 25, 1613/14. Chamberlain had written that one had taken refuge in the Venetian embassy.

4. That he had "had many trials of their knavery or inconstancy." *L. J. C.* I, 508.

5. This reference is puzzling, since in 1601 Savoy had ceded Bresse to France in return for Saluzzo.

6. Henry Purvis was the leading English merchant resident in Venice in this period. "He transmitted money, stored and shipped goods for travellers, and was in close touch with the ambassador." Stoye, *Travellers,* p. 114.

Sir, though I wrote to you the last week, yet I cannot omit to thank you for your last of the 31 of March in that you have therein fully satisfied both your own conjectures and my hopes—that business being brought to a wished end,[1] wherein the difficulties made the conquest the greater and will undoubtedly purchase much love and honor to that noble lord who was so true to himself and his friend in overcoming them. I were now no good servant to the king nor friend to myself if I did not conceive in my heart that full contentment, as I really do, for Mr. Secretary's preferment. The times never required more than now those parts of integrity, constancy, judgment, learning, and experience which are rooted in him, and all have seldom concurred in any one of his predecessors. Touching his successor in the Low Countries I writ nothing to him more than I have done formerly, resting in the same resolution that if it be thought to concur with his majesty's service that I be removed thither I shall embrace the condition most willingly and thankfully, reputing it an argument of confidence in his majesty to be employed in a place of so much use to the state and of favor in Mr. Secretary in that he prefers me before so many others, who I know will be suitors for it. But neither in his respect nor my own do I desire he should engage himself in suit for me touching this employment, it being no ways proper for him to enter into *contrasto* in the beginning of his charge for a matter which I perceive by his own letter is subject to opposition; and when it is with difficulty obtained I must take the entrance into a new service as a reward for an old and begin in another school, wherein I have not my lesson so perfect and was not otherwise to be preferred before this, wherein I grow an old truant, but in regard of the like accidents, an end which have befallen the last above all his predecessors in that employment which I am not so indiscreet and vain as once to look after. And truly were not I moved with this consideration, that Mr. Secretary, having been there ambassador so many years, knows more perfectly than any

[164]

other possibly can do what belongs to that service, would as well by his judgment direct me as by his friendship and favor protect me in many cross encounters, to which I know that place to be subject, I would not once think of it; for as I said to you once before, though I would be gladly nearer home, yet as long as there is a sea between me and my friends, I am little the nearer, save only for a few days' difference in the delivery of a letter. Will you know in few and plain words my true ambition? It is to have some competent estate at home whereby to live amongst my friends and having rather a desire to see Mr. Secretary once a month than write to him once a week and talk with you *a quattr'occhi,* then *con penna d'oca*; and herein I desire his favor, not despairing to attain to any reasonable condition by the means of so good a friend in such a place, and especially being this much further encouraged by him that neither his majesty nor my lord of Somerset [2] are ill satisfied of me. I cannot tell as yet what to aim at in particular and therefore must refer myself wholly to Mr. Secretary, who knows what there is stirring at any time and what I am capable of. Yet by the way of provision, when you have any idle talk with him, I pray you remember Eton College, which my predecessor here had my late lord treasurer's word to do his best to procure for him when it fell. In the search after it by my lord Wotton for his brother, it was found the king had then passed a grant thereof to Peter Young, yet they despaired not of it since, at Sir H. Savile's late sickness, Peter Young, laying claim to his reversion, Mr. Newton did likewise produce a promise for the same,[3] so as they two were falling out for a dead man's clothes, who, thanks be to God, is yet living, and so I desire he may long do, for I love and reverence him unfeignedly and would rather enjoy him than his place whilst I live; but we have a saying, young men may die and old men must, wherefore since this may fall unexpectedly, I pray you, as I say, prepare Mr. Secretary in it, and to stop their mouths that strive for the bone you know where a good morsel lies recommended to your care, and my brother Williams there shall be another ready upon an hour's warning, both which I shall think well bestowed. In the meantime, here or wheresoever else may be best for his majesty's service, I shall now go on with much alacrity; only, if I continue here, I would desire this further favor of Mr. Secretary, that in regard as I understand Signore Foscarini [4] hath taken the alarm that I am a suitor to be removed into Holland, which he accounts a prejudice to the dignity of his masters, whereby I shall much fall in my reputation amongst these signori, that he will be pleased to let him know it was neither my suit nor his majesty's pleasure, but only the good wishes of some private friends to have me so much nearer home and in so good as that proves to my better preferment. This will be a grateful office in respect of his majesty and recover my credit with advantage here, which, that you may know in particular in what state it stands, I have been dealt with underhand from some of the best not to think of removing from this state and for their satisfaction have the rather resolved of removing to another house. They have quarreled with me of late for demanding no graces of them, wherein they say my predecessor was more free, but my *vale* is *qui beneficium accipit libertate[m] vendit* and am loath to sell my freedom. Yet the two morsels I speak of are put *in lucrum* by such accidents that you may see I not wholly neglect myself. The king's allowance goes wholly to his service, and I am glad when it brings the year about. It is objected against my remove into Holland, my predecessor's refusing of Brussels. If his example of being chosen for France [5] might send me into Spain, a few years might be spent there to better purpose, but my condition is hard in this respect. By his example I must not look lower and my own thoughts will not suffer me to aspire higher. I write so little to Mr. Secretary concerning myself that I will entreat you again at a fit hour to say somewhat to these purposes, and now I do fully *liberare animum*. I shall have the less cause to trouble you so much hereafter in this kind, so I rest [6]

I shall be glad to hear whether the Fabritii be of the Parliament and what bustling they keep. God bless our friend's [Winwood's] proceedings in that place.

1. Chamberlain had written that Winwood was sworn in as principal secretary of state on March 29. *L. J. C.* I, 521.

2. The king's favorite, Robert Carr, recently elevated to the earldom of Somerset.

3. Lord Wotton's brother was, of course, Sir Henry, who ultimately became provost of Eton. Peter Young, a Scot, had been King James's tutor, along with the famous humanist George Buchanan; Adam Newton, dean of Durham, also a Scot, had been tutor to Prince Henry.

4. The Venetian ambassador in London, Antonio Foscarini.

5. It had been rumored that Wotton would be appointed to the embassy in France; the appointment was not made. See Chamberlain's letter of October 27, 1613, *L. J. C.* I, 483.

6. This letter is a copy, not in Carleton's hand; it contains no signature.

Venice, September 6/16 1614

S. P. 99/17, ff. 127–28

Good Mr. Chamberlain, I shall salute you now and once more before I part from hence; for though I have my letters of revocation yet I must not prejudice his majesty's service by an unseasonable remove; howsoever, the winter coming on, the weather is like to prove unseasonable for my journey. I never knew Venice so full of business. Every day one ambassador or other hath audience, and loud words pass on all sides. This state is courted and wooed by the Spaniard and the duke of Savoy like a mistress, which is a strange alteration in that within these few months it was as much scorned and despised of both.[1] The Spanish ambassador would have these signori send such forces as they pay in defense of Montferrat to assail Savoy. Savoy, on the contrary, persuades them by his ministers to arm in the confines of Milan and divert the governor from assailing of Piedmont. They provide for their own security without satisfying either, but more incline to Savoy, having given express order to those forces they pay in Montferrat not to stir from thence upon what pretense soever and have sent 10,000 of their *cernide* to the confines but

[167]

with charge only to stand upon the defensive. There is a truce in Piedmont for all this month, at the end whereof we shall see whether peace or war; meantime both the governor and the duke increase their strength, the one by Swiss and Neapolitans, the other by Swiss and French, and the least of their armies will be 20,000. This greatness of strength on both sides makes it concluded there will be peace because the one hath not means to continue long armed, the other will be loath to run such a fortune as may follow any cross encounter in these parts. The nuncio Savelli [2] travels betwixt them by entreaty of both. This state is likewise desired by themselves to part the fray betwixt them, yet are they so far gone on both sides that they know not how to retire with honor. The Spaniards openly profess their resolute purpose to be to depose the duke of Savoy and place his son in his seat. The duke, apprehending this to be their real intent, had rather try the hazard of war than expose himself disarmed to their practices in time of peace, he having offended them (as he doth imagine and not without cause) beyond all possible hope of reconciliation. Yet (as I say) the opinion is their wars are at an end, and, though the duke of Savoy in this quarrel be wished well by other princes in these parts, his wonted inconstancy hinders their present succors. I must see this treaty *fait* or *failli* before I part from hence, which cannot long be deferred. This week past I have been at Udine and Palma, where I had much good entertainment, having in my company my lord Cromwell (a very civil and ingenuous nobleman), Sir William Candish (who doth likewise make good use of his travels), Mr. Hare, and some other gentlemen.[3] Udine is the best seat and Palma the most perfect fortification that ever I saw. In my journey to the Low Countries I hope to see Mantua if that duke be absent, otherwise his cardinal's hat (which sticks close to his head) will drive me another way. Sir Henry Wotton doth somewhat confound me here in that he writes nothing about his house.[4] I am very loath this where I now dwell (the fairest, most convenient and cheapest of any of the ambasadors') should go to any but the English. The French offers me largely to buy all my stuff at a good rate, to reimburse me the rest of a whole year's rent and to rest with much obligation; yet, I reserve it for my successor, which is more than I owe him considering his dealing with me when he was my predecessor, whereof all the stratagems were not known whilst you were here, and now it will be my luck to fall foul upon him again, both here and where he remains; for I forget private interest when I think what belongs to the public service, in which regard I have a care to accommodate him to my own loss and incommodity. Here is a Savoy ambassador every day expected who hath already sent his stuff and part of his family. The marquis of Urfé (who came from the prince of Condé) hath letters from the state in answer of those he brought and a chain worth 600 crowns.[5] I shall have no cause to brag of any extraordinary present at parting for I know what to look for, but I have so many good words that I wish I could make them over to Signore Foscarini by bill of exchange and share with him in his expectations. Thus with all our kindest remembrances I rest

Yours as ever most assured

1. Carleton had finally received his sought-for appointment to The Hague. He took formal leave of the Venetian government on September 18, but it was to be some time before he left Italy, on account of the renewal of the conflict between Spain and Savoy. Neither Savoy nor Mantua had observed the truce; Lerma's peremptory order to Savoy to submit was rejected, and the war began again in September 1614.

2. The papal nuncio in Savoy, Giulio Savelli.

3. Thomas, fourth Baron Cromwell, eventually became an earl in the Irish peerage. Sir William "Candish" (Cavendish), son of the earl of Devonshire, a young man of 23, was travelling with his tutor, Thomas Hobbes. Nicholas Hare, who lived in Padua, was the son of the recently deceased clerk of the court of wards, who left the office in reversion to him, provided he lived in England, *L. J. C.* I, 457.

4. Wotton had been designated as Carleton's successor in Venice.

5. The marquis of Urfé, in the name of Condé and other French princes, urged the Venetian government to use its influence to annul the Franco-Spanish marriage treaties, on the ground that Spain's only purpose in negotiating them was to drive the Huguenots into rebellion. See *C. S. P. Venetian, 1613–1615*, pp. 188–89.

Good Mr. Chamberlain, I did not expect to have written any more unto you from this place but you will have heard what a stop I have met with, the which did encounter me Tuesday last was sevennight on my way at Padua, where I rested one night with purpose the next morning to have continued my journey, having hired my coaches for Bergamo and abridged all my stuff (save that only which is gone already by sea into Holland) into valises, proper only for carriage; you will then judge with what incommodity I here rest and so am like to do (as I suspect) for all this winter, but Mr. Secretary gives me comfort that this sudden stay proceeds not of any alteration in his majesty's purpose to revoke me from hence and employ me in the Low Countries, which makes me pass over the matter with patience, only I am somewhat distracted how to rejoin myself with this prince, of whom I had taken leave and presented another as his majesty's minister in my place until the coming of my successor. We have only the care as yet of new settling ourselves, which depends upon the courtesy of our neighbors the Jews, and they, seeing my present necessity, make their advantage, not sparing to boast they have now a fleece of me as they had of my predecessor, whom they expect again as their Messiah. There was never less joy in remaining here than now at this present in regard of sickness, which they will not yield is contagious but in one household which you know (that of George Silvester and Robin Hassal) there are six sick at one time, whereof Paulina the fair niece and her husband were the last night both given over for dead; and yet it was my fortune to light on that house without knowing anything whilst my own might be put again into order; but I soon dislodged when I found in what state they stood. Knevet, who married the Greek courtesan, died lately of the same disease, which turned at the last with him into the smallpox. A young fellow who hath a house and shop in London and accompanied Sir Richard Musgrave into these parts sickened of it at Padua about three weeks since and died frantic. That knight took Denis [paper torn] his place to travel with him to Naples. They went in company of Sir William Ca[ve]ndish and Henry Purvis, who passed by Rome at such time as the new Venetian ambassador [Simone] Contarini made his entry, and at his first audience H. Purvis had the especial grace to kiss the Pope's *petitoes*. The same day that Contarini made his entry there, his brother left the world here of this popular disease. Here is gone an ambassador [Ranier Zen] from hence as ordinary to the duke of Savoy and extraordinary to the governor of Milan, with a train of 70 persons, which he doth purpose so much to increase by the way that on what side soever he be, he will furnish the army with a complete company. He is of the family of the *podestà* we met with at Crema and is a very sufficient gentleman. This state doth rest in hope he will come in a good conjuncture to bring them the honor of accommodating the differences of those parts, the duke of Savoy being pressed by his necessities and the Spaniard with diversion in many other places; but the matter is like to be disputed this whole winter, and betwixt this and next spring *multa cadunt*. For the present they remain in the selfsame state as they do in the Low Countries, the Spaniard fortifying and the duke looking on without giving him molestation. This Spanish ambassador hath had a meeting lately with the duke of Mantua at the Lago di Garda, from whom he hath brought a hatband with buttons of 1000 crowns' value. His errand was to persuade that duke to assail Piedmont on the side of Montferrat, to which if he yield he is sure to lose the assistance he hath continually from this state, in that they here profess to be his friends, but for the defensive only. Monsieur de Rambouillet,[2] we hear, is come into Piedmont but as yet understand nothing of his negotiation. It is said he persuades the duke to disarm upon any conditions and that if persuasions will not prevail he is to use threatenings. The Venetian ambassador is to concur with the duke in his own cautions of *riputazione* and *sicurezza,* and yet they esteem themselves more interested in the peace of these parts than France can be. I will not fail to write to you of the success, as I must desire you to resume your part of

[171]

our wonted correspondence, and so with all our kindest remembrances, I ever rest

Yours most affectionately

I must not omit to let you know the extraordinary kindness of one of these citizens, Bartolomeo del Calici, he that doth so much beautify the carnival with his divers suits of cloth of gold, by which token you may remember him. He sent unto me Pompeo the apothecary of the two Mores the first day of my return hither to offer me a complete furniture of my whole house, specifying hangings, plate, beds, and linen and all this *sènza interèsse,* only because I was minister to a prince so well beloved of the state to which he is subject, and I must believe he hath some such public respect in that he is a man with whom I never yet exchanged word. But I understand these kindnesses to be as civilly refused as they are courteously offered; and yet the duke of Mantua having an offer made him by the same person in his late occasion of a loan of 50000 crowns made no great dainty to accept the same, and it was performed.

1. Carleton arrived in Padua on October 11/21, a Tuesday, which suggests that this letter was written between October 18/28 and October 25/November 4. His orders to stay in Venice were prompted by the war; he was soon to be ordered to go to Savoy and attempt to help mediate a settlement.
2. Charles d'Angennes, marquis of Rambouillet, was the French ambassador to Savoy. He and Carleton got along very badly.

Venice, January 5, 1614/15

S. P. 99/18, ff. 176–77

Good Mr. Chamberlain, I could not by the last ordinary make answer to your two letters of the 24 of November and first of December (both which I received at one time) being at that present cast down with a sharp fit of sickness, which, though I have not yet fully recovered, yet I can no longer defer to thank you for them and particularly for the later part of the latter, wherein I approve of your opinion in the generalities, though for the particular occasions I think I may truly say to you, *tu si hic esses aliter sentires*.[1] But it seems you could allow of our doings, so it were in an active age, and if that be the scruple, I assure you these parts are at the present, and so have been for the most part of the year past, generally in action, more than hath been known in the age of any that now lives, all being busied either in preparations for war, treaties of peace, or negotiations of leagues and amities, amongst which (I must confess unto you) as occasions have been any way presented, for his majesty's service or the common good I have not forborne, with Diogenes, to roll my tun, or rather to suffer it to be rolled by others, for so hath it fallen out that whatsoever I have entered into hath been rather entertained than sought; so as it were hard if I came into danger of faults of commission, since I could no ways have excused those of omission. The particular occasion which you found specified in Mr. Secretary's letter [2] had a delay at that time which I am not sorry for because, as I have not since revived it, so now I am resolved it shall die. I assure you no one occasion doth more move me to desire my remove to an employment nearer home than this; that, at this distance, if I attend to govern myself by instructions, I lose opportunities; if I embrace opportunities, I subject myself to construction. Fabritio doth boast himself that my stay here is by order, not to interrupt him, and that if he find himself well where he is, which (he sayth) he will demur upon, that I must content myself where I am. I know no greater misfortune than thus still to fall cross upon that man; and to mend the matter I find myself and Mr. Wake drawn into print by his vanities, there being a foolish pamphlet lately published in Germany in answer of the apology touching the definition of *legatus,* wherein our old English saying is verified that a liar is no better than a thief; you may happily hear of it under the title of *Legat a latro*.[3] The ring you write for for my lady Rich [4] I send with this letter, and another to bestow where you will. They grow into great request in all places and are for the price, as they say in Spain of their *Juego de toros poco per veras* and *troppo per burlas*. We are yet here at a stand touching the affairs of Milan and Piedmont, in that the answer of the treaty of Asti[5] (made the first of December) is not come out of Spain; but, by what is gathered from the Spanish ministers, it will not be accepted, so as either the French ambassador and the nuncio Savelli must patch up a new accord or else in the spring they will fall to wars. The Spaniards arm this winter in great diligence, and, though they have lost many men by sickness, they make account with the levies they are now making in the states of other princes in Italy to have 30,000 men in the field, which number they will be able to furnish but speak of double as many. They have lately published a proclamation against the duke of Savoy for Asti and Santhià, as places held of the duchy of Milan and, in regard of his being entered into hostility against Spain, devolved unto that state. The Genoese make a great noise of their touching their treasure of Saint George[6] upon this occasion, and if they can purchase anything of the Spaniard hereby it is well; but otherwise they are cried out of by all other princes in Italy for more forwardness than needed. Florence, being demanded by the Spaniards to furnish 4000 men, to which that duke is bound in regard of Siena, hath made a discreet answer, that when the Spaniard is put to the defensive the men shall be in readiness. This state continues still in neutrality. I have even now received your last of the 15th of December and by those I have from other hands understand I am in danger to make a journey into Piedmont.[7] You say it is a pleasure to deal in great and high matters; and I must confess I have that taste of them when I can any way foresee by probability how to advance the king's contentment and service. But I wish the cards turned and my predecessor with his Italian in Piedmont and I in Holland. Yet God may so bless this occasion that I may not repent myself of it, and in this hope, when the order comes (which as yet I have not), I shall go on with all alacrity, though I have some cause to mutiny in that I am embarked *sènza biscotto*. Thus with all our kindest remembrances I rest

Yours as ever most affectionately

1. Chamberlain (*L. J. C.* I, 560–62) had written a cautionary letter, warning Carleton that if his dealings in the confused Italian situation "should not succeed à souhait," he would be held responsible, "specially if there be not sufficient warrant for every particular." Carleton's reply indicates that he was not afraid of responsibility.

2. The letter was from Carleton to Winwood, dealing with the complex diplomatic situation which threatened to delay—as it did—Carleton's departure from Venice. Chamberlain had mentioned that Winwood had discussed the letter with him. *L. J. C.* I, 561.

3. A pun on *legate a latere*. Wotton was ambassador extraordinary to The Hague, the post in which Carleton was slated to be resident. Wotton's famous definition of an ambassador had been made first in Latin; hence the reference to *legatus*.

4. Carleton had sent a ring to Chamberlain to deliver to George Rooke. Chamberlain had shown it to Lady Rich (née Isabel Cope) and her mother, Sir Walter Cope's widow. Lady Rich was anxious to have one like it. Her husband, Henry Rich, the future earl of Holland, was the second son of the earl of Warwick; his mother was the famous Penelope Rich.

5. A temporary agreement had been worked out at Asti by the mediation of the French ambassador and the nuncio in Savoy. The Spaniards did not ratify it, and the fighting resumed in the spring.

6. The bank of Saint George was the major Genoese banking corporation for purposes of external financial dealings, of which there were many. It was well managed and prosperous.

7. He was, in fact, about to make it. Chamberlain in his letter of December 15 had said that Spain's attitude toward Savoy "is very unwelcome hither and much detested." *L. J. C.* I, 562–64.

Venice, January 27, 1614/15
S. P. 99/18, ff. 273–74

Good Mr. Chamberlain, the last night was my first of the carnival, whereof I spent the most part at *Non nobis* in the Canale Grande at the wedding of young Correro the cavalier's son, who hath 40,000 ducats with a fair *nouizza*[?] of the Ca Gritti. This occasion hath made my day shorter and less leisure to write, yet that I have I cannot bestow better than in thanking you for yours

[175]

of the 5th of this present and chiefly for your good advice in the conclusion, which you can well judge of what use it is to those who are so far from home and knowledge of home affairs.[1] By my last I sent you two rings, the one for Kensington, if you thought fit; the other for whom you pleased. Here enclosed you shall receive a letter of Mr. Pory's which I desire you to show my lady Cope that she may see how well the money I disbursed for Sir W. Cope was bestowed in that they were delivered hereby from further charge and their old servant provided for in a place of preferment.[2] They write from thence that the Grand Signor prepares by land against the next summer for the wars of Persia and by sea with 120 galleys for revenge of his late losses upon the Spaniard. To this purpose he makes all fair weather with the emperor not to be diverted by his means and hath sent him a present, which savors little of that barbarism which we lay to their charge, the note whereof I send you herewith. Here is newly arrived in this town the count of Villamediana, son to Taxis, who was ambassador in England.[3] He was yesterday at the feast unmasked but so basely apparelled both himself and his company that they turned his name to *mèdia villano*. His errand hither is to recover a debt of 13000 ducats which he won of Priuli, the Venetian ambassador who died in Spain, and is like to prove a desperate debt. Here is at this present an example of great severity showed upon one Priuli, an ancient senator of almost 80 years of age, who hath run through the chief offices of this state and was at this time *savio grande,* from which place he was taken the last week and committed to close and dark prison by the council of ten, and, since, all the favor he can obtain is to be removed into the light. His imputation is that being three years since proveditor at Raspo and inquisitor general, he sold the surplusage of corn which was allowed him for his provision at a higher rate than the market did yield and forced the subjects of this state to buy the same, wherein it is thought he will acquit himself well but hath many, and those heavy, enemies for the rigor he used to divers gentlemen both in that and other charges, for which they give him the *soprannome* of Attila. I know not what to say of my journey into Piedmont, which I cannot expect will hold unless it be (as they say here) *dopo la morte il mèdico,* wherein, you know, there is small comfort. Mr. Morton [4] arrived there a week since and tomorrow comes the ordinary, by whom I shall know more; meantime, I stand at his discretion. They are there in feasts and triumphs, and here we pass our time as well as we can, the French ambassador having led the way into a course of good fellowship by bidding himself to supper unto me, where he met the Savoy ambassadors, and on Sunday last he invited us all to a great supper, where besides much amends in good cheer, he paid me back the money he won of me at cards, with some advantage. The Spanish ambassador makes himself merry at this correspondency and pleaseth himself with a conceit he had formerly of the duke of Savoy, that he was like a man who had an ill process and from one court in law would still gain time by appealing to another; so as he had already run through the Swiss, the Venetians, the Pope, and the French king, and was now come to his last appeal wi[paper torn] the king of England, which the French ambassador will not allow of, saying that they have already cast him *hors de court et de procès.* You may make Mr. Secretary, if you find him in a good mood, as merry with this as they are here; and thus with all our kindest remembrances, I commit you to God's protection.

Yours as ever most assuredly

I pray you acquaint my father Savile with as much of Mr. Pory's letters as concerns his books, and, though the price of them be returned in commodities, I will be accountable to him for the money; but as yet I have received nothing from Mr. Pindar.

1. Chamberlain had written (*L. J. C.* I, 569) that some people were intriguing to be appointed ambassador to The Hague. Winwood had told him this and had added that he had been definite with James that Carleton was the best choice. It was clear, however, that Carleton would have to stay in Italy till the crisis over Savoy had ended. Chamberlain concluded by advising Carleton not to rely too heavily on the fair words of people who might play him false.

2. Sir Walter Cope had died in 1614, deep in debt; John Pory, who had

been one of his entourage, was now in Constantinople, where, among other things, he was buying books for Carleton's scholarly father-in-law, as the postscript to this letter indicates. Carleton had helped Pory by recommending him to Sir Paul Pindar, the English ambassador in Constantinople. Chamberlain, in reporting Cope's death (*L. J. C.* I, 554) wrote that before he died Cope had wanted to close his accounts with Carleton, who, so Pory had written, had given him £20 on Cope's word that he would reimburse Carleton for his expenditures.

3. Don Juan de Taxis, count of Villamediana, had been the working head of the Spanish delegation which negotiated the peace treaty of 1604 in London.

4. Albertus Morton, Wotton's nephew, had been appointed resident ambassador in Savoy. He did not remain in the position very long; he was on his way home by June, owing to bad health.

Turin, April 13, 1615 [1]

S. P. 92/2, ff. 323–24

Good Mr. Chamberlain, I have received your letter wherein you write of your going to Cambridge, and now I expect with great devotion your next with relation of the king's entertainment.[2] In these parts [3] they begin to leave sport and fall to earnest, this duke being gone suddenly into the field to Cherasco, Cortemiglia, and those parts where the Spaniard and he are at ketch as ketch may for certain imperial *feudi* which lie in Montferrat, the Spaniard having taken from him Roccaverano, wherein the duke had garrison, and slain in entering of the town 15 or 16 Frenchmen. The duke hath 8000 men with 7 fieldpieces, whereof the English which came with Eston [4] have still the charge, and every one of them, at their going from hence, in their caps and feathers put a jacobus piece for a jewel; which shows these poor mens' good mind towards their prince and country, to which they have done as much honor as comes to have their names in a gazzetta and to be sung about Lombardy in ballads. The princes, Victorio and Tomaso, are each of them with 6000 men, the one at Vercelli the other at Asti. The governor of Milan was to come to Alessandria the 7/17 of this present, where he hath assembled much provision of artillery and all other necessaries for the field, but his men are raised so hardly and come forward so slowly that he is not thought at this time stronger than the duke; though before the end of the next month he expects to have double the number. The Pope hath proposed to this duke from the king of Spain certain articles of peace, that the duke must absolutely disarm without further capitulations, promise not to molest Mantua, and refer his pretensions to the arbitrament of the emperor. Touching Mantua he willingly consents and hath showed in his passage by Alba and other towns in Montferrat that he means no more to offend him. But the other two conditions he professeth he will hazard all rather than admit; in that, for the one, he will not stand at the mercy of the Spaniard but will either have an equal disarming or none; and for the other, he will not make the same prince judge and party. In these manifests (which I send you in print) you will perceive this new proposition of the Pope's to be the same as was formerly treated at Milan and laid aside, and by the last of them you will see how well the duke doth answer the emperor. If his strength were answerable to his mind or to the justice of his cause (as time and accidents have brought the matter about), he would find the Spaniards as troublesome a piece of work as they have met with this many a day, but, in conclusion, without help from others he must stoop to his necessities. The count Scarnafes [5] will be with the king as ambassador by that time this letter can be with you. The count Carlo Moretta, with the Senator [Giovanni] Pescina, who was in Venice, go into France. Others are assigned to go into Germany and to the States and so have long been, but dispatches are slow in this court and so uncertain that they often put our brains *a partito,* not knowing what judgment to make of their proceeding. The prince cardinal [6] is left here in Turin with his sisters the infantas and a garrison of ambassadors who look one upon another at very good leisure. Mr. Morton [7] continues sickly and longing after the hot baths; I thirst as much after the cold ones in respect of the stone, of which within these three days I have had another very sharp fit. How I shall be disposed of I cannot conjecture, but seeing no use of my longer abode here (where there is more work for soldiers than ambassadors) I pray you make my desire known to Mr. Secretary, that if it be his majesty's pleasure I should go into Holland that I may in the way spend some time at the Spa; if [I] return to Venice that I may have the like favor, as all other that are now abroad have had, to go first into England, and in the way to take the waters of Poogues, which have the like virtue as those of Spa.[8] The last course is returning absolutely into England, which you know in what ill state I am to think of, but now I am fallen on the rhyme *servire et non gradire*; and on the reason that since wants are such at home that necessary charges abroad cannot be supplied and therefore it is best to live where the shame of my want shall only light on myself, I shall very willingly and gladly submit myself to anything shall be resolved; and when we meet I will show you as a friend the reason of somewhat which hath passed my hands in these parts which, when you know all circumstances, I persuade myself you will admit; though I forbear for many respects troubling others with apologies. I expect this week my wife and my sister [9] from Venice, with the rest that I left there, whom I sent for as well to free them from solitariness as likewise to be ready to take such part as I shall do when I know how I shall be disposed of. Thus with my best wishes I commit you to God's protection resting ever

Yours most assuredly

Since the writing hereof I have received your letter of the 16th of March with the relation of your Cambridge entertainment and questions. My lord Roos in gone safe through the Grisons and Swiss towards the Low Countries, so for England. He purposed to have returned from hence to Milan, but an affront offered him at Novara by searching his chamber with an officer and 40 soldiers at three hours at night for his Spanish servant Diego (who, upon an item I gave him of some such danger [whereof I had news] left him at Vercelli) made him forbear going any further into that state.

1. Carleton's pen slipped in recording the year date; he dated it 1614.
2. Chamberlain had written on March 2 (*L. J. C.* I, 583) that he was

going to Cambridge at the urging of Winwood and Bishop Andrewes to be an observer at the royal visit. He did not disappoint Carleton: his letter of March 16 gave a full account of the visit. *L. J. C.* I, 586–89.

3. Carleton had left Venice for Savoy at the beginning of February with instructions to mediate the dispute between Savoy and Spain in co-operation with the ambassadors of other powers, notably Venice and France.

4. Peter Eston was an English pirate now in the service of Savoy.

5. Count Antonio Scarnafes made three trips to England in the years 1614 and 1615 in search of a league and a marriage alliance between Savoy and England.

6. Maurice, third son of Duke Charles Emmanuel.

7. Albertus Morton, the English resident.

8. Spa is the famous German resort, where Carleton hoped to find relief from the stone; "Poogues" is presumably Pougues-les-Eaux, near the town of Nevers, in central France.

9. Alice, who had been in Venice with her brother throughout his stay.

Varie, June 6/16–11/21, 1615

S. P. 92/3, ff. 149–53

Good Mr. Chamberlain, I have received your letter of the 3rd of the last by the way of Lyons and find therein the continuance of your friendship by the good offices you do me with Mr. Secretary, with whom I must acknowledge you did first sow the seeds of that favor he hath always showed me, which you have since cultivated upon all occasions; and now it rests that I may reap that fruit which I have ever promised myself of him in the place to which his merit hath called him; and though my endeavors since his coming to that charge have been ever blasted either by my indiscretion or others' misinterpretation, yet knowing his constancy to his friends I doubt not but with good industry to recover myself, wherein truly in my own conscience I have not failed hitherto of the respect I owe him, considering the charge I have for the address of such packets as concern his majesty's service, which I must continue until I have order to the contrary, not out of faction or making of court (which occupation I understand not nor am willing to learn), but out of obedience as long as I am in a public charge to do that which I am directly told is his majesty's mind, a rule which Mr. Secretary himself, when he was in these employments, would never transgress. That which you write me of his coldness of late towards me [1] I understand from others of my good friends and find the effects thereof many ways, but your counsel of patience prevails the more with me in that it agrees with my own disposition, though I must confess these cross encounters did somewhat mortify me for the present in that I found blame and reprehension in place of the good acceptance I promised myself and a course taken, which, as it was without example, so I hope (for the good of all that shall serve his majesty in these foreign employments) it shall be no precedent. I am now in a place much more subject to misinterpretation and our proceedings so fantastical that I am very much apprehensive of the event, in regard of my own particular, if so be I shall be censured by methodical rules and not by the present occasions. I am here employed in a treaty of peace by those that will not treat one with the other, the Spaniards refusing absolutely to treat with this duke. I am commanded to join with other ministers of princes in this treaty without order taken that they should join with me, and the French ambassador, [2] who hath the chief authority, doth avoid any partner (the nuncio only excepted) as much as he may. Occasions offer themselves to treat with the governor of Milan, to whom I have no letters of credence and in conclusion not a penny of money I have heard of, for some months before I left Venice. These things I know you will compassionate, but I excuse them all, partly in consideration of other great affairs which may divert those which are in place from thinking of that which is convenient for me, who, having nothing else to do, observe particularly what is omitted, and partly out of the want at home which causeth all to suffer abroad. That which doth most molest me is that I have lost my credit with all my private friends, who condemn me generally, by that they hear out of Mr. Secretary's family, of follies and *mancamenti*. In one word, if I did neglect him to whom I have so much obligation, they had cause to complain of me, or if I should leave him to adhere to any new favorite I might be taken for a courtier; but seeing I only continue the course wherein he found me and that I cannot change it until I have order to the contrary and which (unless I am mistaken) is observed by other of my profession, I may be the better excused.[3] You write me I must return to Venice, which I shall do willingly in hope my residence there will not be long. I sent for my wife and sister from thence to deliver them from solitude, having so small company of strangers and continuing more strangeness betwixt themselves than I wish. At Turin they have much good society. I have been here in the duke's camp for this fortnight past, being lodged in a castle a mile distant from Asti, where the Venetian ambassador and the nuncio are likewise quartered. The French ambassador, for better commodity of lodging, remains further off. My first accident after my coming to this place was that, sending Mr. Brent [4] with a French gentleman who belongs to the Prince Palatine and had here borne arms under the duke and one of my servants to the French ambassador on a visit, they were all taken in the way by the enemy, but upon my letter delivered with their horses and all their things; only the soldiers having taken away their swords the governor gave them good ones in place of bad ones, and my man, for staying longer than was fit for his livery, had ten crowns given him for recompense, which cost me a better reward to him that restored it. I dined with the governor upon occasion of business on Whitsun Monday and had courteous entertainment of him and all the chief of his army. We are now drawing towards a conclusion of peace, which, notwithstanding, will hardly be brought to pass betwixt the Spanish stiffness and this duke's volubility. But so stands the state at this present with this duke that, as some by diligent following a suit in law make their cause just in the end which was not so in the beginning, so hath he managed his affairs that he hath at the present the right on his side, and I cannot but allow of what he wrote lately to me to Turin, *Dieu sera de mon côté, puisque la raison y est.* He hath yet his town of Asti in good state, which hath been now besieged a full month. His trenches without, towards the enemy, are so large that he can cover his whole army in them of 12000 foot and 1000 horse with security, having the advantage of a hill for their defense. He now wants no men nor

[183]

victuals. Money here is none stirring and munition is not very plentiful. His courage overcomes all difficulties and defects, and he hath often a speech of the late French king's in his mouth that he recovered his kingdom *sans argent et sans hommes*. The Spanish camp is reckoned 25000. The expense of it is 300,000 crowns a month. Their trenches and caution in their proceedings is such as if they stood on the defensive and this duke were the assailant. His loss of men in their approaches to the place where they are now lodged proceeded always of temerity, wherein now he saith he will be more moderate, yet yesterday whilst we were treating *in campagna* a skirmish was entertained in our sights, begun by the duke's side, which took him from us until the enemy was retired into their trenches. Our place of audience is an entrenchment where, in the reading of a leaf of paper, we have had three or four parentheses made by the cannon. There hath none of the ambassadors been in the duke's trenches or the town since it was besieged but myself, who was once led through them by the duke, the gates being shut against all the rest in regard of the French ambassador, who the duke mistrusts will debauch those he hath in his service of that nation. The gates of the town in this regard (as I say) are always shut this way towards the duke's country unless it be for the receiving in of provision, but towards the enemy there are three breaches made in the wall for the duke's soldiers to go freely into their trenches. The English pirates have a platform for their artillery in the most eminent place of the town and fittest to annoy the enemy, which is called the English battery. There have been exchanged in this time of siege 3000 cannon shot and no great hurt done. No man of quality hath been slain on this side with artillery save only the baron of Serra, a Savoyard, who had his thigh shot off and his man killed by him as he was seeing his horse shoed. We hear of many extravagant accidents. The Venetian secretary Scaramelli, who was in England,[5] rising earlier one morning than was usual with him, was no sooner out of his bed but a cannon shot came in his place. An inhabitant of Asti, carrying his son behind him on horseback to see a skirmish, had his son shot from behind him and he untouched. The duke hath had his house divers times shot through, yet changeth not his lodging. Whilst any ambassador is with the enemy, as we go commonly by turns, but most of all the French ambassador, the shooting ceaseth for that day. Whether peace or war, as near as we are to conclusion, which is expected shall be this night, I cannot yet say, but if the war go on they will both, before this town be taken, heartily repent themselves of the bargain. I write you not the particularities of the skirmishes in the Spaniard's approaches because you have them in the gazzetta. Mr. Morton left me here three days since with purpose to go with the best diligence he may toward England, though I yet hear he is at Turin. I have had of him since my coming hither very good and friendly company. Mr. Wake,[6] I imagine, is on the way, and therefore I write not to him. If he be still with you I pray you give him part of this letter. Let my brother Williams have his share likewise, to whom I write not, nor to any private friend but yourself. So with my most affectionate remembrance, I ever rest

Yours most assuredly to dispose of

From Varie this 6/16 of June 1615

The protracting our business from day to day hath stayed my courier so long that I have since the date hereof received yours of the 20th of the last which came in 12 days, whereas this post who runs or rather stands like a post was 20 days on his way hither.

This night the duke hath given upon a work of the enemy, from which he beat them and burnt their *gabbione,* but lost 25 men and had as many more hurt, amongst which the count Guido San Georgio is shot in the right arm. Once more adieu

Yours as ever

this 11/21 of June 1615

1. Winwood was a member of the anti-Howard faction and was currently promoting the career of George Villiers, the future duke of Buckingham, as a rival to the reigning favorite Rochester, whose fortunes were beginning to fade. Carleton, after Salisbury's death, had been instructed by the king to communicate with Rochester; he continued to do this after Winwood became secretary because, as he said, he had no instructions to the contrary. Hence

[185]

Winwood's coldness. Chamberlain put it this way to his friend: "I doubt you have leaned too long upon a broken staff, that cannot or will not, or (I am sure) hitherto hath not given support to any that relied upon it, and in respect thereof neglected those that in all occasions would have stood more firmly to you." *L. J. C.* I, 592.

2. The marquis of Rambouillet.

3. Chamberlain, in his reply to this letter, wrote that Winwood complained only of Carleton on this point; both Wotton and Edmondes sent their dispatches to Winwood, Edmondes having taken the precaution of asking James for instructions. *L. J. C.* I, 605–606.

4. Nathaniel Brent was one of Carleton's staff; after Carleton's transfer to The Hague he was considered for appointment as Carleton's secretary. Like so many of Carleton's associates, he was a fellow of Merton College and ultimately became its warden, in which position he had a long and controversial tenure. See *L. J. C.* II, 425, 430.

5. Giovanni Scaramelli was Venetian agent in England in 1603, at the time of James's accession.

6. Isaac Wake, Carleton's secretary, had accompanied Carleton to Turin and had been sent to England late in March. See April 6/16, 1615, Antonio Foscarini to the doge and senate, *C. S. P. Venetian 1613–1615,* pp. 417–18.

Venice, September 8/18, 1615

S. P. 99/13, ff. 221–22

Good Mr. Chamberlain, it is now a long space that I have not heard anything out of England, though I was never in greater expectation, but my hope is the good endeavors of my best friends, in furthering my speedy remove from hence, do supply the defect of writing, having understood that Sir Henry Wotton is revoked out of Holland,[1] though certain of these grave senators, hearing of my expectation and desire to be gone, have wished me to set my heart at rest for this winter, in that the business in which I was lately employed hath a coda left, which they would fain have cut off and the affairs of these parts better settled before my departure. But I hope, since the marquis of Rambouillet, who chiefly treated this business, is long since returned into France and the Venetian ambassador at Turin upon his revocation, who had his part likewise in it, and since the governor of Milan (whose promise we are only to rely upon) is sent for into Spain, that I only shall not be tied to this coda, in that it may as much import his majesty to have his minister in these parts changed upon this occasion (in regard of the doubtful success thereof) as it doth other princes. But I am fully persuaded the peace of these parts will be continued, though there be small appearance of perfect reconcilement betwixt Savoy and Mantua, who were the beginners of the troubles. The Spanish army is not yet dissolved in the state of Milan, but rather reinforced upon occasion of opposition against the marriages in France.[2] A great part of it is lately removed from the Cremonese and other parts confining with this state towards the Astigiana, which I take to be done to a double end, first to free this state of jealousy and next to hold the duke of Savoy in suspense, whereby to hinder him from giving assistance to the princes in France. This state (as I think I wrote to you about a fortnight since) hath lately taken and sacked Novi in Dalmatia, an usual retreat of the *Uscocchi,* and hath since burnt certain mills of salt, having ravaged the country likewise and cut up the greatest part of their vines about Trieste, which, though it be done in revenge of wrongs done by the *Uscocchi,* yet the *Austriaci* complain of it much as a notable affront to their greatness. The Jesuits have with much importunity crept into Gorizia, from whence they have been long kept by the people, who were much affected to the reformed religion. This state is no whit pleased with their so near neighborhood. Here is a great question betwixt the patriarch and the temporal authority in this town touching a priest who hath gotten one of these gentlemen's daughters, of the house of Pisani, with child, the patriarch requiring the knowledge of the cause by reason of the calling of the offender and the temporal justice claiming as much in regard of the quality of the offense. The parents endeavor to prove it a rape, which might have some color if the wench were not at woman's estate, and the priest in his justification shows he hath no more ravished his young mistress than her *massaia* who is with child by him likewise. Don Verginio Ursino died the 9th of this present, at Rome, suddenly as he sat at dinner. He was of liberal diet and could use no exercise by reason of the gout, which caused his end. His debts (if the account be not mistaken by a cipher) are 800,000 crowns. There is a certain civilian monk at Rome (who hath the style of the Pope's historiographer and is in much grace with him) that hath an ambition of erecting a convent of English friars in Rome in imitation of the Jesuits' college, which is opposed by the Jesuits, both English and others, with that earnestness, as if they fought *pro aris et focis*. Here in this town we see the effects continually of the intemperance of this summer, which makes pestilent fevers very common and dangerous, though for a while they were somewhat ceased. This last week there was buried in one family the father, mother, two children, and the *massaia*. All my sick are recovered, one only excepted, whom I brought sick from Turin, and is in some danger. Robin Hassall is going to Turin to make merry with his old friend. Some nearest me here are in doubt lest our new agent [3] there will be too active with them in absence, as they accuse him to have been in presence and for prevention (as they tell me) have written unto you touching a particularity which might do me no good if in matters of such moment the hen should crow louder than the cock, but unless you hear the matter spoken of, I pray you let it rest. [4] The party may well be suspected for divers misdemeanors and some tricks of malice whilst he was in house with us, which I was long informed of, but, in regard of his long service and those good parts which are in him, chose rather to set him in the course of a preferment than to bring myself and him upon the stage with Foscarini and Muscorno, both of which are like to pay dear for their brabbles in England, the one being still in close prison and so like to continue until the arrival of the other, who will assuredly be called in question for his many extravagances. [5] Barbarigo should be by this time arrived in England, who hath left his treaty with the Grisons as he found it and that with the Swiss unperfect by reason of a dispute concerning passage betwixt the Swiss and the Grisons, which the Grisons will not yield without terms of greater advantage than will be afforded by this state.[6] Thus, with all our kindest remembrance, I ever rest

Yours most affectionately

1. Wotton was slated to succeed Carleton in Venice, now that his special mission in the United Provinces was ended.

2. This refers to the famous double marriage agreement between Spain and France, by which the eldest daughter of Philip III was to marry Louis XIII, and Louis' eldest sister, Philip's heir. The treaty was significant because it marked the final abandonment by Marie de' Medici of the anti-Spanish policy of Henri IV; it was, therefore, most distasteful to anti-Habsburg Europe, including the governments of England and Venice.

3. Isaac Wake was left behind in Turin to act as English resident, a post he filled for about fifteen years. There is an account of Wake's career in Stoye, *Travellers,* pp. 161–68.

4. Carleton's wife and possibly his sister were evidently at odds with Wake.

5. Antonio Foscarini was the Venetian ambassador in England; he had quarreled bitterly with the embassy secretary, Giulio Muscorno. The quarrel was public knowledge and, according to Muscorno's successor, Giovanni Rizzardo, divided the court into two parties, *C. S. P. Venetian 1613–1615,* p. 467. See also pp. 481–83. Foscarini accused Muscorno of treasonable dealings with the Spanish ambassador and of plotting against King James. Muscorno accused Foscarini of planning to have him murdered. Muscorno had been recalled and was in prison; in July, Foscarini was recalled, and on August 3/13 it was resolved to arrest him on his return. *Ibid.,* p. 556. Foscarini's career never recovered from this setback; in 1622 he was executed for treason on charges which turned out to be false. Bouwsma, *Venice,* p. 509.

6. Gregorio Barbarigo, Foscarini's successor in England, spent the better part of two years attempting to shore up Venice's alliance with the Grisons and with various Swiss cantons, notably Zurich and Berne. He had some success; that he did not have more was owing in part to the opposition of France, whose Italian policy at this juncture was designed to avoid anything which might offend Spain.

Good Mr. Chamberlain, I thought my last week's letter would have been an epilogue to our play upon this stage, but a heavy accident *in extremo actu* was like to have changed our comedy into a tragedy and we are not yet free of the danger. Poor Phil Lytton [1] hath been all this week past at death's door by an unfortunate mischance of hitting his head against a nail in a wall, which pierced his skull and the *membrana* so as at the first dressing a small quantity of his brains were found in the wound, but the *membrana* was again closed. He took his hurt on Tuesday was sevennight but concealed it until Saturday for shame of the occasion, which was the fault of another drunken companion more than his, for he is not given to that vice, though now he was overgone. Yesterday he had a great flux of blood out of the wound, which put us all in a fear, but now he is in better state and hath no fever, so as we are in good hope, though his physicians and surgeons dare not warrant him. He hath the best in this town of both kinds and if he escape he will go amongst their miraculous cures. I hope to see him past danger before my departure, and I will then leave him in the hands of such friends with such order that he shall want nothing. This place is unfit for him for many respects, so as when it pleaseth God he may recover I advise him to go into England; meantime, it were convenient his friends would think of some course for him that he may not grow idle upon his coming home, which he will hardly shake off again. This accident shows he will be unfit for the place where I am going, but I would be glad the occasion thereof might be concealed from his friends, though his mischance and danger they must needs hear of. I cannot take my leave of this duke, who is taking his leave of the world,[2] but yesterday I did bid them farewell in the college, and now our Frankfort martmen being returned I have horses for Augusta, which were wanting until this day, so as I think to set forward on Sunday next at the furthest. I pray you let Sir William Smith [3] know that I find more trouble in a money business of his than I expected, in that his creditor's father goes from his word, but I take the best course I may to procure him satisfaction before my departure. My brother Williams will advise with you touching a domestical business wherein I pray you assist him and all of us. So with our kindest remembrances I bid you farewell until I have the happiness to see you, and ever rest

Yours most affectionately

1. Philip Lytton was Carleton's rather alcohol-prone nephew, who had been with him some time.
2. The doge, Marc Antonio Memmo, died before the end of the year.
3. Sir William Smith was a friend of Sir Walter Cope's and later sheriff of Essex.

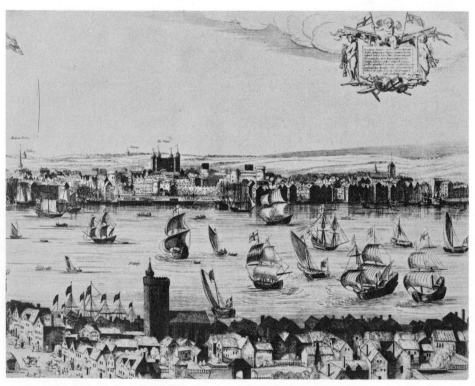

View of London in 1616. Engraved by C. J. Visscher. *Courtesy of the Folger Shakespeare Library, Washington, D.C.*

III

AMBASSADOR AT THE HAGUE

1616–1624

The Hague, March 29/April 8, 1616
S. P. 84/72, ff. 42–43

Good Mr. Chamberlain, I saluted you from Flushing with a few
lines by the captain of the ship who conducted us thither; from
thence to Rotterdam we were as long upon the water as betwixt
Margate and that place, having the wind always so contrary that,
coming within a league of Dort (when continuing in the east it
might have served us from thence), it then shifted into the west
so as we had nothing but the benefit of spring tides and fair
weather to help us during the whole voyage. At Rotterdam I
stayed no longer than might serve for the unshipping my stuff
and finding commodity to transport it hither so as the same day I
landed (which was the 24 of the last sto. no.) I came to The
Hague, where I was defrayed by the state for the space of fourteen
days, in which time I had commodity to settle myself and my
family and dispatched all ceremonies and compliments after the
accustomed form. The States are most of them absent in their
several provinces, and Monsieur Barnevelt[1] being sick, here is
very little doing, only the soldiers have an alarm of the marching
of Spinola's troops to Wesel and making a bridge over the Rhine
at Berg [Rheinberg] which makes them believe they shall have
some stirring this summer.[2] The restitution of the cautionary
towns[3] is a thing much spoken of and desired by this people; so
is it as much hearkened after and wished on the archduke's[4] side.
If it be so with you in England, surely *non carebit effectu quod
voluere* so many. However it succeed, I pray God it may turn to
the good of his majesty and this state, which will hardly be if the
reasons which the other part allegeth for their hopes be of any

[194]

validity. They discourse that this restitution must needs argue a disgust betwixt his majesty and this state, which may be followed with an open rupture, that these provinces shall hereby much enfeeble themselves, seeing they shall in redeeming the towns disoblige his majesty from sending them succors or at least much lessen his affection and care to preserve their state, of which hitherto he hath in some kind been a member and now shall lose that interest. Whilst we are busy in these cogitations there is a sharp execution committed at Frankfort and another threatened at Aquisgrane, of both which you have heard.[5] This shows the *Austriaci*[6] take courage at the peaceable disposition of other princes. The day before my arrival in this place here was a jeweler of Amsterdam found murdered and robbed of jewels to the value of 10000 pound sterling. His body was taken in a dust heap within the court gates, where it is conjectured he was laid but the night before, though in all likelihood he had then been murdered three days. The authors are not yet discovered, though much search is made after them. I send you certain letters from Venice which concern Phil Lytton, wherewith I pray you acquaint his brother as far as is needful to procure Signore Nys's satisfaction.[7] If you can give Gregorio[8] any comfort I shall be very glad, for the poor man doth much languish after it. I do exceedingly lament with you the loss of Sir Henry Fanshawe, whom neither his family, his friends, nor his country could have spared these many years, though the constitution of his body did not promise long life. If the partaking in grief may give ease to those that are chiefly interested, I pray you assure my lady no friend he hath did more love and honor him whilst he lived nor sorrow more for his death than I do, which I will witness whilst I live by any service I may do my lady or any of his. I pray you commend me and my wife to our friends in Hertfordshire.[9] My sister Alice caused an ominous token to be delivered [to] my wife at her first coming, an empty purse, which I doubt by reason of the company and good fellowship of this place we shall bring home with us. Sir Edward Conway came hither this day from The Brill. We expect Sir Edward Cecil the next week, now he hath performed the ceremony of his wife's funeral at Utrecht.[10] Others

[195]

have been here or will come in their turns. I find my house here very commodious and Colwell [11] to answer the recommendation of his first master. I wish I were as well able to satisfy the expectation which Mr. Secretary, in his great love and favor during his abode in these parts, did raise of me both amongst my countrymen and these chief persons, of whom I have received many professions of kindness in his right. I pray you remember my service and my wife's to my lady Winwood and so with our best wishes to yourself I commit you to God.

Yours as ever most assured

1. Johan van Oldenbarnevelt, the most important politician in the United Provinces. His official position was advocate of the States of Holland.

2. Wesel was a fortress in the duchy of Cleves, near the Dutch border; Ambrogio Spinola had occupied it in 1614, and his forces were still there.

3. The towns of Flushing and The Brill. Carleton took up his embassy just in time to take part in the final stages of the negotiation for their restitution to the Dutch in return for liquidation of the Dutch debt to England. The amount England received was a fraction of what was actually owed; James's financial necessities brought about a rather unsatisfactory bargain. The treaty was signed on April 23, 1616; the towns were turned over at the end of May. See below, letter of May 30, 1616.

4. Archduke Albert. He and his wife, Archduchess Isabella, were in theory independent rulers, but their status was less than clear, as their provinces were to revert to Spain if they died childless, which was what eventually happened.

5. In 1614 a Protestant insurrection had taken place in Frankfort, inspired in part by anti-Semitism; the insurrection was suppressed, and in February 1616 the Jews came back to Frankfort under imperial protection. Aachen (Aquisgrane, Roman Aquis Granum) had been governed by the Protestants from 1611 until it was seized by Spinola in 1614. In 1616 the Protestant leaders were punished by execution or exile.

6. The Habsburgs, both Spanish and Austrian, are meant.

7. Daniel Nys was a Dutch merchant in Venice.

8. Gregorio de' Monti was Italian secretary to Wotton and then to Carleton during their years in Venice; he was sufficiently trusted by both of them to be left in charge of the embassy occasionally during their absences. In June of this year, Carleton and Wotton jointly petitioned for a reward for him. There is a biographical note in Smith, *Wotton,* II, 473–74.

9. Sir Henry Fanshawe died early in March. He lived in Hertfordshire; hence the reference.

10. Sir Edward Conway, lieutenant governor of The Brill, was ultimately to become secretary of state, an unusual promotion for a soldier. Sir Edward Cecil, later Viscount Wimbledon, grandson of Lord Burghley, was an experienced but not gifted soldier. He had been in the Low Countries, off and on, for years; he was to play a major part in the ill-fated Cadiz expedition in 1625. His wife was Theodosia Noel, the daughter of a Rutlandshire knight. She was buried in the cathedral at Utrecht.

11. William Colwell (or Colwall), whom Winwood had employed as a steward and occasional secretary in the embassy.

May 1, 1616

S. P. 84/72, ff. 169–70

Good Mr. Chamberlain, I have suffered myself to be surprised by two of your letters, the one of the 6th, the other of the 20th of April, since my last by Andrew,[1] still expecting a fit occasion to dispatch Phil Lytton from hence (who hath now spent almost a fortnight with me) and to write by him. He is come hither without money or clothes, and how he will pay his debts or what course he will take hereafter I must leave to him and his friends, for whose sakes, as well the dead as the living, I cannot but wish him so well that he should have my best furtherance if I knew wherein to assist him. The best course in my opinion which he can take is to address himself to Mr. Secretary Winwood or some other of the lords in best grace and employment about his majesty and, when he knows his star by which to guide his course, then to begin a new voyage and perfect his travel. This is different from the common custom, in that men which go abroad keep themselves free whereby to have the world before them to choose or leave at their return, but at their return they are thereby left to the wide world, and *nemo est qui immittat in piscinam,* wherefore it is good to have one to whom he may make his endeavors known by his letters whilst he is abroad and by whom he may be assisted at his coming home. My sister's seal, which she expected from Venice, I sent in a letter to her by Andrew and have written again to hear of her stuff, which I presume must be come to London before this time because such things as I left when I came from Venice are safely arrived here this week past by way of Amsterdam. It were good Randolph Simmes [2] his principal in London were spoken unto, for to him she left the charge. I am only unfortunate in my drinking glasses, of which there is more than a third part broken in the carriage, and they were very fair. The person [3] who, you write, did relate at a dinner at court my having audience so long before I advertised it myself is the man whom I commended unto you for the good provision he makes for my dinners here, for he holds his wonted correspondency with Mr. Secretary and writes much oftener than I can find subject for, which being discovered unto me I do no ways restrain him, only I have desired him hereafter to let me know when he writes. The reason of my late dispatch at that time was the Easter Holy Days and other impediments which came betwixt my first audience with the States General and my admittance to the council of state, which, being both matters of ceremony, I thought fittest should go together. You know a letter I left behind me in London touching our friend, which was buried in silence unless you have heard more of it since my departure than I have done, though otherwise I hear from him as there is occasion.[4] We are here at a stand in all affairs, expecting now a final end touching the cautionary towns, which is a business most hearkened after. The news of the peace of France came hither the last night, and this day the French ambassador hath given account thereof to the States, with many thanks for their meddling so little in those broils.[5] The murderers of the rich jeweler of Amsterdam are in the end discovered by a second robbery they committed upon one of Count Maurice's [6] secretaries, whom they having made drunk in a bordello took his key out of his pocket and stole away 600 pounds sterling in gold, breaking open an old window towards a back side to have it believed the thieves entered that way but leaving the cobwebs, in which they were caught; for that being discovered to be but a fraud because it was plain no man entered at the window, they were called into question who were known to be last in the *greffier*'s company and, confessing the money upon the torture, with the money was found part of the jewels and by them the rest discovered. The actors of the murder are two Frenchmen, one of Count Maurice's chamber, the other of his guard; they confess to have committed in his excellency's lodgings at such time as he was abroad and so cunningly conveyed themselves presently into other company that they could give the best testimony of themselves of any which belonged to the court. They will be executed within these few days, and a third Frenchman is in the reckoning of the money, who coming in their way *sul fatto* had a share given him to keep silence, but he knew nothing of the murder and therefore may escape. Here is an English gentleman, one Clare of Sir Horace Vere's [7] company, in much trouble how to get out of hold where he was clapped the last week for wounding a burgher in many places of his body upon a quarrel concerning young Mistress Gilpin, by whom Clare is charged to have two children at a birth, and this is the payment he gives the poor fellow (as they say) for the nursing. We are here shrewdly pinched by a very unseasonable cold for this season. My wife's maids complain that their pleasant park here is full of cuckoos and hath no nightingales, and as yet we see very few leaves. The tulip gardens are in their flower, but we are not yet taken with that delight with which they are here so much transported. Michael of Delft [8] hath been with me and remembers you well by a picture of yours I have of Tintoret's hand. My old pieces both he and others do much approve, but for the new, *figulus figulum*. Thus I end with my paper and ever rest

Yours most affectionately

1.   One of the messengers who carried Carleton's letters back and forth across the North Sea. Carleton frequently mentions these messengers by name in his correspondence from The Hague.

2.   Simmes was the agent in Venice of Carleton's shipper. On May 18, Chamberlain wrote that Alice Carleton had heard from Simmes that her goods had just been shipped. *L. J. C.* II, 3.

3.   Chamberlain did not name the man; it was probably William Colwell,

whom Carleton described in his letter of January 1, 1619/20 (see below) as "my steward."

4. Carleton, on his departure, had left a letter of advice for Winwood behind him. It was full of home truths and bluntly critical language and undoubtedly well meant. Winwood took it badly; he was both troubled and angry. Chamberlain, in an attempt to smooth matters over, suggested to Winwood that perhaps Carleton was passing on the criticisms of others. Winwood was not mollified; he was particularly angry because he thought Carleton had shown the letter to other people. *L. J. C.* II, 3.

5. The ambitious and venal prince of Condé had broken into rebellion in alliance with some of the Huguenot aristocracy against the corrupt and incompetent regime of Marie de' Medici and her favorite Concino Concini and had just allowed himself to be bought off. One of the results of this affair was the dismissal of some of the former ministers; one of the replacements was the future cardinal Richelieu.

6. Maurice of Orange, the leading soldier in the United Provinces and Oldenbarnevelt's chief political rival. Carleton frequently refers to him as "his excellency."

7. Sir Horace Vere, like his elder brother Francis (see above, letter of January 15, 1603/1604), was a soldier; he was now governor of The Brill. After the surrender of the cautionary towns he remained in the Dutch service and distinguished himself in the campaigns of the 1620s. At that time he had the greatest military reputation of any Englishman, and he received a peerage in 1624.

8. Michiel von Mierevelt, a fashionable portraitist. He painted Carleton and a good many other prominent personages. See H. Havard, *Michiel van Mierevelt et son gendre* (Paris, 1874).

The Hague, May 24, 1616

S. P. 84/72, ff. 277–78

Sir, the barrenness of this place doth cast me much behindhand with you in so much that I have two letters of yours to answer, whereof the last is of the 18th of this present. You guess not amiss in your former at Sir Edward Conway's ill satisfaction in the recompenses given to the officers of the cautionary towns,[1] not that his part is not very fair and honorable, but because he is put beside his expectation of the regiment, whereof a councillor who had the greatest hand in this business (you know whom I mean) [2] gave his brother Captain Conway this assurance (who went expressly into England to solicit for him), that as sure as he had a company in the States' pay, so sure should Sir Edward have the regiment; whereupon many letters were written unto him out of England and from Sir John Throckmorton [3] for placing and disposing of officers in the regiment, about which he was as busy as now he is in packing up and providing for his departure out of these countries. I have now my last carriages from Venice safely arrived by sea, which were shipped two months after our departure from thence, which makes me much marvel at the stay of my sister's things, but our English merchants are always noted with negligence in anything which concerns not themselves. I pray you show or send her this enclosed letter, by which she will see what is become of a good acquaintance of hers,[4] who died suddenly, and (as Gregorio writes me) of a fume of the *sbiacca*[?] she lodging over the furnace, which took her in a melancholy fit of her husband using his wench, who dwelt near her nose, more kindly and lovingly than ordinary. I shall be glad to hear from you whether Sir Henry Wotton signed the letter in Gregorio's favor or let the suit fall, which I rather believe. Touching the other letter,[5] I nothing marvel at the cross construction made thereof, since all my actions of late have been subject to that unhappiness. The assurance you gave in my behalf you might safely do, for I never had the vanity of publishing papers; and to have done this had been villainy. My hope is that it will have the effect, as they say of the river Borysthenes (where the words are frozen in winter and melted and understood the next summer) and that time will make it appear no unfriendly nor unnecessary advice, though, when I think well of the matter, I conclude I might have been wiser. I have written to Ned Sherburne to get the most he can for my chains and to lose no more time.[6] We have here a great embassage of the Hanse towns, whereof every one hath sent deputies to determine of their several contributions and other particulars concerning their late contracted alliance with this state.

Meantime, whilst we are here in the midst of our consultations they are on the other side as busy in preparations; they attending only the return of the count of Bucquoy [7] out of Spain to put their army into the field as is supposed, and their first enterprise (it is thought) will be the siege of Juliers, which they think they may undertake under the emperor's banners without breach of the truce: [8] but it will not be so here understood, for Count Maurice saith that a blow on the pate is all one and will be as well felt under a felt hat made in Dutchland as under a Spanish *montero*. The Venetians have not yet compounded their affairs with the archduke Ferdinand, in which respect they increase daily their army and by men out of Candia, Corfu, and the coast of Dalmatia, which help up a number but are so little practiced in wars that if the quarrel go on and the Spaniard engage himself (which must follow in consequence) they will have a very ill match of it. They have chosen the procurator Priuli their general, which is an unusual course in that commonwealth, which never admitted any but strangers to that charge. What is done in Savoy I hear not, for my old friend [Isaac Wake] and I have no correspondence. Our English here want doings, which causeth many quarrels amongst themselves. A son of my lord Chief Justice Coke [9] coming lately out of England to Dort, fell out there with one Liggon, a gentleman of Sir Horace Vere's company, and fought with him at Gorcum [Gorinchem] where he hurt him in the arm, of which he is since dead. Before he left Dort he had another quarrel, with one Croker, and afterwards at Breda another with Ensign Yorke, which Yorke and Croker were at strife whose turn should be first served with Coke; whereupon Croker sent one Manners to Gertruydenberg (where Coke then was) to let him know he was his first man. At some words of comparison in the letter of challenge which Manners carried, Coke assailed him in the streets with his sword drawn, which Manners avoiding, ran him almost through the body in the midst of the breast, but such is his good fortune that he escapes that desperate hurt, whereas poor Liggon died of a very light one. We are here very backward in our season by reason of the colds which still continue and have killed all the fruits. The oaks in the park are not yet covered with leaves, which is strange in the month of June, [in the] style of the place. I have nothing more to say but God have you in his keeping.

Yours as ever most assured

1. Chamberlain's comment on the rewards was "the old proverb is verified, that there never was so plentiful a feast but some went away hungry." *L. J. C.* I, 625.

2. Possibly Lord Treasurer Suffolk.

3. Sir John Throckmorton was lieutenant governor of Flushing. The correspondence with his superior, Viscount Lisle, is printed in W. A. Shaw and G. D. Owen, eds., *Manuscripts of Lord De L'Isle and Dudley,* vols. III–V, (H. M. C., London, 1936–62).

4. Signora Scala, a dog. See below, letter of July 1, 1616.

5. A reference to Carleton's letter of advice to Winwood; see above, letter of May 1, 1616, n. 3.

6. Edward Sherburne had formerly been one of Salisbury's secretaries. He was now acting as Carleton's financial agent in London. The chains were some gold ones which Carleton had left with Chamberlain. *L. J. C.* I, 621.

7. Charles Bonaventure de Longueval, count of Bucquoy, a Fleming, a Habsburg general whose most noteworthy military feat was his share in the victory of White Mountain.

8. Juliers (Jülich) was in the hands of the Dutch, whose occupation of the town had been denounced by the emperor. Hence the notion that the archduke could attack it without violating the twelve years' truce with the Dutch.

9. The violent and unattractive Clement Coke. He avoided trouble on this occasion, partly because, as Carleton put it to Winwood on May 30, Liggon "died rather by the fault of his surgeons, than the danger of his hurt." *Letters, Holland,* p. 27.

The Hague, May 30, 1616

S. P. 84/72, f. 301

Sir, to add a word to the enclosed, which hath stayed long for a messenger, I would entreat your furtherance with Mr. Secretary for leave that I may make a step some time this summer to the

Spa, for which purpose I have written unto him, and you can particularly inform him what need I have.[1] True it is, that since my being at Augusta [Augsburg] I had no fit of the stone, but there is such a quarry settled and confirmed in my kidneys that upon any the least exercise either on horseback or afoot, I am put in mind of that which they call the black water in Ireland, for no other comes from me, and unless I look for remedy in time I must look for no other than a painful and short life. I was once of the mind not to have moved Mr. Secretary this summer but to have attended the next, by reason of my new settling in this service, but I think of the rule, *sero medicina parat* [illegible], when the disease is too much settled, and I make doubt whether the next summer will be so quiet for travellers as this and withal whether I shall have so good leisure. We hear of a bloody accident on the archduke's side, where two men came masked into a midwife's house and carried her away, partly by force, partly by persuasion, to a woman in childbed, whom she found likewise masked, and, after she had done her office, the child was presently taken by those fellows and cast into a fire which was made in the chamber for that purpose and consumed to ashes, the mother crying out and exclaiming upon them for that cruelty, which she said, in the midwife's hearing, was the fifth time they had used in like sort upon her children. This will not quit your Mistress Vincent because, though these men were barbarous, the woman was in some sort compassionate, but I expect before long to hear your Catholic gentlewoman put into the number of saints as well as Garnett and his companion, whose pictures and names I saw in the Jesuits' legend at Augusta.[2] Sir Horace Vere is come to The Brill, and tomorrow is the doomsday of our cautionary towns. His excellency [Count Maurice] is gone towards Zeeland to make his entry into his town of Flushing, where, and in Flanders, with the frontier towns in Brabant and Gelderland, he will spend five or six weeks. Our English captains are most of them here to meet their colonel, and Sir John Ogle[3] with his lady came yesterday from Utrecht, so as we lack no good company. Thus with my best wishes I commit you to God.

Yours most assuredly

[204]

1. On June 17 Winwood informed Carleton of the king's consent to his journey, with the instruction to keep an eye on the English he found there: "I fear many of them worse affected in their mind to the service of the state, than in body for their health." Carleton was also instructed to see if there was an English seminary in Liège, if he passed that way. *Letters, Holland,* p. 41. As the next letter shows, Carleton went via Liège; his report to Winwood, dated August 2, is in *ibid.,* pp. 43–44.

2. Chamberlain in his letter of May 18 had told a story of a woman convicted of the murder of her two children. She was a Catholic; her husband urged her to conform and have the children raised as Anglicans. But "she took this course to rid them out of the world rather than to have them brought up in our religion." *L. J. C.* II, 1–2. Henry Garnett, the Jesuit, was the most famous cleric executed for his share in the Gunpowder Plot.

3. Sir John Ogle was colonel of a regiment in Dutch service and was at present governor of Utrecht for Count Maurice. He returned to England after being replaced as governor in 1618. His wife was Dutch.

The Hague, July 1, 1616
S. P. 84/73, ff. 57–58

Good Mr. Chamberlain, I must give you many thanks for your two (as Mr. Gent was wont to call them) very good letters of the 8th and 22 of the last, and particularly for your care in finding me out so good a merchant for my chains, as likewise for your soliciting my leave to go to the Spa, which took that effect (notwithstanding that no note was taken to you of my letter to that purpose) that first I had notice from Mr. John More [1] that I might put myself in readiness for my journey and since from Mr. Secretary himself that the king had granted me license, so as, having ended some businesses (which were now upon the upshot and would fall to the ground or *recule* by my absence), I purpose, God willing, to take my journey, and on Tuesday or Wednesday next I set forward, having my wife with me (who the physicians say hath no less need than myself), and Sir Horace Vere, who was once of the mind to send for the Spa waters hither, hath changed that purpose and resolves to keep us company. Sir Henry

Carew,[2] a kinsman of my wife's and friend of Sir Horace Vere, goeth with us for good fellowship, unless the sickness of his brother's wife stay him at Gorcum, whither he is suddenly called from us as if he should see her no more alive. In recompense of my sister's grief for la Signora Scala (who, indeed, as Gregorio writes, drunk of the wrong cup) I pray you let her know that another of her acquaintances, Madonna Fortuna, hath five little ones, whereof I mean to send her the likest to the dam for a token and should write her many strange stories of this nursery, were it not that she is two letters in my debt since I came hither, and I have never one word in answer. Sir Henry Wotton, having refused my house before he came to Venice, at his coming thither so disliked that which his servant, whom he sent before, provided for him, that he was a whole week there before he demanded audience, which was thought strange by that state, considering the present condition of their affairs, which required the help of reputation, and that is the most we can give them. I thank the Spanish ambassador for fitting us with so just a character of Don Quixote's,[3] but I am little beholden to him and others of his coat, though I commend their diligence, for putting speeches into my mouth since my coming hither, as if I had moved the States to relinquish the towns they have in possession in Juliers and Cleves and leave them to the emperor—a thing they have generally divulged in Italy and particularly in the state of Venice, whereby to make appear the favor is lent in all places to the House of Austria, and have wrought so strong a persuasion thereof at Paris that even there (as near as it is) it is believed, though the chief ministers of state there have both my propositions and the States' answers, whereby they may see the contrary. Thus may you see what sirens those are to sound that into our ears, which makes us not believe our own eyes—which makes one, in a lamentable letter to me from Venice upon that subject, conclude, *in somma quella parte non può essere più desta, et vigilante in non trascurar còsa pur minima, e l'opposita non può essere piu pigra, irresoluta et sonnachiosa.* The passage through the Grisons is still kept shut by the industry of the Spagnolized French, and, whereas the Venetians served themselves in these occasions of soldiers out of the

Turk's dominions, the doubloons distributed betwixt the pasha and sanjaks of Bosnia have stopped that way likewise, so as they are now in great want of men and the more in regard of a contagious sickness in their camp, which wants little of the plague. They send money in assistance to the duke of Savoy *alla scopèrta* so as we see the rupture in those parts unfeigned and for the present unaccommodable; and if we or this state owed the Spaniards and the House of Austria any spite this were the time to pay it. This being past we shall not live to see the rusty Italian swords drawn again, and we must bear the burden alone in these parts of those who cannot live nor maintain their possessions and reputations without seeking to increase them. To leave these speculations, I have here had a troublesome business about 82 English, Scottish, and Irish who were taken at sea for pirates by two of the States' men-of-war near the islands of Orkney and conducted to their admiralty at Rotterdam and Delft, where the people were so hot upon the poor men that they could scarce be brought alive betwixt their ships and their prisons. By searching into them I found and made it appear to the States that these were soldiers sent out by the governors of the north in Ireland under the command of an officer, one Andrew Westcote, ensign to Sir Thomas Philips, for the apprehension of a young rebel Sawerby McDonell,[4] and for this purpose were fitted with two small barks out of Londonderry and with victual and munition for their voyage, having letters and instructions how to govern themselves. Hereupon they are returned back as passengers, not as prisoners, and all their things whereof they were spoiled are to be restored by inventory, which cost me much wrangling with the lords of their fishery here, who sat upon their lives, in that they could hardly be persuaded nor cannot to this hour (though these men are thus delivered by the States' authority) but that they came with a purpose to rob their fishers because they were found without victuals and upon that foundation to build greater piracies. Other affairs of this kind and the settling our new English regiment in the States' service have found me no small work. His excellency is returned out of Flanders and Brabant and sets forward into Gelderland about the same business of viewing their garrisons and fortifications, about ten days hence. Thus I rest as ever

Yours most assured

1. John More was one of Winwood's confidants and had been his London man of business during Winwood's tenure at The Hague.

2. Sir Henry Carew was probably a brother of Sir Matthew Carew, master in chancery, who is described in the *D. N. B.* as being one of nineteen children.

3. Chamberlain had written that Don Diego Sarmiento de Acuna, count of Gondomar, the Spanish ambassador in England, commenting on the "sudden mutations without any *intermedium*" at the English court, had exclaimed, "Voto a Dios que la Corte d'Inglatierra es como un libro de cavalleros andantes." *L. J. C.* II, 11.

4. Sawerby (or Surley) McDonell was a member of a Scots-Irish family whose activities in northern Ireland gave the English government a great deal of trouble. He was wanted on a charge of piracy; on July 13, Winwood informed Carleton that William Trumbull, the resident in Brussels, was being instructed to ask the archduke to extradite him. *C. S. P. Domestic 1611–1618*, p. 381.

Spa, August 2, 1616
S. P. 84/73, ff. 130–31

Sir, our doctors of the Spa forbid us writing and reading, and therefore I may say of letters as of verses, *non scribuntur aquae potoribus*, yet cannot I fail to salute you from this place and give you an account of our journey. We were upon the way seven days without staying above a night only in a place, having a convoy of 20 horse from Gertruydenberg to Liège and 30 in our company. Here we found the town full of men, women, and children of all ages, of all conditions, of all nations in Europe, for all sorts of diseases, but most for that whereof I suffer, and at our arrival the English did equal in number all other strangers, who were of three ranks, some which came for diseases of the body, others of the mind, the rest for good fellowship. The countess of Pembroke we found here, who complains chiefly of a common disease and much troublesome to fair women, *Senectus,* otherwise we see nothing amiss in her.[1] She hath met with a fit companion, the countess of Barlemont, whose husband is governor of Luxemburg, and they are so like of disposition and humor that whilst the men entertain themselves at pick-staff (a game proper to this place) they shoot at marks with pistols. This lady Barlemont hath with her two fair daughters, one a young widow, the countess of Hoog-straeten, whose husband lived but a month; the other a *devota* designed to a convent. Their lodging is the court of the English for play, dancing, and all entertainments; and so much have they learned of the language as to bid all comers welcome and of our fashions as to take tobacco, so as it seemed strange unto her at our coming that all our company forbore it, as if in her conceit all English had drawn no other breath. Here is the count Fred-erick Vandenberg's lady, who lives more retired, having with her a young son (who shall be one of the greatest heirs in all the seventeen provinces), not above nine years old, and his companion of seven, both pitifully tormented with the stone. My old acquaintance and friend Tobie Matthew and his inseparable companion Gage[2] were here deep in the waters before our coming. Sir Arthur Ingram[3] was here settled likewise, who besides the good company of five or six of his friends came laden with provisions of gammons of bacon, cheeses, red deer pies, English beer, and such like stuff of easy digestion. Now the English regiment begins to disband, there being gone in one troop twenty at least who are fixed in the archduke's provinces, amongst which are four women, the lady Crofts, who was Lovell the cofferer's widow,[4] an old woman, Mrs. Fortescue and two pert young dames, the one a wife with her husband, Mistress Camden, the other a maid, Mistress Woodrowes of the north. We had here three English Jesuits, two of Liège and one of Louvain, and three Jesuitesses of Saint-Omer, where they train up young wenches to that religion. Now to the point which your affection assures me you most hearken after. I cannot tell what effect to promise you of this water, which they say I must look for hereafter; for the

[209]

present I drink it without difficulty, and it passeth without pain or inconvenience either to my appetite or rest but dwells so long with me that it seems, and so the physicians say, it meets, with rocks in the way, which must be worn away *non vi sed saepe cadendo*. My wife cannot so well agree with the waters, and there is the less hurt because she hath less need. Sir Horace Vere finds they do much weaken him (he takes them for the spleen), yet he continues them and so may (as they all assure him) without danger, for though many make doubt whether they do any good, all conclude they can do no hurt. The season this year, by reason of wet and cold, is very unproper, and I doubt it will remove us from hence sooner than we intended. We shall take the way back by Louvain, Mechlin, and Antwerp, by reason that the way through those places is safe and the other not passable without convoy, which cannot be so conveniently had. Thus (for aught I know) I shall bid you farewell until we come so much nearer you, and I must desire you to let my brother Carleton and my sisters near you, with our other good friends, know of our well-being, to whose healths we drink every morning in fifteen cups of water each of a wine pint. If you would pledge us in as many at the Mitre in Bread Street you would be a merry company. So I rest as ever

Yours most affectionately

Tobie Matthew is a suitor for leave to go into England to recover a debt of £1000, which Sir Henry Goodier doth unfriendly detain from him.[5] He spake to me to write in his behalf to Mr. Secretary Winwood, which friendship, I must confess, I owe him and would have done it in regard I find his edge of disputing and arguing in religion quite taken off, yet for many respects I have rather wished him to be his own solicitor by a letter, which he hath written and sent, and if it lie right in your way I pray you further him with a good word. If he behave not himself well in England he may be as well and as soon sent back as recalled. The paper I send herewith contains the reasons which he allegeth for his license to return, and I shall be glad to hear from you if it be like to take place.

1. Countess Mary Herbert, widow of the second earl, was Sir Philip Sidney's sister and a well-known patroness of literary men. She was about sixty at this time.

2. For Tobie Matthew and his "fidus Achates" George Gage see above, letters of November 10/20, 1605, and August 14, 1612.

3. Sir Arthur Ingram was the well-known financial operator. Chamberlain did not like him: "a scandalous fellow," he called him, (*L. J. C.* I, 584–85). R. H. Tawney, who did not like Chamberlain, "a garrulous snob" in his view, had even harsher words for Ingram: "gross predatory animal." *Business and Politics under James I* (Cambridge, 1958), pp. 83–84. Carleton evidently found time to discuss his own affairs with Ingram; in October Edward Sherburne wrote that Ingram had spoken to the lord treasurer about Carleton's allowances, "which are promised." *C. S. P. Domestic 1611–1618,* p. 400. The best work on Ingram is A. F. Upton, *Sir Arthur Ingram* (London, 1961).

4. Gregory Lovell, cofferer of the household to Elizabeth. He died in 1597.

5. Sir Henry Goodier was a close friend of John Donne's and a patron of literary men and artists; he was friendly with Ben Jonson and Inigo Jones. He was also constantly in financial trouble, which may explain why he was "detain[ing]" Matthew's £1000—he probably did not have £1000.

The Hague, September 5/15, 1616
S. P. 84/73, ff. 201–204

Good Mr. Chamberlain, I left with you at the Spa the 12/22 of the last, from whence we parted within two or three days, taking the way of Maestricht as well to avoid an ill encounter which was threatened us at Liège (whereof I wrote unto you) as likewise to see a new town and country which are very ill matched, the town being very poor and desolate and the country both rich and pleasant. From thence we came the next day to Saint-Trond where by the way we were encountered with a troop of the bishop of Cologne's [1] horse, who, having made good cheer in the town whither we were going and half drunk (as it seemed), came towards us with their pieces and petronels in their hands after the manner of a charge, to see, belike, if they could make us afraid or by some disorder give them occasion of assailing and robbing us, which we

[211]

the rather believe because, by one I sent about an hour before, they knew who we were and lay in ambush for us in an open field behind a hill until we came to a fit distance for their bravado, but Sir Horace Vere and myself, whom they met with first, keeping on our way without alteration, after some words they left us to our journey. From Saint-Trond we came the next day to Louvain, where Mr. Trumbull [2] met us and giving us to understand of the archduke and infanta's [3] absence from Brussels, we took that place in our way, where we dined with Mr. Trumbull and lodged that night at Mechlin, whither he conducted us in company of Mr. Tobie Matthew, who found us at Louvain, or rather we him (for there is his residence), and left us not until we came to Antwerp. At Louvain we saw nothing remarkable but the duke of Ascot's [4] chapel, an English mile distant from the town, where those of that house have their monuments, and it is a great rarity for a family under the condition of absolute princes. At Brussels we had the full sight of the court, where the hall and chapel are exceeding fair, and the park within the walls of a town is a singularity; the grotto and gardens very perfect and pleasant; the whole house and furniture rather commodious than suitable to the palace of a prince. The seat of the town was all we could consider in so short time, which is the most pleasant that I have seen anywhere. The English nuns took it unkindly to be left unvisited, who take themselves to be such precious pieces (and so are set out and magnified by our English Catholics, whereof there we found many) that they think they should not have been so slighted, but we had neither time nor much desire to use that ceremony. Mechlin, both for the ways and gardens near it and the fairness of the streets and buildings, was absolutely the best town we saw in Brabant until we came to Antwerp, which I must confess exceeds any I ever saw anywhere else for the beauty and uniformity of buildings, height and largeness of streets, and strength and fairness of the ramparts. We stayed there (as in all other places) one night only, having an afternoon and morning to see the town, which we performed in friends' coaches, whereby to give our own rest, and left nothing of moment unseen, but I must tell you the state of this town in a word so as you take it literally, *magna*

[212]

civitas magna solitudo, for in the whole time we spent there I could never set my eyes in the whole length of a street upon 40 persons at once; I never met coach nor saw man on horseback; none of our company (though both were workdays) saw one pennyworth of ware either in shops or in streets bought or sold. Two walking peddlers and one ballad-seller will carry as much on their backs at once as was in that royal exchange either above or below. The English house is filled with schoolboys under the Jesuits' discipline and the Easterlings' stands empty.[5] In many places grass grows in the streets, yet (that which is rare in such solitariness) the building are all kept in perfect reparation. Their condition is much worse (which may seem strange) since the truce than it was before, and the whole country of Brabant was suitable to this town, *splendida paupertas,* fair and miserable. We soon found the contrary qualities in the first step we made into the territory of this state, which is rich and unpleasant, and this we imputed rather to the nature of the government than of the soil (for Brabant was never accounted poor) and thereof observed this manifest reason, that it proceeded of the quality rather of the stranger-soldier than the inhabitant, in that on that side the soldier is a master over the state (the Spaniard I mean), on this side (of what nation soever) a servant. At Breda (which both for the town and castle is a place worth the sight) we were both lodged and defrayed by the governor, as we were at Gertruydenberg in our going and saw both the garrisons, as well horse as foot, in arms. At Gorcum and Turgoe [probably Gouda] (which way we returned to avoid shipping of our horses), we had the like entertainment of the burghers, as we had likewise at Dort in our going; but Rotterdam makes profession of laying aside all such courtesy. At our return hither we found all in state as we left it; only some alteration in my house to the better, which the States, by changing the hall stairs and adding a piece of building in our absence, have made more commodious. For our healths I find myself (I thank God) much better for the present and hope well for the future. Sir Horace Vere is much lightened and eased of the spleen. A waiting maid of my wife's hath shaken off in this journey a quartern ague which hath held her a year, and these are three diverse

[213]

effects of the same cause, for we all drunk the same waters and used the same diet. I send you a book of the Spa made by one of the most experienced doctors of that quarter. And to leave this subject and itinerary, herewith I send you a letter which I met with here at my return, from Gregorio at Venice, by which you will see in what ill state the poor man stands and how much he fares the worse for his friends' recommendation. He is now out of my jurisdiction so as I should incur blame to be a suitor for him; otherwise I should not fail to remember to Mr. Secretary Winwood how ten years' faithful and diligent service under his majesty's ministers and twice six months by himself, during my abode at Turin and since in the interim of our ambassadors at Venice, deserves some remembrance. Here is passed by my Lord Dingwall [6] from Venice as free a man as he went thither, save only that he came away loaded with a gold chain worth 2000 ducats (as he saith himself), having seen their camp in Friuli and received good entertainment. The relation he makes shows they hearken rather after treaties of peace than provide for any great exploits in the wars. We have here a secretary from Venice employed upon these occasions, and by his seeking of a house he would make us believe he shall be here resident, but these sad signors will see him settled before they send one in like manner to Venice, which is a thing that state looks after. The French king hath sent hither to Count Maurice and his brother Henry a present of six lean and old Spanish horses, with fair clothes of blue velvet laced with gold, which were conducted by Pluvinel,[7] the king's chief rider, and much ceremony used in the delivery. About a day or two after, we had news of the prince of Condé's [8] imprisonment at Paris, which makes an ill interpretation of this message and present, as if it were to purchase friends against a day of need. *Imitantur hamos dona,* so saith an old poet upon the like occasion. The States of Holland are here assembled about their questions of religion and contributions, in both which they are much distracted. What you do at home I have not heard a great while by reason of the progress and my absence from hence. Tom Carew [9] went from me at the Spa to seek a fortune amongst our new councillors, where I shall be glad he may speed; for he proves much fitter for such a service than either for this place or me. I wrote to you by him and desired you to assist him with your advice, but I have ever observed that absence lays open faults and close knaveries which are of so high a nature in him as you would little imagine, and therefore as I will leave him hereafter to himself, so I wish you would, notwithstanding that as I wrote before and thus much I though necessary to say to you misdoubting his insinuations. Sir Horace Vere returns for England about ten days hence. Sir Edward Cecil went by the way of Antwerp a week since, having first shipped his daughters with his sister, the lady Tufton,[10] at The Brill, whose husband we left at the Spa, and there I leave you where I began with you, resting ever

Yours most affectionately

1. Saint-Trond was in the bishopric of Liège. Liège and Cologne were both held by Ferdinand, brother of Duke Maxmilian of Bavaria.

2. William Trumbull was the English resident at the court of Archduke Albert, having served his apprenticeship as secretary of the embassy during Sir Thomas Edmondes' tenure as ambassador. When Edmondes was recalled in 1609, Trumbull was promoted to resident and remained in the post for sixteen years, until the open rupture with Spain in 1625.

3. The archduke's wife, Infanta Isabella, was the daughter of Philip II.

4. *Aerschot* is meant—one of the oldest and wealthiest noble families in the Netherlands.

5. The reference is to commercial houses. *Easterling* was the common term for the Hansa.

6. Richard Preston, Lord Dingwall, one of James's Scottish favorites, who received his peerage in 1609. He is not memorable.

7. Antoine de Pluvinel was a famous trainer of horses as well as the king's equerry.

8. The new ministers installed as a consequence of Condé's recent rebellion (see above, letter of May 1, 1616) had plucked up their courage and ordered his imprisonment.

9. Thomas Carew, another of the Merton College set, and a cousin of Carleton's wife, had been in Carleton's service for about three years. He was an idle and dissolute young man who became a poet. He and Carleton did not get on, as this letter indicates.

10. Frances, the daughter of Thomas Cecil, earl of Exeter, was the wife of Sir Nicholas Tufton, who ultimately became earl of Thanet.

The Hague, September 11/21, 1616
S. P. 84/73, ff. 229–30

Sir, betwixt the sealing and sending the enclosed I have received yours of the 24th of the last; when the reversion you wrote of [1] was put into my mind I did cast with myself all objections before I wrote to you of it; and, touching those who you say aim at it, I imagined that since this man put into possession they had laid by any further pretention as scorning to attend the time of being served after him. If he that is nearest in place and credit can keep the reversion from being bestowed and so advantage himself or prefer the other when it shall fall, I have then done, not being so presumptuous as to march with them in concurrence. But as this unknown person got a grant secretly, which was afterwards maintained nothwithstanding all the opposition could be made, so will some other (unless I am deceived) step in before long by recommendation of some great person about the king and then *addio l'aspettativa.* I am not wedded to this nor anything else, only in this quick world I would be glad to catch with others at somewhat which might serve for a retreat. For in this place I already find I shall eat my corn in the grass, my allowances out of the exchequer being so ill-furnished that the merchant and shopkeeper who give me credit reap the fruits of my labors, so as I cannot deal upon so sure ground as Mr. Secretary did in this place, who saying here still by his own means and the king's allowance (which was then well paid) was sure to make a fortune and removing went to a present preferment. Besides I cannot propose to myself such windfalls as he very luckily met with, since in the transaction of the cautionary towns (a business whereof the like heretofore turned to the benefit of princes' ministers which were on the place) the matter was so handled that (though my father

Savile did congratulate my good fortune of coming hither so opportunely) I not only reaped no imaginable benefit by it but want my quarterly provision, though the supply of his majesty's wants come from the place where I serve. I am glad of any good that cometh to Sir Thomas Edmondes, yet I cannot but find it strange that the money which goeth from hence should skip over my head, who am on the place, and pay his provision in France.[2] Thus I disburden myself to you, to the end you may be contented to advise me without making other use of what I write, for I find that complaints with some do rather stir spleen than compassion. Sir Horace Vere went yesterday towards England, who, whilst we were at Spa, saw you sometimes in your letters and doth much love you. This bearer will deliver you two Spa staffs, which I will pray you to present Mr. Secretary and his lady to walk withal in Ditton Park and if, when time serves, he will procure I may walk by him as his poor neighbor at Eton, I will say to you again *addio l'aspettativa* and all other ambitions. You shall hear from me again very shortly by Martin the post, until whose going I defer writing to Mr. Secretary. So with my very best wishes I commend you to God and ever rest

Yours most affectionately

I cannot but thank my lady Fanshawe for her kind invitement, which I do in some sort better satisfy than her neighbors, in that I am often at Ware Park in conceit and wishes, which have not yet carried me to the other place.

1. The reference here is not altogether clear. Chamberlain's letter of August 24 (*L. J. C.* II, 19) suggests that the chancellorship of the duchy of Lancaster, which had just changed hands, might be in question. What Carleton really wanted, as the end of the letter makes clear, was the provostship of Eton.

2. Edmondes, who was now ambassador in France, was evidently receiving money from the payments the Dutch were making for the cautionary towns.

Good Mr. Chamberlain, I am now again returned from a petty progress, having taken the opportunity of his excellency's [Count Maurice's] absence and a vacation of affairs to visit Haarlem, Amsterdam, Utrecht, and Leyden, in which journey I spent six days, choosing rather to acquaint myself with these places in the beginning of my residence here, whereby the knowledge of them might be of some use, than (as many do) at parting, to find talk when they come home. I found at Haarlem a whole town so neat and cleanly and all things so regular and in that good order as if it had been all but one house. The painters were the chiefest curiosity, whereof there is one Cornelius for figures who doth excel in coloring but errs in proportions. Vroom hath a great name for representing of ships and all things belonging to the sea, wherein indeed he is very rare, as may appear by the prices of his works when a burgher of Alkmaar gave him for the fight which Greenfield made in the *Revenge* £200 sterling and his son for the *bataille* of Lepanto (which is not above a yard and a half long and a yard broad) doth demand and stick hard at £120. Goltzius is yet living but not like to last out another winter, and his art decays with his body.[1] At Amsterdam I saw many good pieces but few good painters, that place being in this commodity as in others the warehouse rather than the workhouse. The plague grows hot there, which made my stay the less, yet I saw the whole town and observed this difference from Antwerp, that there was a town without people and here a people as it were without a town. Such are the numbers of all nations, of all professions and all religions there assembled, but for one business only, of merchandise. Their new town goeth up apace, which they make account will be finished and filled within the space of two years. I was in their East India House, where the governors expressed unto me their desire of joining themselves in society with our merchants of the same trade,[2] whereby the charge should be equally borne as each should equally partake of the profit, for which they pretend

[218]

this reason, that they were first at the cost of expelling the Portugals out of many places and after of making fortresses and paying garrisons to secure their trade, for which they say they have in those parts, as well in their forts as their ships which are there at this present, 10000 men. It seems our men have no mind to part stakes with them, and I doubt we shall hear of greater difference in those parts betwixt our men and theirs than betwixt them and the Portugals, so stiff are they here in their resolution to hinder our trade if we do not contribute rateably to the charge. They have three ships lately come from the East Indies to Rotterdam and Middleburg, whereof I send you the bills of lading. To return to my journey. At Utrecht I saw eleven companies of the king's subjects in arms, which was more than any town in these 17 provinces can show of one language, or I may well say any town in Europe, and they are all very good men. At Leyden I only stayed a dining time, having the commodity to see that place at leisure, and yet I must note as a singularity the common inn where we dined, which hath diverse rooms hung with tapestry and some furnished with pictures of the best hands. Here at my return I found your letter of the 3rd of the last, for which I give you many thanks, as likewise for the enclosed, in requital whereof I send you my last from Venice, from whence I hear weekly and cannot but as much marvel at Fabritio's diligence in writing as at Isaac Wake's negligence, he being the man whom it hath been my fortune to do so much good for as would have obliged another as good as himself all the days of his life. It may be he stands upon the punctilio that because I came last abroad I must write first, which our agents in Spain and at Brussels (though with one of them I have small acquaintance) did not stick at, so as we hold good correspondency. We say here the world goeth ill with the duke of Savoy and that the governor of Milan's army is lodged in Piedmont. The Venetians (as you will find by these letters) proceed successfully in their wars but hearken likewise to peace, which lest it should not take place they do very providently take care for men against the next spring, which is their chiefest want, they having obtained a levy in these united provinces of 3100 foot, which shall be commanded by Count John

Ernest of Nassau, a kinsman of his excellency's, who hath charge here under the States. He hath already touched 40000 ducats for the raising of the men and the conduct, in which he doth now so bestir himself that it is the chiefest business of this place, but as well before as after he hath his men on board he will find many difficulties and I doubt will scarce show half his number upon Saint Mark's Place, which is appointed for their landing. His captains, like his soldiers, are of diverse nations and of them two English, Sir John Vere and Captain Woodows.[3] Others offer themselves if they might be entertained. We have here the deputy with three or four others of our English merchants at Middelburg treating with those of this province of Holland touching the revocation of a placard by which the sale of their dyed and dressed cloths is forbidden, wherein I believe there will be some good course taken for their contentment, though not all yielded to which is demanded.[4] Count Maurice is returned from his progress into Gelderland and those frontiers, where his half-sister, the countess of Hollock, died whilst he was near her but not present at Buren when she departed on Monday night last. The 13/23 of this present he goeth to her funeral at Buren, where the prince of Orange[5] doth meet him from Breda and the rest of the house from other places. Thus I end with my paper and rest

Yours most assuredly

1. Cornelis Cornelisz painted in the Italian style, but not very well; his work and that of Hendrik Vroom, whose chief products were pictures of sea fights, are virtually unknown today. "Greenfield" is Sir Richard Grenville. The famous sea fight, in which Grenville withstood a Spanish squadron, took place in 1591. See A. L. Rowse, *Sir Richard Grenville of the Revenge, an Elizabethan Hero* (London, 1949). Hendrik Goltzius, who did indeed die in 1617, is somewhat better known as a portraitist and etcher, but his work could hardly be called exciting.

2. In 1613, and again in 1615, conferences had taken place between English and Dutch commissioners on the matter of a possible union of the two East India companies. The Dutch were almost certainly being disingenuous; they had no intention of sharing the Eastern trade with the English or anybody else, and their purpose was to induce the English to join them in an attack

on Spanish holdings and shipping there. The fullest account of the conferences is in G. N. Clark and W. J. M. Van Eysinga, *The Colonial Conferences between England and the Netherlands in 1613 and 1615* (Leyden, E. J. Brill, 1940).

3. Sir John Vere was the bastard nephew of Sir Horace Vere and fought in his regiment; in April 1617 he arrived in Venice as commander of 600 English troops under Count John of Nassau. Henry Wotton unsuccessfully recommended him for promotion after Count John's death. Smith, *Wotton* II, 111–12. Captain Henry Woodows later acquitted himself well in the fighting against the Uskoks before Gradisca d'Isonzo. P. R. O., S. P. 84/77, f. 54.

4. One of the consequences of the disastrous Cockayne project, for which see below, letter of November 26–December 2, 1616, n. 3, was a Dutch embargo on the importation of English dyed cloth. Cockayne's scheme was on the verge of collapse, and the English cloth-traders were trying to salvage what they could from the wreckage.

5. Maurice was the son of William the Silent by his second wife; he had numerous half-sisters, the children of his father's third wife. His elder brother Philip William was prince of Orange; Maurice succeeded to the title on Philip William's death in 1618. The latter was such a nonentity that Maurice was sometimes called prince of Orange before 1618, but not by Carleton, who was always correct.

The Hague, October 24, 1616

S. P. 84/74, ff. 109–10

Sir, your letter of the 12th of this present came so richly fraught with stuff of all kind and all of the best that I thought not fit to make you so scant and slender a return as the hasty dispatch of my last messenger would suffer, and therefore I took more day for better provision, of which I will now discharge myself at large. I send you back your letters [from Wake] from Turin, having now newly received from the same hand one of the same date as your last and of the same substance, wherein he doth accuse divers others written unto me by the way of Venice and Heidelberg, which I take as an excuse of silence, in that I hear

[221]

from both those places weekly and therefore see not how his letters should fail. This hath given me occasion of expostulating some old matters with him, which will make him believe my sister and I conspire in a quarrel, and he will love us both alike now he hath so little need of us, which is the rule of his friendship.[1] Tobie Matthew had heard (as I perceive by him) of Mr. Secretary's recomending his suit, but not of the answer. I doubt his stiffness in refusing the oath is rather more confirmed than altered with time, only his heat in disputing is qualified, which would make his being for a small space in England to dispatch his affairs less dangerous if it might be admitted. You give me much comfort concerning myself of Mr. Secretary's good will towards me, which I was never doubtful would be recovered in time, knowing his real disposition and my constant resolution to deserve no other but well of him, but I should be glad rather to procure somewhat by his means whilst I have so good a friend in place than to expect his reversion, because this unusual constellation of preferring foreign ministers to places at home will be out before my turn come to be served. You gave me a rule in one of your former letters, *semper tibi pendeat hamus,* and by my next I shall show you somewhat *quo minime credis gurgite,* wherein you may have your share if you think it worth the catching. I do not marvel that the lord you write of [2] be already weary of his father-in-law because he could never endure his own father, but it is very strange how he could insinuate himself where he loves so little and where he is so well known. It seems there is somewhat which continues the ancient property of taking *hominesque Deosque,* but I hope our good friend will be wise and wary enough for being overtaken. The malignant planet for diseases reigns hot in these parts, of which Mr. Trumbull hath suffered lately and very hardly escaped with life. One of our English merchants (the treasurer of the company at Middelburg), who was here about the business of clothing, died very unexpectedly in this place, being found dead in the morning in his bed without giving any warning to those who lay in the same chamber. His excellency's treasurer died the last week of two days' sickness, and two others of good account in a manner suddenly. His excellency is returned from the burial at

Buren and for fear of these dangerous times is entered into a course of physic. The princess of Orange [3] came yesterday from Breda, where she hath been with the prince of Orange and his lady for the space of a month. Count Henry's [4] marriage with the landgrave of Hesse's daughter is at length fully concluded, and before the new year he is to meet his bride at Arnheim and so bring her hither to lodge in the same house with his mother the princess, which will much increase that court. The French king hath demanded by his ambassador here resident assistance of the States of five men-of-war for the siege of Blaye by Bordeaux, which they have here readily promised in case the siege proceed. [5] Our Venetian levy is increased by one French company, so as they are now 3250. Rocquelor, a Frenchman, is the second colonel after much pursuit. Some of the companies are now mustering and embarking by Texel, they going separately for fear of giving jealousy to the Spaniard. The Venetian war upon the archduke Ferdinand and the Spanish upon the duke of Savoy proceed hitherto with like success, both having gained ground upon their enemies with loss of their best men, Pompeo Giustiniani being killed by a shot as he was viewing a passage over the Isonzo on the Venetian side, and Gambaloita of the Spanish, who was shot in the head (as you see in your letters) and is since dead of his wound. The count of Sulst, general of the high Dutch, is dead of sickness at Turin. A Spanish captain, Vives, son to the Spanish ambassador resident at Genoa, is taken prisoner by the Savoyards, whom Don Pedro sought to release by setting at liberty freely without ransom a secretary of the prince Thomas and 20 poor Savoyards then newly taken, but the duke in requital gave him a poor old Spaniard only, upon his word that Don Pedro did esteem him more than twice twenty Savoyards; but Vives lies by it. Hitherto all goeth well but I fear what *serus vesper* will bring, that poor duke having so potent an enemy lodged in his country and nothing but his courage to support him. The Spaniard hath taken and fortified Santhia and was set down the 5/15 of this month with cannon before Saint Germain, which is a place of small defense; and my sister can tell you how near it is to Turin because my wife and she dined there and lodged at Turin the same night.

That place being taken Vercelli is environed round with the enemy and will be the next besieged. There is great cruelty used on both sides, especially with fire, there being no open place near the armies left unburnt. I do much pity the duke, who doth *jouir à tout perdre* and is faintly seconded by friends. Here we dispute of religion. In England you make merry. In Germany they talk and do nothing. France during the nonage is not considerable. The Turk is engaged far off with the Persian; so as the Spaniard never had *si beau jeu,* since he may proceed against a weak enemy without fear or apprehension. But it is strange we apprehend no more the consequence of an old enemy both to our religion and state with a victorious army.[6] In this sad contemplation, I leave you, ever resting

Yours most assured

1. Carleton was evidently disenchanted with Isaac Wake.
2. William Cecil, Lord Roos, whose father, was William, eldest son of Thomas Cecil, earl of Exeter. His father-in-law was Sir Thomas Lake, Winwood's colleague as secretary; Chamberlain had written that Roos was currying favor with Winwood. For Roos see above, letter of August 14, 1612, n. 3.
3. The dowager princess, Louise de Coligny, William the Silent's last wife.
4. Frederick Henry, Maurice's half-brother and successor.
5. The French ambassador in the United Provinces, Aubrey du Maurier, asked for aid on the ground that the governor of Blaye was in rebellion against the state.
6. The recurrent war between Spain and Savoy broke out again in September 1616. This installment was to last for a year, and result in the capture of Vercelli by Don Pedro de Toledo, the governor of Milan.

The Hague, November 26–December 2, 1616

S. P. 84/75, ff. 22–23

Sir, I wrote to you lately by a post who went in company of the archbishop of Spalato,[1] but my letter was only concerning that person, so as I made no mention of the receipt of yours of the 26th of October and 9th of this present, since which time your other of the 14th is come to my hands, though not by the messenger you name; by which means I am brought into great arrearage; but you have the advantage of the bank, for from thence all is good payment, whereas I must confess I find little here which can pass for current, yet since you can be content with the gazettas you shall have them by every messenger and you need not send them back, though I will desire you to keep them, in that I make (and so have done a long time) a collection of them as some do of almanacs to know the certainty of the weather, yet not with so great diligence as the duke of Urbino, who hath them in process of time from great antiquity. Mr. Morton [2] is newly passed this way towards Heidelberg in better state of health than I could have expected of his crazy constitution. He brought one brother with him and met another here, who have conducted him on his way. Our Venetian soldiers are not yet embarked but are ready for the first wind, and we hear from the archduke's side that they are as diligently laid for in the straits by the Spaniards as they are expected by the Venetians with great devotion. Yet I doubt more of their answering expectations when they come there than of any danger by the way, their general being a man of no great experience, though a gentleman of good valor and courage, and most of the captains young men. The soldiers are better than happens ordinary [sic] with levies of voluntaries, and in the whole troops it is thought there are at least 600 English who have borne arms though there be two captains only of our nation, and those are esteemed the best of the two regiments. I know not what will be the issue of our cloth business,[3] which gives me somewhat to do here as I perceive it finds you discourse at home, but my hope is there will be moderation on both sides to prevent the inconveniences which will follow the change of our merchants' residence, who are wooed by the archduke's side with very large offers to come from Middelburg to Antwerp, and I know not how it falls out, but so it is that though they do here see and know the loss they shall sustain by their remove, yet they are not forward to use any great invitements to stay them, but rather provide to set their people on work if the worst should happen than to seek to prevent the inconvenience.[4] The States of Holland are again

[225]

assembled here at The Hague touching their differences about religion, which I doubt they will hardly end because they come with such limited instructions from their town without leaving anything to deliberation, and time hath rather kindled than quenched their dispute. I hear say Doctor Carleton hath written somewhat concerning Arminius' doctrine, which hath gotten oversea and infected our universities. If he fare no better for this than for other his labors he were better take his ease in his old age, but his diligence is to be commended though others go away with the preferments.[5] Poor Gregorio hath written unto me that he is lately married and he saith he chose his wife chiefly for two qualities, she being *pòvera* and *brutta,* the first whereof made her humble and the second freed him from jealousy, but these rules do not hold always; meantime it seems the poor man hath little to brag of. The nuncio at Venice hath bought up all the archbishop of Spalato's manifests and obtained a sentence of the Inquisition against printing or publishing any more. The papists in this place (whereof here are some very passionate) have raised many scandalous reports against him, some saying that he had a wife and children at Venice, which made him fly from thence, and this they gather out of a text of Saint Ambrose which he cites in his manifest *nec patriae contuitu, nec parentum filiorumque gratia nec uxoris contemplatione revocari debemus ab executione preceptorum coelestium,* etc. Others charge the poor old man with an Italian peccadillo and will have it that he forsook his country for the love of Robin Barnes, who they saw here so diligent and serviceable about him; but some are otherwise affected by his manifest, whereof one professed in an open assembly his mind in these words: *si ce qu'il dit est dit de bonne conscience, sans interests humains, je le suiverai.* I have received a letter from Mr. Tobie Matthew, whereby he doth acknowledge much obligation to Mr. Secretary Winwood and to you for the furtherance of his suit, though it hath not succeeded according to his desire. My wife doth always desire to be kindly remembered unto you, though I often forget her commissions. So I rest as ever

Yours most assured

Hague this 26 of November, 1616, *sto. vet.*

Sir, the weather hath been so tempestuous and the wind so contrary that I have stayed my messenger a whole week, in which time nothing is happened to enlarge my letter, unless it be with thanks for another of yours of the 23rd of the last, which I received yesterday. I perceive by what you write as likewise by what I understand from Mr. Brent that no butter will stick to my bread for that poor place in Ireland; since Sir Dudley Norton was in execution of it, I did not imagine there would have been so quick carving; otherwise I should have made better provision in time.[6] Thus once more I bid you farewell resting ever

Yours most assured

Hague this 2nd of December, 1616, *sto. vet.*

1. Marc Antonio de Dominis, archbishop of Spalato (Split), who came to England because he quarrelled with his ecclesiastical superiors over a tax question. He became dean of Windsor, but eventually left England and reverted to the ancient faith.

2. Albertus Morton, Wotton's nephew. He was on his way to Heidelberg to serve Princess Elizabeth as her secretary. *Letters, Holland,* p. 68.

3. The "cloth business" was the attempt by the syndicate headed by alderman Cockayne to undercut the Merchant Adventurers by undertaking to dye white cloth in England, thus bypassing the Dutch dyers. The United Provinces retaliated by prohibiting the importation of dyed cloth, and since Cockayne's group could not handle the dyeing of the huge stocks of white cloth, the English export business underwent a major crisis. This was the so-called "Cockayne project"; there is a large-scale account in A. Friis, *Alderman Cockayne's Project and the Cloth Trade* (London, 1927).

4. The Merchant Adventurers' staple port was Middelburg, in Zeeland; there were frequent suggestions from cities in Holland like Amsterdam, as well as from Antwerp, where they had been located till 1568, that they move.

5. George Carleton, Dudley's cousin, another fellow of Merton, had just missed the bishopric of Carlisle. In 1618 he became bishop of Llandaff and was one of the English delegates to the synod of Dort, where he argued for the doctrine of the apostolic succession. He was translated to Chichester in 1619.

6. The "poor place in Ireland" was one of the secretaryships there, to which Carleton had once been appointed. The job was vacant, and Carleton was hoping either to profit from it or get it for Nathaniel Brent. He was successful in neither; Sir Dudley Norton, the other Irish secretary, got the position for Sir Francis Onslow. See *C. S. P. Domestic 1611–1618,* pp. 406, 427.

Sir, Our messengers into England have been for a long time wind-bound and our news of these parts frozen, though as yet we are free from frost, which is a miracle in the midst of Christmas. The Venetian troops lie still in the haven; yet not so still but that those in the Texel have suffered much by being both sea-beaten and weather-beaten as they ride at anchor; but this long stay makes them go better accompanied, there being many good merchants' ships from Amsterdam which will pass the straits with them *in conserva,* from whence news comes daily what strict guard is laid for them. My gazetta fails me this week, in place whereof I send you an abstract of a particular letter from Venice. I believe you will see before long in England Ottavian Bon,[1] the extraordinary Venetian ambassador who hath been long in France; and from thence we shall have him here, to make these parts of the world capable of the Spanish designs on the other side of the mountains,[2] where the progress they shall make will in the end light on these provinces though the danger be far remote, and of this they are here sensible enough, but the remedy is not so easily found as the disease foreseen. They think here they do not a little assist both the Venetians and the duke of Savoy in diverting so great a part of the Spanish forces as they do both in their own respect as likewise in regard of their neighbors in Cleves and Juliers. At least they will pick some thanks of those princes in this consideration, though what they do is for their own interest. The treaty of Xanten[3] is again *sur le bureau,* but many accidents since the framing thereof and change of affairs of the world makes it a difficult business. You will have commissioners in England touching the merchants' affairs from the States, if you can stay their leisure,[4] which it seems our men, for their desire of novelties, can hardly do; and how to make these men hasten their pace in a business which universally concerns their provinces I see not any means, wherefore as the change of the wonted trade began with us I would be glad we might attend the accustomed means of reconciling such differences, which is now in the way to proceed from hence. We expect here within few days from Breda the prince of Orange with his lady, who will stay here till towards Lent. The princess of Ligne with her fair unmarried daughter Ernestina went from hence the last week towards Brussels and before her departure bid herself very friendly and confidently to dinner to my wife and brought with her the widow princess of Orange, the duke of Holstein, and Count Henry [5] but left all their trains behind them; so as we had no more guests than I have named persons, and they made themselves very merry. At their passing from Rotterdam it was their fortune or curiosity to go near the ships of soldiers now bound for Venice, of whom they received the accustomed salutations of this country, whore, whore, whore; and to be sure not to miss them they cried out Spanish whore, French whore, Neapolitans' whore, Brabant's whore, and as many more as they could devise to come near the fashion of their attires. I hope the good old bishop [6] be safely got over to you, though he hath had the wind still contrary. At Rome his books are already forbidden, and the next work will be to burn him in effigy for a breviary of his which the nuncio at Venice, searching his study since his departure, found amongst some other books (which he left with one that married his niece), wherein he had cancelled the names of all the canonized saints and made a great reformation with his own pen. We have his manifest here translated into all languages, and it doth much good as well in regard of the common enemy as the private disputes and schisms in this church, wherein he doth use arguments of temper and moderation. Fabritio gives this good old man the title of my spiritual son, and I shall be glad he may so prove that I may own him. I write at this present very earnestly to Mr. Secretary to be a means for better payment of my allowance, which part of my letter I send you that you may (if you so please, and so I desire you will) lend me a good word in conformity thereunto. Thus I wish you and our Hertfordshire friends in all places a merry new year and ever rest

Yours most assuredly

The gazetta is come very opportunely to make up my packet.

1. Bon, a veteran diplomat, was slated at one point in the summer of 1617 to go to England on a special mission, but never did.

2. This was a reference to the current installment of the continuing struggle between Savoy and the Spanish viceroy in Milan, which Carleton, and many others, regarded as part of a deep-seated plan for Spanish aggrandizement.

3. The treaty of Xanten, signed in November 1614, had arranged for a temporary settlement of the disputes between Spain and the Dutch over the disposition of the Cleves inheritance pending a final decision on the fate of the duchies. Almost immediately the argument broke out again, over the implementation of the newly signed treaty. Winwood had recently informed Carleton of a statement by Gondomar to the effect that, if the treaty were not executed by the end of February 1617, the Spanish would remain in permanent occupation of the territory they held in the duchies. The Dutch were not moved.

4. The "merchants' affairs" referred to were the disruptions in the cloth trade caused by the Cockayne project, which was about to collapse completely.

5. Count Henry was the only son of the widowed princess of Orange, fourth wife of William the Silent. Duke Joachim Ernest of Holstein Sunderberg had recently offered to take service with the Venetian republic.

6. The archbishop of Spalato, who arrived in England a few days before Carleton wrote this letter.

The Hague, February 5/15, 1616/17

S. P. 84/76, ff. 128–29

Sir, I believe you will be long without my letters, the wind holding so contrary that all our messengers fail of their passage, and indeed there hath not been such a winter in many's memory, no frost as yet appearing save only for a day or two in September last; whereby this country (whereof the profit chiefly consists in quick and often returns at sea) doth suffer much; a plague is feared, which hath already taken four houses in this town, and a famine will hardly be escaped by reason the corn in the ground is usually consumed with numbers of mice when they are not killed with the frost. The doubt hereof hath caused the States of Holland to recall many ships, which being laden with corn have lain for these two months outbound and wind-bound with the Venetians in the Texel, and it so falls out, by reason of the enhancing of the market in this time, that they have made a better return back betwixt the Texel and Amsterdam than if they had performed their voyage. We have another whale-fish cast on shore here by Katwyk and one in Friesland, which find more work for our Dutch diviners; but if they grow so common they will cease to be wonders. Our fishers complain much that they have chased the cableaw [codfish] and all the good fish out of these coasts; and indeed we that are housekeepers find the markets ill served. These questions in religion grow every day to greater heat.[1] At The Brill they were in arms on Friday last to seek out a minister of the Contraremonstrants and at Rotterdam the Sunday before the people were using some violence to an assembly of that party which had a sermon in a private house, whilst in the meantime, at Amsterdam, there being the like meeting of the Remonstrants, the windows were broken down in sermon time and the preacher hardly escaped from being flung into the canal. We expect within eight or ten days another assembly of the States of Holland, which unless it take a final order, the real news I shall send you will be that they are all together by the ears, which is the more to be feared because the magistrates themselves are as much kindled in this cause one against another as the common people. Monsieur de la Noue hath made his proposition, which was an apology of the administration in France both during the king's minority and since; which he concluded with a request not to assist the princes but the king and queen in case of necessity.[2] He is lodged and defrayed according to the ordinary use of extraordinary ambassadors, though here is a speech he shall take the place of resident from du Maurier, who is now going into France. We have news of peace betwixt the Muscovite and the Swede, of wars in hand betwixt the Swede and the Polack, and of preparation both at sea and land by the king of Denmark, whereof Lübeck and Hamburg are very jealous.[3] I was on Saturday last invited by the University of Leyden to a tragedy of *Troas* [*Troades*] in Seneca, which they began at two of the clock in the afternoon and ended at five, so as I went and came back the same day, which made the play so much the better, being both short and sweet; and to give them their due, if their outsides for their dressing and apparel (most of the parts being women) had been answerable to their pronunciation and action, they might compare with our universities. My sister Williams hath invited by way of provision either me or my wife to christen my nephew Anthony's next child, which he looks for shortly; and if it be a boy I will entreat you to assist at the christening in my behalf to give it the name which the mother likes best. Ned Sherburne hath charge for the rest to make purchase of a piece of plate, wherein I have stinted him at ten pound; but you must make the choice. This pains I will pray you to take though it prove a girl, in which case my wife will entreat my sister Alice to be her deputy.[4] I have received your last of the 18th of January. With this I send you a letter from our honest French doctor at Venice [5] and so commit you to God's protection.

Yours most assured

The doctor's letter is *smarrita,* in place whereof you must be content at this time with the gazetta.

1. The quarrel between the Remonstrants, the followers of Arminius, dominant in the States of Holland (though not in Amsterdam) and the Contraremonstrants, the orthodox Calvinists, powerful outside of Holland, was coming to a head. Oldenbarnevelt was the key figure in the Remonstrant party; Maurice had just thrown in his lot with the other. Carleton's letters for the next two years are full of this quarrel, which finally resulted in the triumph of the Contraremonstrants and the execution of Oldenbarnevelt on trumped-up treason charges. Carleton supported the Contraremonstrants out of a combination of instructions and conviction. There is a good account of the dispute in P. Geyl, *The Netherlands in the Seventeenth Century* I (London, 1961), 38–83.

2. Domestic trouble had once more broken out in France; the government of Marie de' Medici sent special embassies to both England and the United Provinces to prevent them, if possible, from siding with the dissidents, which included most of the great Huguenot aristocrats. The ambassador, Odet de la Noue, was the son of François de la Noue, a Huguenot companion-in-arms of Henri IV's.

3. The peace of Stolbovo between Sweden and Russia was signed in Febru-

ary 1617, thanks in part to the mediation of James's agent, the merchant Sir John Mericke. War between Sweden and Poland was almost continuous in this period, owing to the efforts of the Catholic Sigismund III of Poland to recover the Swedish throne, which he had held between 1592 and 1604. James was sympathetic to Sweden for religious reasons but did not take sides openly owing to the large English trade with Poland. See his letter of December 14, 1617, to Carleton, P. R. O., S. P. 95/2, f. 42. Military activity by the belli-cose Christian IV of Denmark, James's brother-in-law, always made the free cities of North Germany nervous.

4. It turned out to be a boy and was named Dudley. Chamberlain spent 9 pounds, 15 shillings, on a pair of silver candlesticks. *L. J. C.* II, 61.

5. Jacques Asselinau. See above, letter of April 24, 1612, n. 3.

The Hague, April 26, 1617

S. P. 84/77, ff. 63–64

Good Mr. Chamberlain, your letter of the 29 of the last required rather thanks than answer, only I would gladly see a copy (if it were possible) of Doctor Donne's sermon whereof you make mention, which being in so great an audience and so generally well liked methinks should be hearkened after.[1] Your last of the 5th of this present confirms that which I understood before of Ned Sherburne's applying himself to my lord keeper,[2] whereof he hath written to me himself, with offer notwithstanding to continue my affairs, which (if those he hath about my lord be no greater than they are like to be at first, with one that is so well followed) I canot deny but he may very well do; and yet the difficulty of recovering money out of the exchequer (which is his chief business for me) would require a whole man, to be every day seeking and giving, and all little enough. But I am very well content to go on with my former course with him, so long as I find he neglects not my business, which hitherto I believe he hath not done, notwith-standing that the effects of his diligence have not followed as I expected. Touching the new assurance which he endeavors to procure since the death of his father-in-law, that which he offers

[233]

is so little that I had rather trust to himself. *Fides obligat fidem*; and I have that confidence in his honesty that he will discharge himself well towards me; only I require this of him, that he will acquaint you so particularly with his own estate and mine, that in case either of us or both should die, each of us or our friends may know where and how to have our own; and for that which is past he will either bring or send me with the first commodity a just account. I hear that Sir John Bennet is come to Antwerp at a time when the archdukes are in their devotions at Sichem; so as he hath entertained himself with Mr. Trumbull in his company in that good town ever since his arrival. His wife is expected here in her way to Amsterdam, whither she makes a progress to see her friends, but I know not whether we shall see him or not; howsoever I expect Mr. Brent very shortly.[3] We have been here lately much distracted concerning the succors which were demanded by these French ambassadors and urged with much eagerness as a due by right of treaties betwixt that king and this state, to which the chief here inclined and showed their greatness by swaying the matter against the minds of the most, who did well distinguish betwixt the interest of the king and the faction of the court. But before all was concluded the news came in lucky hour of the death of the marshal d'Ancre, which hath delivered them here as well as the rest of the world, of much pain; and here they participate of the universal joy which is advertised from Paris, for which it cannot be denied but that there is just subject, and yet I cannot be without apprehension to see a young king's hands bathed in blood and the proceeding so extolled and magnified. *Quamquam ille dignus hac contumelia,* yet it had been fitter for a king to proceed by way of justice than *par voie de fait*; which he might have done, this being no duke of Guise; and the law took hold of a Marshal Biron.[4] But what needs (say you) this discourse. To come home to our own affairs. Our questions about religion draw towards an exigent, most of the provinces having given order to their deputies, and some sent express commissioners, to treat with those of Holland and persuade them to have a greater care of the public quiet; counselling them to a course which is likewise advised by his majesty by a letter (whereof I send you a printed copy) which is to call a national synod.⁵ This is likely will be the conclusion, but the difficulty is for the interim, the people growing daily into greater impatience, as on Wednesday last was sevennight it appeared at Oudewater, where the magistrates being assembled in their statehouse to suppress (as was suspected) one Lidias, a preacher of the Contraremonstrants' party, the people broke in upon them with their hands upon their knives yet close in their pocket and forced them to subscribe to an act of toleration, that Lidias and his audience should have the first use of the church and celebrate the Lord's Supper with all other church rites apart from the rest, which is a thing of dangerous example and will (if matters be not soon ended) come to blood. We hear of all our mens' safe arrival at Venice, three captains only excepted, which are thought to be in the gulf. The entertainment of their general you will see in the enclosed from Sir Henry Wotton, which when you have read you will return unto me. Thus with my kindest remembrances I commit you to God, ever resting

Yours most assuredly

1. Chamberlain wrote that Donne, at Paul's Cross, "made . . . a daintie sermon upon the eleventh verse of the 22th of Proverbs" and praised Queen Elizabeth to an audience which contained Archbishop George Abbot, Sir Francis Bacon, Winwood, and others. *L. J. C.* II, 67. The sermon was preached on March 24, the anniversary of James's accession; the text was, "He that loveth pureness of heart, for the grace of his lips, the king shall be his friend." It is printed in G. R. Potter and E. M. Simpson, eds., *The Sermons of John Donne* I (Berkeley, 1953), 183–222.

2. Sherburne, Carleton's financial agent in London, was about to take service with Lord Keeper Bacon. Chamberlain had written on April 5 that Sherburne's father-in-law, John Stanley, the auditor of the mint, had died; he was surety in the amount of £1,000 for Sherburne's honesty in handling Carleton's affairs. Sherburne was unable to find anyone to replace him but offered to get a number of people to be surety for £100 apiece. *L. J. C.* II, 67–68. Carleton, as this letter indicates, did not think this was necessary.

3. Sir John Bennet, judge of the prerogative court of Canterbury and grandfather of the earl of Arlington, Charles II's secretary of state, was sent to Brussels to complain of the publication of a pamphlet, *Corona regis,* which

satirized King James He got no satisfaction. Nathaniel Brent was in his entourage. Albert and his wife were often referred to as "the archdukes."

4. On April 14/24, 1617, the captain of Louis XIII's guard, on orders from the king's favorite Luynes, shot Marie de' Medici's favorite, Concino Concini, marquis of Ancre, to death. The Dutch government hoped that this would mean the end of factionalism in France and also of the pro-Spanish policy followed by Marie de' Medici; hence their rejoicing. The duke of Guise, who probably could not have been removed in any other way, was assassinated by order of Henri III, who shortly thereafter was himself assassinated in retaliation. Charles de Gontaut, duke of Biron, was convicted of treason and executed by the government of Henri IV, the latter part of whose reign was beginning to appear to English diplomatists as a peaceful interlude between periods of domestic turmoil.

5. The policy of the national synod, favored by James, was that of the Contraremonstrants; Oldenbarnevelt and the dominant faction in the States of Holland were to fight it bitterly and, in the end, unsuccessfully.

The Hague, June 13/23, 1617

S. P. 84/77, ff. 208–209

Good Mr. Chamberlain, I have had nothing this many a fair day worth the writing into England, which hath made me use silence with you as with all others; and now I send you a large packet in requital of your three letters, whereof two came by this bearer Diston,[1] whom I dispatched before another post, who hath long waited here because you give so good a report of him and he of us here, which I shall endeavor to deserve of all which are of that house to which he belongs. Your packet is the greater by three letters besides your gazettas which come from the same place, and though one of them be of a stale date yet I send it with the rest that you may see whether more be to be picked out of them than out of Fabritio's conceits; but I must desire you for some good respects to keep them to yourself until you return them to me. Mr. Morton passed this way on Monday last from Heidelberg to find the king in Scotland, which errand he hath picked out of a letter from Fabritio wherein he advertiseth some matter of danger to the king's person, and withal hath sent a certain Jesuit of Milan into England as the discoverer, whereof at Heidelberg they have reason to inquire after the news.[2] He lighted here very opportunely to a wedding feast of a Dutch man which serveth me and hath gotten a pretty young wife with £900 portion, besides the charge of the wedding, which continued in drinking and dancing, dancing and drinking, three whole days and nights. My lady Bennet would not vouchsafe all the while she was in Holland nor yet going or coming to Amsterdam to visit The Hague, but she had soon enough of that good town, though she was in a nest of her friends and kindred by reason of the boys and wenches, who much wondered at her huge vardugals[3] and fine gowns, and saluted her at every turn of a street with their usual caresses of whore, whore, and she was the more exposed to view because when she would go closely in a covered wagon about the town she could not because there was no possible means to hide half her vardugal. Some of Sir John's train is come hither from Brussels as Mr. Brent amongst the rest, who do not much brag of their entertainment amongst those Dons. Mr. Trumbull writes me he is like speedily to be called away and no more to be sent in his place, which I shall be no gladder of than the cardinal's muleteer was when his master was made Pope because my work will be the more, to write the news of that side likewise, of which I was now well discharged. We are here busy in deliberation about giving assistance to the duke of Savoy, wherein somewhat will be done, and if the princes of the Union follow the example (as they are like to do), it will be to good purpose.[4] But they [sic] delay is in danger to make it *soccorso di Pisa*. Here is a German count [John] of Levestein who hath lain these seven weeks at Amsterdam treating and negotiating with shippers for the transport of his 3000 men to Venice, wherein he cannot agree upon the bargain; meantime he runs into so large detriments in his inn that on Sunday was sevennight his host presented him a bill of £500 sterling, which would have gone well towards the difference which is betwixt them for the freight. We can yet come to no end of our disputes about religion nor so much as enter into the way to this long journey's end, the course of synod, which is recommended by all other Protestant churches and by the most of the provinces, being violently withstood by the greatest part of these of Holland. Yet in the conclusion *volentes nolentes* they must either do that or worse. Excuse I pray you my hasty scribbling when I write and silence when I have nothing worth your knowledge. So for the present I commit you to God's holy protection ever resting

Yours most affectionately

Diston hath partly in kind heart to his fellow post, who hath long waited, and partly for business given over his interest in this dispatch and attends the next. Your letters shall come hereafter directly unto you as this doth, but they shall go on my account and therefore you need not trouble yourself with postage.

1. William Diston was a courier employed by Winwood to carry dispatches between London and The Hague and a favorite of his. Carleton kept him on in the same capacity.

2. Morton was currently the English resident at the court of the elector palatine as well as secretary to Princess Elizabeth. The Jesuit was one Tommaso Cerronio, who had a story about a plot to kill the king and subvert the state. He reached England accompanied by a couple of Wotton's staff; his tale proved utterly baseless. Chamberlain commented that "I doubt this *legatus peregre missus* will make goode his *mentiendi causa,*" referring to Wotton's famous epigram. *L. J. C.* II, 93–94. See also Smith, *Wotton,* II, 114–18, 122–23. James was currently on his one visit to Scotland since his accession to the English throne; he arrived in Edinburgh in May and returned to London in mid-September.

3. Farthingales. Lady Bennet was apparently about as huge as her costume.

4. The duke of Savoy was once again at war with Spain. This installment began in September 1616 and lasted for a year. The "Union" was the Protestant Union, the league of Protestant German princes.

Sir, I wrote to you by the two last posts, Herman and Diston, since whose departure I have not heard from you. Your gazettas go accompanied with an honest friend's letter, which will tell you no more news than you know already; yet is it worth the reading at an hour of leisure. The postscript of Monsieur Asselinau's letter which you had with my last is not verified, nor any further news out of the gulf [of Venice], though both the Venetian and Spanish fleet are there in readiness for fight and make many bravados. The siege of Rubia continues without any great progress by reason of the excessive rains, which the Spaniards say have likewise hindered them from taking of Vercelli.[1] But I remember an answer of Count Maurice to the count of Bucquoy, who being prisoner and passing upon the Rhine with his excellency, *"ces rivières"* (said he) *"vous servent bien de rempart. Et à vous"* (answered his excellency) *"d'excuse."* The Venetians do much commend our men, but complain of the captains for withholding the soldiers' pay; so as it seems they want our Dutch commissaries. That state hath made stay of all the Hollands' ships, which is not ill taken here because it is done out of caution that they should not fall into the hands of the Spaniards, whereby this country would suffer and that state likewise. They have here written expostulatory letters to Brussels (of which our door-warder John Hindrickson is the messenger) for arresting these country ships and merchandise in Spain, Naples, and Sicily. Out of the East Indies here are newly come two great ships richly laden to the value of two millions and a half of florins, conducted by Spilbergh,[2] who hath now made three voyages thither, and this last through the Strait of Magellan. In his company is come one La Mer, a merchant of North Holland, who saith he hath made a new discovery of a passage into *mare pacificum* and that he went that way, two degrees beyond the Strait of Magellan, the passage being (as he reports) 7 leagues in breadth and 7 only in length, so as it may be sailed through in less than a day. But this is too great a rarity to be too quickly believed. The last letters out of Spain say that the Hollanders have utterly defeated the Spanish and Portugal fleet at the Manilas,[3] of which we must likewise expect the confirmation. The duke of Savoy hath in the end obtained an assistance of money from hence: 50000 florins monthly, for the four next months in case the war continue so long with him. His ambassador is going to the duke of Saxony and the princes of the Union to seek their assistance, whilst in France he hath others for the same purpose, who want no men if they could tell where to have money. We thought we should have had here some scuffling the last week about our churches but all passed quietly, the Contraremonstrants being settled in the new church in the Voorhout, which is far the greater assembly, and the place both spacious and commodious. I send you the copy of a prayer which the chief apostle of the Remonstrants, Utenbogaert,[4] amongst other bills for the sick and distressed, read openly in the church; at which finding much offence to be taken, he unprayed it again the next sermon following, saying that he was abused by some who thrust the paper into his hands with others and that he read it at unawares, which we must believe in charity of a man of his profession, though his enemies say he brought it in upon malice and that some great man is glanced at therein. Howsoever our pretty young friesters[?] of The Hague rest much scandalized that they should be thought not to be able to keep their maidenheads without the prayers of the parish. I believe Mr. Secretary Winwood sets forward this day toward Scotland, and I take this time to write that a packet may overtake him (as it will do by computation) when he comes to the king, though we have no extraordinary affairs, as will appear unto you; yet it is good to know as well what there is as what there is not. The world is much confused in conjecture at Fabritio's late dispatches, which strangers write hither, out of his letters to his friends, are matters of the greatest moment that ever *Legatus peregre missus,* etc., sent to his prince. I am here driven to great straits, my Dutch secretary (who helped me in English, which he copied well and perfectly like Carpenter) having the excuse in the gospel *uxorem duxit,* which makes him neglect my service. Mr. Brent finds himself too far spent in the

[240]

world to wait for an after harvest and flatters himself much with hopes of my lord of Buckingham, whose kinsman, young Sir H. Butler, he hath here in his charge.[5] Colwell is laid up of the sciatica, so as I must look about me for some fit man whose pen and head I may use for my own ease; and if you could be as lucky in finding one for me here as you were for my business in England you might much pleasure me.[6] But this inquiry I will desire you to make with some secrecy because some there are who desire to come to me for whom this place is not good enough. In all my affairs you have part of the trouble, which I pray you excuse. So I rest

Yours most affectionately

1. The siege of Rubia, in Friuli, was an episode in the war between Venice and Archduke Ferdinand. Vercelli, in Piedmont, was shortly to fall to the Spaniards.

2. Admiral Joris van Spilbergh, one of the more humane Dutch officials.

3. The report was inaccurate. The Dutch attempts in this period to weaken Spanish power in the area at its source by attacking the Philippines were uniformly unsuccessful.

4. Johannes Utenbogaert was the leading Remonstrant theologian and the principal preacher at The Hague. In July 1617 the Contraremonstrants, after some months of walking to Ryswick every Sunday to hear a preacher to their taste, seized a church, and the Remonstrants, confronted by the newly declared hostility of Maurice acquiesced.

5. Sir Henry Boteler, son of Sir John Boteler and Elizabeth Compton, who was Buckingham's half-sister. Chamberlain, in his answer to this letter, reported that young Sir Henry was to accompany Sir John Digby to Spain, "which may prove a good viage in curing the disease of drinking." *L. J. C.* II, 87–88. Buckingham's relatives were an unappetizing lot.

6. Chamberlain's only suggestion was their old acquaintance, John Pory, who was allegedly on his way to The Hague. *L. J. C.* II, 87. Given Pory's penchant for the bottle, this was a rather unsatisfactory proposal.

Sir, I received your farewell to London about ten days since, being
then in the country about two hours' distance from this place (according to the Dutch phrase, and travelling) at a house with which
Count Henry did pleasure me, where we had his company often,
the prince of Orange's once, Sir Henry Carew's [1] (my wife's
kinsman) always, and hunting and fishing better than any else
this country yields. It fell out very luckily the second day after
our arrival there that a fat buck came to me out of England
tamquam ex machina, an honest soldier bringing it along—who
told me he found it waiting for a passage at Margate accompanied with a little letter, which showed that I was beholden for
this courtesy to honest Sir Peter Manwood. Since, I have had a
stag from Sir Robert Sidney [2] which proved not altogether so
good; yet hath it been well hunted by Count Henry and other good
company, whereof we have store at this present by reason of certain extraordinary deputies from most of the provinces, who are
here arrived to determine of a national synod. How that business
will proceed is yet doubtful by reason of the opposition of the
Arminian faction, which is strongest in Holland, sways all in
Utrecht, and is *mipartie* in Overyssell. All which hath been hitherto
endeavored by the rest of the provinces is to persuade Holland
to reassemble the States, whereby to consult of this course as the
only remedy to the present disorders; to which those which have
chief authority lend a deaf ear, insisting upon the resolution taken
in their last assembly, which was a flat exclusion of a national
synod unless a provincial might precede and that framed in that
manner as is noways practicable. Monsieur Barnevelt, against the
time of arrival of these deputies, absented himself to Vianen, for
change of air (as he pretended) and since, under color of taking
physic, stays at Utrecht and thereabouts, notwithstanding that he
hath been often desired by letters and once by two express deputies
from the council of Holland to return. Divers imagine (and upon
great presumptions) that he will give over the managing of affairs

[242]

and leave The Hague; but unless things go worse than they have hitherto done, and from words come to blows, I am not of that mind, for in that case he will remain where he is best assured; but matters proceeding (as I hope they will) to be determined by treaty, it were a madness for him to abandon the authority he actually enjoyeth in the state in maintenance of a cause whereof the first ground (which is this dispute of predestination) is (as he hath solemnly protested unto me) against his conscience; he being (as he saith) of the opinion of the Contraremonstrants though he holds for the Remonstrants, in that he thinks and maintains there may be a toleration of both, which the Contraremonstrants cannot admit; and *hinc illae lacrimae*, he and his faction striving to effect this toleration without separation in the Church, by absolute authority, and the others continuing separate until the toleration (or what course else is thought best) shall be determined by synod. For maintenance of this authority here are in several towns of Holland certain soldiers raised to depend wholly upon the magistrates without reference to Count Maurice or the States General; and at Utrecht they have now during his abode levied six companies of hundreds for the same purpose and after the same manner, which the States General do much dislike of and have sent four of the council of state to persuade them to desist from that course; but it is likely they will proceed, and hereupon great disorders will follow amongst their soldiers and in their finances, so as the state is like to grow hereby into as great confusion as the Church. Here are many broad speeches upon these occasions, as on the one side that Count Maurice doth aim at the sovereignty of the country, and on the other that the Arminians have a design to call in the Spaniard, both which I account scandals; yet we find many things to fall out in execution which were not in the first intention, and therefore the sooner they can get out of these straits betwixt Scylla and Charybdis it will be much the better, for time doth rather augment than diminish their animosities. We have news of some stirring of the enemy[3] and of a new levy of 1500 horse and three regiments of foot under the emperor's title and with Spanish money; but their rendezvous being in Alsace shows they shall march into Germany; and they say as far as Gradisca [4] to raise that siege, so as we do no more here than only give all the horse warning to be ready to march upon the first alarum. The Venetian President Sorian [5] is gone to Delfzyl to pass muster of the count Levestein's troops, which will be within few days ready to set forward for Venice. The knights of Malta have built a goodly ship of 1200 ton at Amsterdam after the English model, which is now in the Texel waiting the first wind. Mr. Pory had the good luck to see her, taking that way to this place, which was somewhat a long voyage; and after he had his packet he stayed from Wednesday till Monday in London for want of wings, there being no money to pay the port. And now he was not so slow in coming but he makes as much haste to be gone, having too many irons in the fire to think of any settled course in this place; so as I have said nothing to him concerning the matter you wot of,[6] and I will have patience until I may be fitted to my mind. To go on in answer of your last from Ware Park of the 27 of August I like best to defer the matter which concerns myself until Sir Thomas Edmondes' coming over;[7] and then I would be glad (as occasions may be offered) you would speak both with him and our friend, but as a motion of your own: for, besides that it is a business wherein none should be their own spokesman, I find myself subject with my best friends to the censure of intrusion, which I must yield to thus far that I am, indeed, more ready to look about me and conceive better hopes, now I have so good friends in place, than if they were strangers; and this makes me write freely to you and sometimes desire you to speak to them as anything comes to mind either at home or abroad. In this there is no danger in stay, and it may be things will so settle here that I need not desire change. You may remember how I have long had an eye upon the reversion of Eton, which is come by mischance to my father Savile's knowledge; but he seems not to take it ill, having offered my brother Harrison in my behalf to do his best to get the king's promise; and if he continue in the good mind I pray you add your helping hand with Mr. Secretary Winwood; for betwixt the two it might be easily compassed; and though the promise of a place which is elective be no assurance, yet having the good will of the fellows (which I will not despair of) I should have a great advantage above other pretenders. You have commended in two letters the affairs of one Sherman, who married Doctor Burgess' daughter,[8] who hath been (as I understand) lately in this country but not here at The Hague; when I can see him or hear particularly of his business I will not fail to give him my best furtherance. I have had lately a troublesome expostulatory business command me by the lords of the council concerning one Brown a Scottishman, who, being an officer to my lord duke of Lennox as admiral of that kingdom and collecting certain rights due of the herring fishers to that crown, was brought away prisoner by the States' men-of-war; which hath given me occasion to write to their lordships and to send them my proposition in that subject; and if you meet with Mr. Clement Edmondes,[9] from whose hand I received by directions, I shall be glad to understand whether the lords allow of my proceedings. We are all well here (I thank God) within doors, though the plague continue in the town and is hot in other places but lights most upon children and young folk. In so much that at Amsterdam in one place where a hundred were lately buried there were two only which exceeded twenty years. I have had lately a kind letter from the archbishop of Spalato with three of his books,[10] whereof two I caused to be presented in his name, the one to the States, the other to his excellency, to which he hath kind answers, and a fair gilt cup worth £40 from the States for a token. You shall see by an abstract of his letter to me his opinion of our universities and the country he passed through in that journey; and if I can recover the copy of the States' letter in time you shall have it as a thing wherewith I believe the good old man will be much encouraged, as he hath been with a very good letter from the king out of Scotland, whereof I send you the copy though it may be you have it already. My wife is not a little proud that her token was so acceptable unto you; and so with both our kind remembrances to yourself and our service to the lady Fanshawe if this find you at Ware Park, I rest as ever

Yours most affectionately

I send you my freshest gazettas only, leaving out the oldest with Fabritio's schedules (wherein he still puts me off to new day of payment) not to engross your packet, which my nephew Will Williams comes opportunely to carry after 4 days' waiting for a fit messenger.

1. See above, letter of July 1, 1616, n. 2.

2. Sir Robert Sidney, the son of Robert Sidney, Viscount Lisle, former governor of Flushing, was colonel of a regiment in Dutch service, although only twenty-two.

3. The Habsburgs.

4. Gradisca was just across the Venetian frontier in Habsburg territory; its siege was an episode in the war over Archduke Ferdinand's protection of the Uskoks.

5. Cristofforo Sorian was the Venetian representative in the United Provinces.

6. The reference is to becoming Carleton's secretary, a proposal which Carleton found dubious. See above, letter of July 7, 1617, n. 6. Carleton had written that he was quite willing that Pory stay with him for a while, if he could "stay *saldo* against the pot (which is hard in this country)." P. R. O., S. P. 48/78, f. 160.

7. Carleton in his previous letter had written that he had heard that Edmondes was to be recalled from France, and he asked Chamberlain to suggest to Winwood that he, Carleton, be transferred from The Hague to Paris. Chamberlain replied that Winwood had told him that the government's financial plight might lead to the replacement of ambassadors with residents when their terms expired; he suggested that Carleton get in touch with Edmondes and persuade him to urge Carleton's request on Winwood. *L. J. C.* II, 97–98. This Carleton was unwilling to do.

8. John Burgess, Sherman's father-in-law, was a prominent Puritan clergyman. He had refused to subscribe to the canons of 1604, had gone to Leyden and studied medicine. In 1616 he subscribed and resumed his clerical career. He was attractive to the ladies and had powerful friends, among them the wives of Winwood and of Sir Horace Vere, whom he had known in the Netherlands. *L. J. C.* II, 86.

9. Clement Edmondes was the clerk of the privy council.

10. The archbishop published several works while he was in England, including the first part of a large book, *De republica ecclesiastica,* in 1617.

Good Mr. Chamberlain, your letter of the 31 of the last was the last of many which I have received concerning the sad news of Mr. Secretary Winwood's decease,[1] but the particularities thereof made it the most welcome; and if the concurrence in grief for his loss of many here may any way assuage yours there I do not think any one of our nation since the death of that nobleman to whom Mr. Secretary once belonged (the news whereof I received by your letter being then in this town) hath been so generally lamented.[2] I would say thus much to his virtuous and sorrowful lady and add such comforts as pass usually betwixt friends in such occasions if I thought her grief were usual and to be eased by words; but I fear a contrary effect and therefore will desire you to say that for me which is necessary in assurance of my service as a due to his memory, who is with God, and to herself and hers. I thank you very much for that you write me of my lord of Ely, which makes it plain unto me with what fictions and fancies some busy brains and one in particular whom you name do delude the people.[3] Malre[4] in Zeeland died the last Tuesday; he and Barnevelt have been competitors all their lives, in which time what he wanted in reputation of his opposite he will gain in their ends, unless he that is living correct himself quickly in his headstrong courses, of which I yet see small appearance; and he is not likely to last long, having kept his house without looking out of doors ever since his return from Utrecht. Touching myself, who am (as I find by many letters and from some whom I never knew before) brought upon the stage amongst other candidates, you shall know in few words *petitionis nostrae rationem*. The archbishop of Spalato and Mr. Brent assure me of my lord of Canterbury, Sherburne of my lord keeper Bacon, Rudier of my lord chamberlain, Master Pory of my lady Elisabeth Hatton, others of other lords and ladies, and Sir Horace Vere gives me good hope of my lord of Arundel; but the principal verb wants all this while, who unless he be made unto me by some of these before mentioned, I have no hope, being a stranger to

[247]

him and absent.[5] Amongst all the pretenders you name I give way nothwithstanding to none but Sir Thomas Edmondes, with whom it is not fit for me to enter into competition; but, if he be contented with his place he hath already, I pray you advise with him of the fittest means for my good, which if he undertake, he hath knowledge and dexterity to set all these wheels going,[6] which may carry me further than my own hopes, with which I flatter myself very little for all the great encouragements I receive from my friends. I send a letter herewith to Mr. Pory, which I pray you convey speedily unto him, he being lodged in the Strand, but I know not where, save only by description at the next house [to] where Sir Bernard Dewhurst died.[7] If my father Savile be in London, I pray you visit him upon this occasion and acquaint him with my *broglio*. We are at a stand here for news, save only of the peace of Italy, which, being concluded with an incursion on the duke of Savoy's part into the state of Milan and of Don Pedro's into the Venetian territory, is like one of those farces whereof we have seen many, which end always with bastinados, Harlequin beginning still, with Captain Spavento, and the Spanish Captain revenging himself upon the Pantalon.[8] I send you a letter of the honest French doctor's whose turn I have done with this state for *Chechini*[?], with which I shall make him a glad man; and thus with my kindest remembrance I commit you to God.

Yours most assuredly

1. Winwood died on October 28. Chamberlain's letter of the 31st described his death and the terms of his will. *L. J. C.* II, 108–10.

2. Robert Devereux, earl of Essex, who was executed on February 25, 1601. Winwood began his career as a follower of Essex. For the Dutch reaction to Essex's death see above, Introduction, p. 7.

3. Chamberlain had written that Andrewes had said that Hugo Grotius, after eating twice with him, "gave out and fathered many things upon him that were neither so nor so." *L. J. C.* II, 111.

4. Sir James de Maldere, president of the States of Zeeland, an office comparable to that held by Oldenbarnevelt in Holland.

5. The "principal verb" was Buckingham, whom Carleton did not know. The lord chamberlain was William Herbert, earl of Pembroke; Lady Hatton

was Burghley's granddaughter and the wife of Sir Edward Coke. At this moment she was in high favor at court. Her daughter having been married off, over her bitter opposition, to Buckingham's weak-minded younger brother, the favorite—and the king—were intent on extracting as much property as possible from her. There is an account of this unedifying business in Gardiner, *History,* III, 85 ff.

6. The others Chamberlain mentioned as competitors for the secretaryship were Wotton, Sir John Bennet, Sir Humphrey May, and Sir Robert Naunton. May and Naunton were Buckingham's men and had the inside track. Naunton got the secretaryship in January 1618; May shortly thereafter was consoled with the chancellorship of the duchy of Lancaster. The others got nothing.

7. The death of Sir Bernard Dewhurst, dean of the arches, had been reported to Carleton in October. *C. S. P. Domestic 1611–1618,* p. 487.

8. Peace between Spain and Savoy was signed in Madrid in September 1617. "Don Pedro" was Don Pedro de Toledo, now governor of Milan.

The Hague, December 2, 1617

S. P. 84/81, ff. 12–13

Good Mr. Chamberlain, your letters of late are late in coming (your last of the 15th of November having been full a fortnight on the way) but are ever most welcome. The unkindness our good friend [Winwood] conceived against me was of more ancient continuance than my departure out of England and deeper rooted than the letter he mentioned; for I have been informed, since my coming on this side of the seas, his old master,[1] upon some dislike he took at my slender seconding his desire of correspondency by letters when I was at Venice, had bred ill impressions not only in him but in some others (with whom he had credit) against me; but they are now both with God; and if they had lived I should not have doubted but to have recovered their good opinions, for they were both real and honest, and that being their natural disposition whatsoever was accidental was subject to mutation. Yet I must confess since my coming to this employment to have found small signs of relenting in our good friend but rather a hard hand in all affairs according to the nature of them; for all things that would be gracious here had their dispatch continually without my knowledge in England, and here I had nothing but *commissions ruineusses*; which to one that would not be ill seen where he doth reside (as in a place rather *habitandi* than *commorandi*) is a hard condition. And further I had some ill measure in concealing my endeavors from his majesty; as that speech which you approved well [2] was never showed the king until (long after the time that I sent the same in writing) a printed copy was casually presented to him, of which he gave allowance both for the matter and manner thereof; and this was the first and only word of encouragement, and that from a second hand, which I received since my coming into these parts; which consideration being added to the ill furnishing my provisions from home and the cross constitution of affairs here abroad will make you soon see (unless his condition had been better) what small reason he had to wish himself here again, especially the cautionary towns being gone, which were the supporters of the reputation of this charge; and for profit, the golden age ended with his time. Thus you see how I stood then and, though my condition might have been much better if he had been better inclined towards me, yet I protest unfeignedly unto you I am much sensible of his loss; for what I wanted of his love I reposed in his honesty and sincerity, which would have kept me from wrong, though he might (as I say) have done me more right. But *transeat cum caeteris erroribus*: he had small errors and imperfections but many great virtues. I have had much ado for this fortnight past about a public act which the States' government decreed to make by way of placard against the book which hath been here printed against me; [3] but the Arminian faction hath cast so many traverses in the way that hitherto the placard is not published, and their hope is (as I am informed) to have some word from the king (to which purpose they have written to their instruments about him) that he doth not take the matter so heinously as I persuade them he will; and in this confidence they have showed themselves in this cause very boldly. The States of Holland are newly assembled; and we shall soon see what effect Count Maurice's progress amongst their towns hath wrought, who spoke at large in their common councils and left his speeches in writing, which were all to the same effect: first, in answer to those ill aspersions which are cast abroad against him and in justification of his proceedings; next in condemnation of the resolutions of the assembly of the States of Holland in August last; then in recommendation of the national synod, noting the necessity thereof by the inconveniences as well in Church and state as particularly by the disorders in execution of justice, by the new levies of soldiers, by exacting new oaths and promises of the old, etc., and lastly by way of advice that their deputies in their assemblies should not take resolutions in such weighty cases but upon report first made to their councils and receiving thereupon their orders. To the like purpose he wrote particular letters to such towns as the shortness of the time would not suffer him to visit. Count Henry hath received a curst message from the landgravine of Hesse for his being so cold a suitor to her daughter, which hath broken off that match. We have news from Lübeck of the death of the grand duke of Muscovy and of a great victory upon those people obtained by the son of the king of Poland.[4] For the affairs on the other side of the mountains I refer you to those which go herewith, whereby you will see how Fabritio at last lets down not only his milk but his cream too; and yet I must confess to you I find more taste in my old correspondent. Thus with my very kind remembrance I commit you to God.

Yours most assuredly

1. Sir Henry Neville; Winwood's first diplomatic appointment was as Neville's secretary when Neville was ambassador in France. Neville died in 1615.

2. On October 25 Chamberlain had written in praise of Carleton's speech, which was made to the States General, one of many he made on the subject of the synod. *L. J. C.* II, 106.

3. This was an Arminian book written by Grotius, which attacked not only Carleton but also James and which, rather inconsistently, tried to win the king's favor by comparing the Arminians' opponents to the Puritans, an argument Carleton found specious. For Carleton's account of the contents of the book,

see his letter of November 22/December 2 to Secretary Lake, *Letters, Holland,* pp. 205–11.

4. The report of the death of Michael Romanov was untrue; however, the Polish invasion, which began in September 1617, was still going well. Vladislav, the son of Sigismund III of Poland, was attempting to make good a claim to the Russian throne.

The Hague, February 3/13, 1617/18

S. P. 84/82, ff. 136–37

Good Mr. Chamberlain, we are here much incommodated at this present both for writing and sending, our rivers and ink being frozen up, which is somewhat unseasonable for the midst of February, and our affairs are as cold and suitable to the weather, so as I have much ado in all respects to return you so much as a bare answer, and therefore you must expect a poor return for your two letters of the 10th and 17th of the last, which came, both of them, well freighted with plenty and variety; but the former arrived here five days after the latter (the one coming to my hands the 22 the other the 27) and yet gives me the more subject of writing, for which here is an unexpected opportunity of one Baskerville, a Muscovy merchant, who being (as it seems) hardened in that country, makes his passage in an open boat from Scheveningen; and because I have recommended unto him divers letters (though I have not seen him, but only heard of his waiting there for a wind) I shall be glad to hear from you, particularly of his arrival. By him (but under cover to others) I do congratulate with our new lord chancellor and secretary;[1] with the latter of which I pass further than in ordinary compliment in giving him an account of the state of these troublesome affairs, which it seems you can be content likewise to understand, and therefore I send you the copy of a letter, which (having looked over my minutes) I conceive to be that you inquire after; but it being like a process, with reference to divers evidences against Monsieur le Balancier,[2] you will find small taste therein, unless you had likewise *le sac des pièces,* which would make too enormous a packet, and, howsoever, you would see yourself much abused in the report, because there is nothing in the letter to satisfy curiosity, it being enough for me if I can serve necessity; and indeed my study is, in all which passeth my hand, rather to set out the matter than the writer, which is the essential difference betwixt me and Fabritio. And because you have patience to overlook papers I send you a speech I made since in the assembly of the States General in consequence of this letter, wherein for that which belongs to our English church I helped myself by *Tortura Torti;* [3] and I know not how to put these novelists to a greater torture than to convince them so manifestly of falsehood. Yet thereby I incur the inconvenience which the apostle complains of, *inimicus factus sum vobis vera dicens.* This appears besides their animosities here by the charities they seek to lend me at home, Grotius (a busy brain and an instrument for the rest of the Arminians) having dispatched not long since an express agent into England with letters of credence to the archbishop of Spalato and the bishops of Ely and Coventry complaining by name against me and desiring by their means to have both the man and the matter carried to his majesty.[4] The poor old archbishop was so suddenly surprised that he spake of the matter to the king, but finding how ill it was there relished refused to return any answer to Grotius either by letter or message, for which he gives me this reason (*perchè mi pareva còsa indegna l'acerbità che lui mostrava contra il ragionamento pubblico di V. Ecc. dove ella ha con infinità soddisfazione seguito l'ordine di S. Maestà*); and indeed he did herein very discreetly, because the end of this pedantical fellow is nothing but to draw answers from men of place and authority in England with which to stuff his pamphlets and by wresting the words to his corrupt sense to advantage an ill cause. This hath been done often; and now lately in a Dutch book which is entitled (*A Necessary Answer,* etc.), wherein, having raked our martyrs out of their graves and run through all Foxe's book to find out men of their opinions, they afterwards name one Loeus of Oxford, Barrow and Tomson of Cambridge and spare not my lord of Coventry for some letters they got from him in answer to Grotius, when he was dean of Paul's, which they set down with his name.[5] There are likewise two extracts of letters, the one of the 20th of June 1514, the other of the 16th of May 1513, the names of the authors of which they will seem willingly to forbear, but because they are so bold with others they are taken to be forged. There is nothing cited from my lord of Ely, which confirms what you advertised me long since, that they have nothing of his, and I should be sorry they should shroud their brainsick humors and pernicious designs under the authority of so learned and reverend a person. Wherefore my hope is they have at this time no more from his hand than before, for it is impossible to write with such reservation as not to have ill use made of every line which doth not in direct words condemn them, wherein it may be my lord would be as sparing. I know not how I have been drawn along in this matter, but the truth is, we have nothing else to think of. In opinion that the Pope's determination betwixt the Franciscans and the Jacobins was common with you in England I forbore the sending thereof; but you have it herewith, and because it suits somewhat with our business I would be glad you would return it. I send you a letter I lately received from my cousin Rowland Lytton, who with his father's name hath much of his spirit and more gratitude for small matters than some of his friends for greater. In place of thanks I wish I might not be paid with discourtesy and charged with debts, which is an unworthy proceeding for gentlemen if they were not my near kinsmen. I am weekly called upon by Monsieur Nys from Venice to procure him payment of that which is owing him by my cousin Philip or to satisfy it myself, which I must and will do, but if it lie in your way I pray you free me from it. Thus with my kindest remembrance I rest

Yours most affectionately

You will be sparing in showing the copies of my letter, which goeth herewith, to any but those you well know, which some particularities therein contained you will observe do require, and when you have done with it I pray you burn or [paper torn] it.

1. Bacon was elevated to the chancellorship on January 7; on the next day Sir Robert Naunton became secretary.

2. On January 10 Chamberlain had written asking for a copy of a letter Carleton had written to the king analyzing the situation in the Netherlands. James had praised the letter, and it was passing from hand to hand. The reference to "Monsieur la Balancier" is to the author of a pamphlet called *The Balance,* which, in attacking one of Carleton's speeches to the States General, also attacked the king. James was angry and insisted that the States General offer a reward for the detection of the author. Carleton at first thought that Grotius had written it; it later became clear that the author was a Remonstrant preacher in Utrecht named Jacobus Taurinus. See below, letter of September 28, 1618.

3. *Tortura Torti,* published in 1609, was a massive (and virtually unreadable) contribution by Lancelot Andrewes to the controversy between King James and Cardinal Bellarmine which began over the oath of allegiance. A full and rather slanted account can be found in J. Brodrick, *The Life and Work of Blessed Robert Francis Cardinal Bellarmine, S.J.* (New York, 1928), II, ch. 23.

4. Grotius was an unpopular figure in England, for both his political and religious views. James very much disliked *Mare liberum.* The bishop of Lichfield and Coventry was John Overall, who worked on the King James version.

5. James was not impressed by the allegations against Overall; in May 1618 he translated him to Norwich.

The Hague, August 28, 1618

S. P. 84/85, ff. 236–38

Good Mr. Chamberlain, you have well guessed in both your letters (the one of the 8th which I found at Middelburg, the other of the 15th of this present, which found me in this place) at the tediousness of my passage; [1] for, though I am an old traveller and (I think) have crossed the seas as often as any man, unless it be an ordinary post, I never had the like. You know how long we lay wind-bound at Margate. We were after three days and two nights betwixt that place and Zeeland; and could not then, being

becalmed, recover Flushing unless we would have lain another
night at sea; wherefore with the shallops of our ships we set ourselves on land upon the open strand in the Isle of Walcheren,
where we should have been troubled to have recovered Middelburg but that the magistrates of that town, guessing at that which
fell out, met us at the very landing with six covered wagons and
after lodged and defrayed us with much courtesy. At the English
house [2] we had a very good entertainment given us, with the
magistrates who met us, at a dinner; and the next day, though
Sunday, we set forward from thence; but it was Tuesday night,
by reason of strong contrary winds, before we arrived at this
place, and betwixt this and Rotterdam (where I was met by Sir
Horace Vere and much good company) we were overtaken with
the most terrible tempest of thunder, lightning, and rain that any
man of us had ever met with, so as it was a common speech
amongst us that it must needs prognosticate somewhat; which
fell out the day following, our great man Monsieur Barnevelt
with two of his chief instruments, Hoogerbeets [3] and Grotius, the
one pensioner of Leyden, the other of Rotterdam, being then arrested prisoners in the prince of Orange's lodgings by order of
the States General, where they remained two days until the lodgings in the court, where the *almirante* of Aragon lay last, were
prepared for them. I account it in some regard ill luck to come
à la veille of such a feast, at which though there are many make
good cheer (and I may well say the most in this country) yet
there being likewise some *mal dînés* they lay no small blame upon
me, and so spread it by public voice as if I had given fire to this
mine by certain intercepted letters which I should have brought
with me out of England. Their apprehension proceeded chiefly of
certain new difficulties and traverses they sought to cast in the
way of the national synod after they had offered themselves, at
the prince of Orange's return from Utrecht, to concur with the
States General and his excellency, which they perceiving and that
this business would prove Penelope's web unless these men were
laid hold on, not only took the resolution for them but likewise
for one Ledenberg, [4] the secretary of Utrecht, who had the same
authority in that province as Barnevelt in Holland and was there

laid hold on the day after these were taken. [Cornelis] Vandermile, who married Barnevelt's daughter, was with me at the instant that his father was taken and went from me to the council,
not knowing anything of the matter until the news was publicly
sent to the council by the States General; which may seem very
strange that he, his father, and the rest of that party who had the
chief managing of the affairs should have so small knowledge or
apprehension of what hung over their heads, this course having
been almost a year in speech, and it was known to forty in this
town the night before it was put in execution. Vandermile doth
since play least in sight; some say he is fled into France, and
some that he lies close in this town. These French ambassadors [5]
do *faire bonne mine et mauvais jeu,* for they seem the most contented men in the world though they have small cause in that the
extraordinary [ambassador] leaves his friends in worse state than
he found them, at whose instance he was drawn hither to countenance their party; but not being able to help them he falls upon
their enemies, having made a bitter speech in the assembly of the
States General against young Aerssens,[6] the *greffier*'s son, who
was ambassador in France when we passed that way to Venice,
and demanded to have him personally punished for certain passages in his writings against Vandermile, prejudicial, as the ambassadors say, to the dignity of the king their master and his
council; but the answer Aerssens hath made is admitted by the
States General as just and reasonable, and the ambassadors desired by the States to be contented therewith. The extraordinary
ambassador parts with a chain of £400 value for himself and one
of £60 for either of his two sons. Yesterday the prince of Orange
went to Schoonoven to reform that magistrate, leaving Count William with 500 men in this town to see all safe behind him. Sir
Horace Vere and all our English commanders are gone with his
excellency, Sir Henry Carew only excepted, who stays to keep me
company. I have preferred Christopher [7] (whom you put to me)
to Sir Horace Vere, who gives him good entertainment in his
company at Dort, and there he may do better than in service to
which he cannot apply himself nor never could since he was at
Heidelberg. All our company are well, I thank God, excepting my-

[257]

self, who am followed into all places with my old disease, yet I find my seasickness hath rather helped than hurt me. Bess Dove [8] hath already lost her tawny face. I pray you put our friends in mind when they are in London this next term to get her mother's portion, which they say her father left her by legacy; for her education my wife will take care. And thus with our best wishes and commendations to yourself, desiring you to deliver the like to those wheresoever this letter will find you (for it must be amongst our friends) I commit you to God's protection.

Yours as ever most assured

1. Carleton was returning from a brief visit to England. This is his first letter to Chamberlain in four months.

2. The house of the Merchant Adventurers, whose staple was at Middelburg.

3. Rambout Hoogerbeets, pensionary of Leyden, was one of Oldenbarnevelt's political allies. He—and Grotius—were eventually sentenced to perpetual imprisonment in the Castle of Loevenstein.

4. Gillis van Ledenberg, secretary of the States of Utrecht. For his fate see the next letter.

5. The extraordinary ambassador was Jean de Thumery, lord of Boissise, a veteran French diplomatist; the other ambassador referred to here was the regular resident, Aubrey du Maurier. The French government regarded Oldenbarnevelt as pro-French; hence their concern.

6. François van Aerssens, who had been the Dutch representative in France until Oldenbarnevelt had him replaced in 1614 for intriguing with the discontented aristocracy. Aerssens, now Oldenbarnevelt's bitter enemy, was obviously *persona non grata* to the French government. His father was executive secretary to the States-General.

7. Christopher was Carleton's page.

8. Bess Dove was Carleton's niece, the daughter of his sister Anne, long dead, and of the Reverend John Dove, who had died the previous April. Carleton had brought the girl back with him from England.

Good Mr. Chamberlain, though I have written unto you at large since I heard from you and have less leisure to spare now than ever, yet I cannot but acquaint you with the circumstances of a strange accident here, the news whereof will be carried unto you in gross by common report. Ledenberg, the late secretary of Utrecht (a man of mean birth, but by his wit and industry, chiefly by strict correspondency with Barnevelt and by his countenance, advanced to the like authority in Utrecht as Barnevelt had in Holland and thereby come to great wealth, a thick short man and now within two of threescore years old), hath made a short end of his part which he was to play in this tragedy, having the 18th of this present in the night murdered himself with three mortal wounds; the manner whereof was this. He being conducted some few days before from Utrecht hither to be examined and confronted with Barnevelt and lodged in the same prison but in a room apart, where he had his son to attend him in place of a servant (every one of the prisoners being allowed one for that purpose), he was divers times visited by certain deputies appointed by the States, who found him more reserved than he had been formerly at Utrecht; so as in the end they told him he knew well they had means to make him speak clearly and freely, intimating thereby the rack, though in plain terms he was not threatened therewith; and being pressed to the confession of some men and matters which he had opened at Utrecht but darkly and in doubtful manner, he required one night's space only to bethink himself (which was that of the 18th), promising the next morning to give them full satisfaction. His son finding him much perplexed, when the States were gone, counseled him freely to discharge his conscience, whereby he might purchase favor of God and the world. No, son (said he) there is question now not only of my own life and goods but of condemning likewise my best friends. He supped well, much more than ordinary and drank two pots of wine, one of Rhenish the other of Spanish wine. Before he went to bed he used long prayers with his son according to his custom, which he concluded with this word only extraordinarily, God keep us this night. Being laid, he spake to his son though he should hear him stir in the night not to trouble himself because he thought he should rise to the necessary place. He had for the space of three days before concealed a sharp knife which was brought in with his meat, and the same being missed and found afterwards by his son (when they were alone) hid under the carpet, he wished him not to speak of it to the guards which attended them because it was fit for their use to mend their pens. He had another knife of his own in his pocket, and these two upon all presumptions he used in this manner. First, with his own knife he thrust himself in at the navel up to the haft; then above the navel about two fingers' space he thrust it into his body again up towards his heart as far as the knife would reach, which being done he put it again into the sheath and so into his pocket. Finding the day approaching and his long night not yet come (for of these wounds he might have lived, as the surgeons suppose, two or three days) with the other knife which he had laid within his reach he thrust himself first through the neck near the bone and then cut asunder both throat and windpipe, the noise of which by the gushing of blood awakened his son, who calling the guards they at their entry found him dead. He is bowelled and lightly embalmed whereby to have time to deliberate whether he shall have an ignominious burial or not; as the use of this country bears for those who make away themselves *criminis causa* to bury them under the place of public execution. His lands and goods by strictness of laws are subject to confiscation; but custom doth challenge (which will not be refused his heirs) an easy composition. They are now going in hand with Barnevelt, who hath not been yet examined. Grotius offers to confess all he knows or probably suspects, so as he may be promised favor by the prince of Orange, who is now absent in a progress amongst the Arminian towns to change the magistrates. Hoogerbeets denies all. The synod holds at the appointed time and place. Our extraordinary French ambassador doth *stare a vedere,* waiting all apt occasions to help the Arminians or hinder the synod; and when he can do neither he will *laudare peracta.* Aerssens goeth away with the bucklers against him and Vandermile, who doth *exulari;* and we have a *décret* from the States if he should return not to admit him to our council table. Taurinus, the Balance-maker, is given out for dead, and his friends are in mourning; yet lest this should be a device they proceed here against him and his book, which is well answered in Dutch by a soldier, and if it be translated into French I will send you a copy. Now for your entertainment (as I think you have good leisure in the country) I send you your gazettas where you will find a strange accident lately happened in Valtellina, which I have confirmed by particular letters. I know not whether in my last I wrote anything to you touching John West's kinsman,[1] whom I have placed with Sir Horace Vere, and he is one of those that guards Barnevelt. My page Christopher is sent to his other company at Bommel because it was no decorum for one of my servants to be employed in that business. Commend my service and my wife's (I pray you) to my lady Fanshawe and let us hear from you often both from city and country. Thus I rest

Yours most assured

1. John West was a friend of Chamberlain's who, on the death of his and Carleton's close friend Sir Henry Fanshawe in 1616, became deputy for Fanshawe's son, not yet of age, in his father's office of remembrancer of the exchequer. West's nephew, Henry Sibthorpe, was the kinsman in question.

The Hague, November 14, 1618

S. P. 84/87, f. 36

Good Mr. Chamberlain, it was in this town that I received your letter touching the death of my lord of Essex, which comes to my memory upon the receipt of one I have now from you concerning Sir Walter Raleigh[1] and proves a subject of much contemplation, as they were of several factions and fashions to balance their lives and their ends; and if it be true *finis coronat opus* this latter hath gotten the honor; for it seems he knew better how to die than to live, and his happiest hours were those of his arraignment and execution, which cannot be said of the other, save only that they died both religiously. We have here the news of the death of the archduke Maximilian, of the emperor's being brought *sub tutela* by the new king of Bohemia, and of the disgrace of the duke of Lerma in Spain;[2] which shows a great fatality to hang nowadays over great men. Our *grande* [Oldenbarnevelt] here hath been now nine days under strict examination, which were time enough to make us see what would become of him; but he is extreme tedious in his answers, having liberty to say what he will, and those who have him in hand are sworn to secrecy until all be ended, so as we hear not what passeth in particular, only they say in general that he excuseth himself upon his masters of Holland. But since he assumeth to himself in his printed apology the honor of all the good actions of the state he must likewise answer for the bad; and those upon whom he seeks to discharge himself will rather prove his instruments than he theirs. In the synod at Dort little is yet passed of any consideration, they having given a fortnight's time of appearance to the Remonstrants after insinuation, which is not yet expired. The interim is spent about common *gravamina,* of which the chief is the want of a perfect Dutch translation of Scripture, wherein they have taken a resolution after the example of the English;[3] but there was much dispute about the Apocrypha, and, though it was held in by the strangers, yet those of this country thrust it out to the very end of the Bible, not allowing it the old place betwixt the testaments. Their seance and their names, as well the strangers' and others', with those who are cited, you will pick out of this Dutch catalogue. The bishop of Llandaff's speech[4] hath yet escaped the press. I send you a copy of it, and as anything shall succeed worth my lord bishop of Winchester's[5] knowledge I will pray you to acquaint him therewith and by that means to preserve me in his memory and good opinion. Thus for the present with my wife's kind remembrance I commit you to God.

Yours most assuredly

1. On October 31 Chamberlain wrote to Carleton describing Raleigh's execution, a superb letter frequently quoted (*L. J. C.* II, 175–79). Chamberlain was clearly sympathetic to Raleigh for many reasons, including political ones; he quoted the view of his friend Ned Wymark that it would be well if Raleigh's head and brains were grafted onto the shoulders of Secretary Naunton.

2. The archduke Maximilian was the younger brother of Matthias and a strong supporter of Ferdinand of Styria, who had become king of Bohemia in June 1617 and who had recently seized and imprisoned Matthias's principal adviser, Cardinal Melchior Khlesl. This effectively ended Matthias's political influence. Lerma's long tenure of power ended on October 4 as a result of a coup engineered by his own son, the duke of Uceda. The principal cause was Lerma's mishandling of the economic and financial problems of Spain, which were grave enough to start with and which his feckless policy had exacerbated.

3. A reference to the King James version.

4. The bishop of Llandaff was Carleton's cousin George; he was one of the English representatives at Dort. The speech, *An oration made at the Hage,* was printed the following year.

5. Lancelot Andrewes, who had been translated from Ely in July.

The Hague, March 19, 1618/19

S. P. 84/89, f. 58

Good Mr. Chamberlain, give me leave to salute you in a few words, for much matter I have not, unless I should descant upon your affairs at home: *fecunda culpae saecula.* That is all I will say of them.[1] The businesses of the synod and our prisoners will take up more time than was imagined, and it will be a month after Easter before we see an end of either. Monsieur de Boissise hath taken his leave of the States, finding small use of his remaining here.[2] He requires, in case the king his master have need upon these alterations in France, assistance from this state according to treaties, besides the troops of that nation which are in the States' service. He hath likewise complained of the taking of two French ships in the East Indies near Bantam by those of these provinces and demanded by an express audience satisfaction; which if he will stay for he will break his appointed day, Monday next, which he hath set down for his departure, because the States defer their answer until they receive information of the fact out of those parts. We expect here two of the deputies of the East India Company to relate what hath passed in the treaty in England;[3] which, if it be not the sooner dispatched, is like to find before long much opposition because both France and Spain (from whence ambassadors are going into England) conjoin in hindering the conjunction of our companies. There are levies of 12000 foot and 2000 horse on the archduke's side raised for the emperor against the Bohemians,[4] whom in all reason I should give for lost, but that I have seen in my small experience a duke of Savoy without men or money so well succeed in his affairs that from the most desperate estate of any prince in Europe he is now in that condition that his sons are the most considerable persons in the two courts of France and Spain, and himself is sought unto by the Venetians for alliance, which is concluded and published betwixt them. You will have understood how the fatal planet which reigns over great persons hath confined the duke of Lerma to his house, cast Don Roderigo Calderón into irons, degraded the prime vizier presently upon his return after his conquest against the Persians with some other alterations in that *pòrta*.[5] [paper torn] come to less matters, Abel Barnard's brother[6] appears now at last and we have his business on foot. My wife can yet hardly digest the failing of that small hope she conceived of enjoying her friends, and I cannot tell how to comfort her because I can foresee no possible appearance of any preferment at home, but God provides when man's discourse fails; and to his holy protection I commit you, ever resting

Yours most assuredly

1. The principal *culpae* were those of the earl of Suffolk, who had just been ousted from the treasury on charges of embezzlement, in which his venal wife was deeply involved, and of Sir Thomas Lake and his awful wife and daughter; Chamberlain's letters had recently been full of the sordid details of this scandal.

2. For Boissise's mission see above, letter of Aug. 28, 1618.

3. In November 1618 Dutch commissioners had gone to London to negotiate

over the difficult question of the East India trade. The upshot was the treaty of June 1619 providing for collaboration between the two East India companies and a division of the monopoly, a treaty which proved to be a dead letter.

4. The rebellious Protestant party in Bohemia was now in control of the kingdom, nine months after the Defenestration of Prague.

5. Calderón was one of Lerma's grasping and unscrupulous henchmen; he was eventually executed in 1621 after the death of Philip III and the coming to power of Olivares. Halil Pasha, the grand vizier, was dismissed in January 1619 after a defeat on the Persian border.

6. Abel Barnard, an old friend of Chamberlain's, was in financial trouble, and Carleton was trying to assist him.

The Hague, April 15, 1619

S. P. 84/89, ff. 142–143

Good Mr. Chamberlain, I have received your letter by the way of Zeeland of the 27 of the last, which came to my hands at the very instant when I had express letters by an extraordinary [messenger] of the king's sickness and recovery.[1] Of which we heard in these parts both at once, only a flying report was spread from the archduke's side that he was in great danger, and some said he was dead, which we believed here spoken as they would have it and therefore gave small credit unto it. But it appears the fear was great at home; and that which is familiar with poor men is strange with princes, else vomiting and looseness, which are the common symptoms of the stone, would not be so much spoken of, and if the disease being now known it may breed with his majesty a better *règlement* in diet (which having tried all I find to be the best remedy) this will serve like *plaga salutis* for his health this many a day, which I assure you is as much prayed for here as it can be with you, as well in regard of the scarcity of princes in Europe at this present which are powerful and masters of themselves as for the particular protection this state hath lately found of his majesty. We draw now to a period of our two great businesses of the synod and the prisoners, both which will concur

[265]

with the word *sero sed serio*, and I shall be very glad in many respects the world were once rid of expectations in these regards. We had the last week a solemn fast for the good success of both, which was commanded by letters from the States General serving in place of a manifest concerning the prisoners with commandment to have them read in all churches. In Rotterdam and Leyden some ministers refused to read them, for which they were put out of their charges, and a country minister betwixt Leyden and Haarlem sped somewhat worse, being brought prisoner to this town and laid in the common jail for reading the letters but praying his audience when he had done to believe never a word of them. The States' order for this fast was signified to the prisoners severally without reading the letters to them but with demand whether they would celebrate the same, to which they all consented, every man prohibiting part of his diet; and I have it by good information that they having no correspondence or intelligence with one another yet every one of them with his keeper and servant sung the seventh psalm. You will have the news of Germany, which doth now chiefly entertain us. The election of the new emperor is appointed the midst of July next;² meantime the business of the Bohemians goeth on in the same terms as it did before the emperor's death, the levies on the archduke's side, which are 9000 foot and 2000 horse with four fieldpieces, being now upon their march that way through Lorraine, where they find 2000 foot and 500 horse levied by the duke of Florence to assist them. The Bohemians speak of great troops, and as I hear they want no men, but they have neither money nor good conductors, so as they are like a body without a head or sinews. All I have from Venice you will find in the enclosed, and I send you likewise a kind letter to me from a great lady, by whom I was well wished. Touching ourselves, we wear out the time here as well as we may and remember you often. Mr. Barnard hath a promise of his brother that if anything be gotten for him his turn shall be first served and if all be true that he saith, that he hath been offered £2000 composition, there is likelihood somewhat will be had in the end; but the suit will yet ask time because it must proceed by an orderly and accustomary course. This morning we were upon a match of hunting with Count Henry, who hath lately gotten a kennel of hounds out of England, and though our sport was not very good yet I have this to brag of to you, that after three hours' good riding I was not so ill of my disease as I used to be, when I saw you last, with three turns about my chamber. Thus with my kindest remembrance I commit you to God and my wife's likewise, who will not be forgotten.

Yours most assuredly

1. James had had a bout with the stone, Carleton's old complaint. Chamberlain commented, "I am glad to see the world so tenderly affected toward him, for I assure you all men apprehend what a loss we should have if God should take him from us." *L. J. C.* II, 225–26. These comments, which were not for public consumption, suggest that those historians who maintain that James was held in contempt by the political classes in England may be wide of the mark.

2. Matthias died in mid-March. The election of Ferdinand II took place at the end of August.

The Hague, August 10, 1619

S. P. 84/91, ff. 132–33

Good Mr. Chamberlain, I have received your two letters, the one of the 15th of July, the other of the 31, and with the first your medicine for the stone, which I shall make use of when I shall be troubled with it again, which I must expect sooner or later, though since my late sickness I have had no touch of it. You will say (as many do unto me) that I should use means for prevention; and I confess that is more than necessary, when a man knows his disease (as I do mine) by so long and painful experience; but I am so much in love with health, when I have any, that I cannot find in my heart to interrupt it with anything that is medicinable, though when I am indisposed I take pleasure and find taste in rhubarb; but (as I said) since my fever I never in my life found myself better. I concur with your opinion in letting the suit fall which you wot of;[1] you liken it to a cheese which is spent in parings and I find that no butter sticks to my bread; but if any man but myself were in this place I should wonder that, after so many and so serious endeavors I have used (and all little enough) to press these men to send into England about the treaty of the East Indies, which hath succeeded so well and so much to the contentment of our company as by their liberalities to the commissioners (which you mention) they do sufficiently witness, the prime instrument should be wholly forgotten; as I must tell you I find myself, and I could be content you could let my good friend Mr. Bell [2] understand by one means or other, that I am not unsensible of such a neglect, and sooner or later I may have opportunity to make it appear. Sir Noel Caron [3] (who only gave aim whilst the business lay upon my hands to drive this employment forward in the midst of their distractions here) hath no such cause to complain; but I am not the first that have used the motto: *sic vos non vobis.* I could have wished you had seen Eton when you were at Ditton, where no company would have hindered your welcome; and I believe the conversation of that place would have so well seasoned the retiredness of the other where you remained that both would have been more agreeable unto you. For if Ditton were to you as I found it when the mistress of it [Lady Winwood] entertained me in a mourning habit and as sad and heavy a countenance, there could be nothing *plus triste,* and therefore you must spend time where there is more entertainment. Now for a few days I doubt not but Mr. Wingfield [4] will have store enough for you, whose observations have been as particular as any man's I know; and he hath had the opportunity of seeing much by my lord general Cecil's company, but they have changed their resolution of going to Antwerp. If Abel Barnard come over he shall be welcome; but his brother makes a cold suit of his business, who hath absented himself from hence all this summer. He had my best furtherance whilst he was here, and his affairs were in some forwardness, but when a man is wanting to himself, what remedy? Two days since I sent you a book by Herman, having no time then to write; and you will excuse me when you know that all the leisure I had bestowed on my lord of Winchester, to whom I sent the like book of the acts of our synod and thereupon discoursed

[268]

with him a little of these church affairs, which as they had strong opposition in the reformation so do they find some rubs in the settling; but in conclusion we shall have one church though we may have diverse faiths, and *libertas prophetandi* will cease though not *credendi,* for here is no searching into mens' consciences. All the obstinate Arminian preachers who would not submit themselves to the States' decree of being silenced and living as private men are banished these provinces. So is Vorstius,[5] who stayed the last day of his six weeks' leave, and a tumult was raised in Tergow about the time of his exile by some who would have made Saint Peter of a new preacher, sent thither by the States of this province, in stoning him whilst he was in the pulpit, wherein the most hurt fell upon those fair glass windows through which the stones were flung at the preacher; and this hath drawn a garrison into that town as upon like accidents into others which were of the Arminian confederacy. Of the High Dutch [German] affairs which are now chiefly considerable you will hear by the frequent extraordinaries dispatched by our extraordinary ambassador,[6] to whom these men here say that neither Ferdinand nor the Bohemians will refer themselves nor scarce give audience; which proceeds undoubtedly (if the report be true) of a fear to discredit their affairs by being the first that hearken to overture of peace; but when they are both a little more wearied (as already they complain on both sides of sickness and want), they will then more kindly embrace a mediator. They say the election of the emperor rests upon this point, whether the Bohemian deputies or Ferdinand shall be admitted by those of Frankfort with quality of the seventh elector, which at the date of our last letters was not decided.[7] And thus with my affectionate good wishes I commit you to God.

Yours most assuredly

1. The suit referred to was Carleton's request to succeed his father-in-law as provost of Eton, a project which Carleton had worked on sporadically for years. Chamberlain and others had discouraged him: "the price is much fallen," wrote Chamberlain, "so that if anything were to be given in gratuities, the thing would prove like a Banberie cheese that goes away most in parings." *L. J. C.* II, 252.

2. Robert Bell was an East India Company merchant and gentleman of the bedchamber, who in this year became a director of the company.

3. Caron was the ambassador of the United Provinces in London.

4. Richard Wingfield, one of Chamberlain's fellow Paul's walkers, had come over to the Netherlands in late June to visit his kinsman Sir Edward Cecil; he returned to England in August.

5. Conrad Vorstius was an Arminian-minded theologian who had been prevented from succeeding Arminius in the chair of theology at Leyden by James's vigorous protests to the Dutch government in 1611 and 1612. See *Manuscripts of Lord De L'Isle and Dudley,* V, xxiv–xxxvii.

6. James Hay, Viscount Doncaster, had been sent to mediate the dispute between Ferdinand and his revolted subjects. He had just retired to Spa, after a series of fruitless discussions with Ferdinand at Frankfort, where Ferdinand had gone to be present at the imperial election. For an account of this stage of Doncaster's mission see Gardiner, *History,* III, 300–307.

7. There were three Protestant (Brandenburg, Palatinate, Saxony) and three Catholic (the archbishops of Mainz, Trier, and Cologne) electors; the Bohemian vote might thus be decisive.

The Hague, September 18, 1619

S. P. 84/92, ff. 35–36

Good Mr. Chamberlain, for all my haste in the dispatch of Abel Barnard (whom, for saving his charge, I accompany with a packet), I cannot but lament with you the loss of Sir Christopher Hatton,[1] whom for the interest I am persuaded to have had in his good opinion I am exceeding sorry to be thus untimely deprived of; besides the part I have in your loss in particular of such a friend and others whom, for their affairs which were entrusted to him, we have both cause to compassionate. He was a very worthy gentleman, but, I know not how it falls out, the best goeth first and with us remains the sorrow for their loss. How we are here this bearer will tell you for as much as concerns our particular. Touching the public, true it is (as you say in your last of the 11th of this present) that this business of Bohemia is like to put all Christendom in combustion, but hitherto I do not hear for certain (though the speech hath been very common) that the prince palatine hath accepted the crown. It is said the princes of the Union, who have been assembled at Rothenburg, advise him to it, and here they think that since the revolution of the world is like to carry us out of this peaceable time it is better to begin the change with advantage than with disadvantage; and so will the kingdom of Bohemia be, which being accepted is a matter of great advantage, but being neglected and by consequence suppressed, the princes of the religion adjoining are like to bear the burden of a victorious army, which where it will stay God knows, being pushed on by Jesuits and commanded by the new emperor [Ferdinand II] who flatters himself with prophecies of extirpating the reformed religion and restoring the Roman Church to the ancient greatness. Here are all the States' horse and store of wagons to conduct a certain number of foot under the command of Count Henry into Germany in case the army on the other side should march that way now they have done at Brussels; and his excellency [Maurice] hath a petty army of 7000 or 8000 foot in readiness for the frontier. If you are not in case to do anything now you will be less able hereafter; wherefore as good begin betimes, so it be in a good cause. I hear nothing of Mr. Abbot's,[2] touching whom you wrote in your former; but I am gladder you spake with him than with Bell, who sounds in such cases very faintly. There is now a secretary of this East Indian company in England to set us right again after these new accidents if it be possible. Thus in great haste I rest

Yours most assured

1. Sir Christopher Hatton, of Kirby, Northamptonshire, a kinsman of Elizabeth's lord chancellor, was the husband of Sir Henry Fanshawe's sister Alice and hence one of the circle of Chamberlain's close friends. He died September 10.

2. Maurice Abbot, a director of the East India Company and a brother of the archbishop of Canterbury. Carleton was becoming impatient with Robert Bell's efforts to get a reward for him for his part in the negotiations.

Good Mr. Chamberlain, I was exceeding glad to understand by your letters of the 2nd of this present that my lady Fanshawe hath dispatched her business so well for her son,[1] about which I must confess to you I was in some pain, lest she might suffer of this catching time. Touching the Bohemian affairs it is hoped here that his majesty will have a better consideration of them than that you write, for the deposing of one king and election of another was done by the voices of the whole state and therefore cannot be well said to be a faction. But leaving the reasons of their proceedings to themselves we must weigh the consequences and then think whether it be *e bono publico* to suffer that kingdom [Bohemia] to be made a kingdom of conquest or for his majesty's particular reputation to be more wanting to his son-in-law than the king of Spain will be to his kinsman. If Spain could be entreated to stand still and look on, it were fit his majesty should do so likewise, but since the Spaniards begin already to stir in this quarrel they show his majesty what he hath to do. This state continues forward in assistance of the Bohemians, to whom they have renewed their monthly aid of 50000 florins and promise all further help which lies in their power. Here are letters from Cologne that the prince palatine was to go the 11/22 of this present from Amberg to Prague, which, if it be true, *jacta est alea*; and I must confess it to be *periculosae plenum opus aleae*. But a crown is at stake and therefore good venturing. God send our friends good luck, who go on (chiefly Queen Elizabeth, a name famous for great actions) with good courage. My lord of Doncaster is yet in chase of the emperor, and here we expect him at his return. His secretary Sir Francis Nethersole [2] (who is Sir Albert Morton's successor with her highness in place of secretary and agent to the princes of the Union) lies here in ambush for him with a party of 16 or 17 of his followers come out of England to meet him. The States are sending out 14 men-of-war against the pirates of Algiers, under the command of one Moy Lambert of Rotterdam, which are ready for the first wind. And this is all we have for the present. Here enclosed I send a letter to Mr. Wingfield, who was lately here with us, and it may be hath said somewhat unto you of an unkind parting betwixt Sir Edward Cecil and myself upon an occasion too long to relate unto you; but I may say my usage of him and his deserved better than to be repaid by a quarrel. You will deliver this letter for me, which saith somewhat to this purpose and commend me kindly I pray you to all our friends in Warwick Lane, Ludgate Hill, etc., who am and will ever rest

Yours most affectionately

1. After the death of Sir Henry Fanshawe, his brother-in-law Sir Christopher Hatton had held Fanshawe's office of remembrancer of the exchequer in trust for Fanshawe's son Thomas. Following Hatton's sudden death Lady Fanshawe got her son sworn into the office, as Chamberlain reported on October 2. *L. J. C.* II, 264.

2. Sir Francis Nethersole, formerly the public orator of Cambridge University, resigned that office in 1619 to become Doncaster's secretary. In the previous month James knighted him and appointed him Morton's successor as secretary to the electress Elizabeth and English agent to the Protestant Union. He was to become an enthusiastic champion of the unfortunate Elizabeth.

The Hague, January 1, 1619/20

S. P. 84/94, ff. 5–6

Good Mr. Chamberlain, I am to give you many thanks for your two letters of the 27 of November and 17th of December, with the first of which I received one from Sir Dudley Digges, to which I send you the answer, which contains thanks only for his good will without desiring to have the matter pressed any further, though the saying what I did was by the king's commandment should be no more applied to me than it might have been to the commissioners; and Sir Noel Caron's example cannot be cast in my way, unless affairs in England had been as much embroiled when our commissioners came hither as theirs were here when there was question of sending; at which time if I had not added my private solicitations to my public offices (of which I could have excused myself though I had forborne) it may be things had not gone as they did. But I am far from repenting myself of anything I have done; and my affection to the business is such that I believe whensoever further occasion is presented it is not ingratitude that can make me slack my best endeavors, wherefore the chief of our company may be commended for the choice they have made where to save charges without peril, though otherwise I cannot brag of their bounty; and yet I should have esteemed of a small toy by way of remembrance as much as of a greater matter.[1] In your last you call upon me for an answer to Mr. Wingfield, which you have herewith; and I should have written to him sooner save only for my many affairs of late days, chiefly since my lord of Doncaster's coming to The Hague, who lodged eleven days in my house, whereby I kept a merry Christmas with so good company; and indeed he for himself is *il più compito* and the best of his train, with whom only I had to do (the States having ordained a house for the rest), *il più regolato* that ever I met with. The best entertainment I could give him was the choicest company of this town, which he had with him at all times; and to all he fashioned himself in that sort just and no otherwise as *omnis Aristippum decuit color, et status, et res.* His liberalities at parting were very noble, having given chains of gold and medals to the captain of his excellency's guard and to the master of his horse; the like to Count Henry, Count William, and the prince of Portugal's esquires (whose coaches he used whilst he was here) besides the officers to the States, who had chains and *médailles,* and his excellency's guard, who were put in arms and did their exercise before him, had for drink-gelt 200 crowns; drums, trumpets, musicians, players, coachmen, etc., were rewarded in proportion. In my house he gave Colwell my steward a chain of gold with a *médaille* of 200 guilders' value; to my nephew, Bess Dove, and my wife's woman, each of them, a diamond ring worth 120 guilders; to my coachman 50 guilders; and amongst the rest of my servants 400 guilders. I brought him to Rotterdam on his way, accompanied with our chief

[274]

officers both English and Scottish, where his supper and dinner the next day cost him 1600 guilders. You may marvel what entertainment I could give his lordship in proportion, which was not (indeed) such as I wished, neither did the time serve, we being in the dead of winter, but such as it was he seemed contented with all; and I wish him a good welcome to his majesty as well for his own sake as mine, because he professeth to owe me a good turn; howsoever, the charge of his embassage having been so infinite great I may believe he will have enough to do with his own affairs without troubling himself much with other men's. The States gave his lordship a present of tapestry worth £1000 sterling, to his secretary Sir Francis Nethersole a chain of £50, and to his chaplain, Doctor Donne, such a medal of the synod as was given to the bishop of Llandaff.[2] By this time you have them all (as I hope) in safety with you, the wind having been good ever since Tuesday last that I saw them on shipboard bound for Zeeland, where they intended to make no stay. And now you shall have before long with you the baron of Dohna,[3] brother to him who carried the news of the Bohemians' election of a new king, for whom you must do more than pray or else he will be (as the Jesuits in Germany call him) a king only for a winter. For the rest of the affairs of those parts I refer you to your gazettas. We have here concluded a confederation for fifteen years betwixt the commonwealth of Venice and this state, for which your friend hath had public thanks from both states. My wife is thinking to see England this next spring, and if she might lodge in my brother Williams' house it would be best to both our likings. Hereof I pray you speak to my brother and sister and let me hear from you with the soonest, for our poor domestic affairs grow to that disorder that the sooner she seeth her friends is the better, yet she intends not to go till May next, and she will live whilst she is in London as privately as may be. Thus with both our best wishes of a happy new year I rest

Yours most assured

1. Carleton was still feeling sorry for himself, in that he had received no reward for his part in the successful conclusion of the negotiations between

the two East India companies. Now he, and Chamberlain on his behalf, were using the good offices of Sir Dudley Digges, who was prominent in the East India Company and who, in this year, was to be sent to the Netherlands as part of an embassy to settle various disputes with the Dutch company.

2. John Donne acted as Doncaster's chaplain during his embassy. The bishop cf Llandaff was Carleton's kinsman George Carleton.

3. Achatius Dohna, the brother of Christopher, who was to spend a turbulent and unsuccessful year in England as ambassador from the new king, Frederick of Bohemia.

The Hague, June 10, 1620
S. P. 84/95, ff. 207–208

Good Mr. Chamberlain, all my letters to you of late days consist of thanks and excuses, for which your often and ample and my seldom and scant writing ministers the subject, and now again I am to thank you for your two last of the 13th and 27th of May and to tell you that I have been of late days in the doctor's hands for my accustomed indisposition, which hangs more continually upon me (though not in such extremity of fits) than it was wont. I know not whether stirring and journeying abroad or sitting still in this muddy air will prove better for my health; but by way of provision I have put myself in the best state I can both by physic and good order of diet (which I observe exactly) for going or staying; and I have had a question put to me from a good hand out of England: how I could like of a journey into Germany?— which, since, I hear, is more commonly spoken of, and though I am not very fond of the employment, considering the confusion of those parts, yet I shall embrace the same very readily if his majesty be pleased there to make use of my service, and so I have answered; but Sir Henry Wotton being already resolved of and one more only thought of, I persuade myself there will be enough at home ready to offer themselves, amongst which a better choice will be made.[1] It is true, that which you write me from Mr. Treasurer, that he wished me in a letter to look after the reversion of the Rolls, but he only showed me the golden fruit without telling me how or which way to gather it, and I had heard long before Sir Henry Wotton had such a kind of promise of it that would serve at least for my exclusion, howsoever he could speed with it.[2] I am heartily sorry for the blow our men have received in the East Indies and wish it lay any way in my power to repair it; for howsoever the committees of the company have used me, first by neglect and since by mocking both myself and my friends who sought to have me remembered, yet their discourtesy cannot make me forgetful of the honor of our nation in general nor unsensible of the company's loss in particular; and as I have always done, so shall I continue to further their affairs as if I had an adventure amongst them. I believe we shall hear of more blows before the news of the accord can be with them in the East Indies, for our men will assuredly seek a revenge though they be much weakened by the loss they have received; and God send them that way to make all even, and then hereafter by their harms they will learn how good it is to be friends. Being gone thus far by way of provision I have received order from his majesty to complain of the Hollanders for their doings in the East Indies and to require restitution to our men of their losses,[3] wherein I shall no whit fail of what I told you before of my intention. I have likewise heard of the two ambassadors, the Sir Edwards,[4] with which I am no whit displeased, but rather content myself with this conceit, that if the business go well I shall have my part of the joy, if ill, less of the grief. But the world wags too much towards action to be held back by negotiation; and therefore one good general would do better (as they say here) than two ambassadors. We are here drawing into the field with 120 companies of foot and the whole strength of horse, but shall not stir till we see what the [sic] Spinola doth with his army of 20000 foot and 4000 horse, which we guess will march into Germany and for the first attempt mar Frankfort mart by making themselves masters of that town, upon the same title they have to Wesel.[5] Count William [6] is taken from us by an apoplexy in an unlucky time when the state hath most need of a man of his judgment and sufficiency, both for counsel and command. You will have all foreign news in your gazettas. So with my best wishes I rest

Yours most assuredly

1. The purpose of the proposed embassy was to try to succeed where Doncaster had failed and mediate between Frederick and Ferdinand. Wotton was eventually chosen, and, predictably, he failed.

2. The reversion in question, that of the mastership of the rolls, had already been promised to Wotton. The treasury had been in commission since the ouster of Suffolk in 1618, so "Mr. Treasurer" is probably Sir Thomas Edmondes, who in January 1618 became treasurer of the household.

3. The reference is doubtless to the seizure of Bantam and the capture of some English ships by the Dutch and the expulsion of the English from Java. The word of the Anglo-Dutch agreement in fact reached the Dutch governor general, Jan Coen, in March 1620. It enraged but in no way deterred him.

4. The reference is unclear; Chamberlain's letter of May 10, which may have referred to it, is lost. In July Sir Edward Conway and Sir Richard Weston were sent to Brussels to protest against any contemplated invasion of the Palatinate and to Prague and Vienna to mediate between the emperor and the elector. Like all of the special missions sent out from London in the opening phase of the Thirty Years War, this one was fruitless.

5. That is to say, no title at all. The Spaniards had seized Wesel before the signing of the treaty of Xanten. By the terms of that treaty they were supposed to relinquish it; they never had.

6. Count William Louis of Nassau-Dillenberg, Maurice's cousin and quondam brother-in-law and a very close confidant. He died on June 9.

The Hague, December 6, 1620

S. P. 84/98, ff. 105–106

Good Mr. Chamberlain, you used so much courtesy to my wife during the whole time of her abode in England (of which she hath made me no sparing relation) that I know your love to us both will make you content to hear of our good meeting, which was on Saturday last was sevennight betwixt ten and eleven of the clock at night, when she surprised me being abed and fast asleep, all covered (as she was) with snow in her walk from her boat to my house. I had been at Rotterdam to meet her, where I lay Friday night, but despairing the next day of her coming, returned to The Hague about two hours before her arrival. And now we are here after the old manner, with this change of entertainment, that she hath many stories to tell me of home affairs whereby to divert the cogitation of the unhappy end of this summer abroad, in all places disadvantageous to our friends and in some utterly ruinous. There be who would fain flatter themselves with hopes of restoring the affairs of Bohemia,[1] which for my part I cannot comprehend, *ipsa si velit salus,* unless I could see as vigorous and constant a resolution taken in all parts where the new king and queen have friends for supporting their cause as there hath been a concurrence amongst their enemies as well by invasion as diversion to overthrow them. They are now (as we hear) at Breslau in Silesia, where they say those of that province and Moravia have sent them many comforts, assuring them of their fidelity and wishing them to take heart and encouragement and not to esteem the kingdom of Bohemia lost with the town of Prague; but how long this fidelity of those people will last towards princes in so great affliction I cannot say. The worst is to be feared. I hear of none of our ambassadors or agents in those parts save only of Fabritio, who writes *canzone.* Count Henry, after many changes of resolution, is coming hither back out of the Palatinate to reinforce his horse against the next spring. My lord General Vere [2] is well, many of his company sick, but few dead. Yet I hear one you and William Fanshawe had much care of (young Worsnam) is dead; of which you may let his friends understand, though it will be a grief unto them. My wife commends her kindly unto you and I rest

Yours most assuredly

1. The battle of White Mountain, which brought to pass the Jesuits' prophecy that Frederick would be but a king for a winter, was fought in November 1620.
2. Sir Horace Vere, who was in command of the English troops being used

to defend the Palatinate. Vere and his troops had left England in July; in August Spinola launched his attack.

The Hague, March 20, 1620/21

S. P. 84/100, ff. 70–71

Good Mr. Chamberlain, I find by your letter received by Mr. Salmon that you were much moved in his business, imputing that to malice which was indeed but an error, as my lord of Winchester rightly conceived it; and that was in my translator of the States' act, who interpreted *andere goederen van zin schip,* other goods taken out of the ship, whereas it should have been other goods of, or belonging to, the ship; and hereof I must confess I took not so much note in the haste I sent you the translat[ion] of the act, only observing as much as I underlined, and thought necessary (since it was here required, after their usual forms) to be put into the acquittance; for howsoever the adventurers are therein specified, it is to give a discharge in their names as well as the owners' for no more than either of them might lay claim unto in regard of Mr. Salmon's pretended *dommages.* Now what his pretentions were we had here in writing, and those I have caused to be specified in the acquittance, letting the word which imports adventurers stand; for I never find it good *litigare* and raise new question about words when there is no doubt in the matter; and I hope both my lord of Winchester and yourself will be now as well satisfied as Mr. Salmon is, who by this accident hath received his money a month the sooner.[1] For the rest it is true that you write, and I find it by fresh experience, that the best interpretation is not always made of my advertisements from hence, which some would have sound more harshly than they commonly do.[2] But I must confess my natural disposition, wherein I am somewhat *opiniâtre,* rather to make good reports than bad when the matter will bear it; and by that I govern myself, that is, the judgment I make of the matter; the ground whereof is better known to me, who

[280]

am upon the place, than such as are absent and not so well acquainted with all circumstances, so as I find that many times imputed to *finesse* or malice, of which (God knows) they are here little guilty. Not that I esteem these men saints, nor on the other side I can allow of a word which escaped the pen of a friend of ours lately in these parts to one of his in England that he met here with men to treat with worse than devils. For I no ways find them so black as they are painted, but many times that is imputed to cunning and design which by their natural slowness and other men's precipitation turns to their advantage; and if those you mention in your letter for haste to be at home carried with them *caecos catulos, ipsi viderint*. But I know who had blame for saying all was well, as it was, and to their liking when that was advertised; and I dare undertake if their leisure could have served them to have visited such papers as they took with them afterwards (with which they had no time to make me or so much as themselves acquainted) anything they found amiss should have been rectified. But they knew best what they had to do, and though other men lose patience I am not bound to do likewise, having more matters to deal in than one; and in all I proceed with that sincerity with which you are longest and best acquainted and of which I must give you an account as long as we live together, it being the best comfort I have in a place which is neither for my health nor my wealth nor otherwise much for my contentment, save that I take in acquitting myself honestly in the duty of my charge and finding better and more solid correspondency from this state toward us and our friends abroad than I met with at first or could observe long after; and those which make other judgment (some of them at least) are like such as put to sea and, looking back to land, think the land goeth from them, not they from the land. For I did not think I should ever live to see amongst our men such an alienation from this state, especially at a time when I know them here to apply themselves more unto us than ever they did since they offered Queen Elizabeth the sovereignty of these provinces, and therefore there must be somewhat else in it, which I will not discourse of for fear of coming within compass of the proclamation.[3] And all this is to yourself. We have

[281]

had here this week past a strange proposition made by the archduke's ambassador, sent hither expressly, of which I send you a
translat[ion] with the answer, which seems as strange to him;[4]
and therewith he posted away by four o'clock in the morning,
guarded by twelve musketeers, for fear of the people, of which
he had reason to be apprehensive because of [sic] much rudeness
and incivility was used towards him and his train as he passed
through Delft before his errand was known. For the rest of our
news I refer you to your gazettas and Mr. Salmon's report, who I
pray you suffer not to send any beer, for I have my full provision,
neither will I accept from him any kind of gratification, for it is not
my manner in such cases. Thus I rest

Yours most assured

1. Robert Salmon, the brother-in-law of Lancelot Andrewes, bishop of
Winchester, was one of the owners of a ship wrongfully seized by the Dutch.
Salmon's claim was for compensation for the ordinance, powder, muskets, etc.,
which were part of the ship's equipment, not for the ship's cargo, which was
much more valuable. Salmon, on the basis of the erroneous translation described by Carleton in this letter, thought the Dutch were muddying the waters
in order not to pay.

2. Chamberlain, in his letter of February 27 informing Carleton of Salmon's anger at the supposed dishonesty of the Dutch, pointed out to Carleton
that in England he was acquiring the reputation of an apologist for Dutch
misbehavior. L. J. C. II, 346–47.

3. The proclamation of December 24, 1620, in which the king warned
people to be careful about what they said or wrote about public business and
secrets of state. Steele, Proclamations, I, 153.

4. Pierre Pecquius, chancellor of Brabant, arrived in The Hague on March
12/22, as ambassador from the archduke. The latter proposed a renewal of
the truce, expressed a desire to see the Netherlands united again, and suggested
that the United Provinces recognize their "natural prince," meaning himself.
The Dutch reply was chilly, to say the least. C. S. P. Venetian 1619–1621,
pp. 612, 621. Maurice had carefully lured the Habsburgs into making this
entirely unacceptable proposal in order to provide for a unified enthusiasm
for the renewal of the war. See Gardiner, History, IV, 186–88, and Carter,
Secret Diplomacy, pp. 258–65.

Good Mr. Chamberlain, I was never more beholden to you than of late days for often and ample letters nor never made you worse requital; which fault, though I acknowledge, I cannot mend, having all my time taken up with business for the king and queen of Bohemia, now at their first arrival,[1] which I can spare from the necessary discharge of the duty of my place. They have had here a free and friendly welcome of all sorts of people, and are hitherto defrayed by the States. The queen looks thin after her long and painful journey but is well in health, and so is all the train. We hear from Brussels the king of Spain is dead,[2] which in my opinion will breed no great alteration. As yet, though all passages are stopped and we are here actually (as we understand it) in war, yet are there passed no acts of hostility. This day three of our popish prisoners were beheaded here at The Hague (Mum, Eckenlow and Budberghen) for a practice to surrender Tiel to the enemy, of which you will see the particularities within few days printed.[3] They all died constantly and were as soon dispatched as ever I saw matter of that kind. The queen of Bohemia was sought unto to intercede for them but was too wise to interpose herself. *Cave putes* there is such another in the world for discretion and all things laudable in her sex and rank. I am glad you and my lord of Winchester are contented with what is done in Salmon's business and as sorry for his lordship's indisposition. Thus I rest

Yours most assured

1. Frederick and Elizabeth arrived at The Hague on April 4. Maurice gave them a warm welcome, in the hope of getting England somehow into the war, which, for the United Provinces, was about to resume with the expiration of the truce of Antwerp.

2. Philip III died on March 21.

3. The expiration of the truce was accompanied by a plethora of conspiracies. Carleton was to report on several during the next few years.

Good Mr. Chamberlain, I find by your letter of the 23 of the last,
as likewise by one of the same date from Mr. Lock, that there
is an opinion at home, and in the best place, that I fail of my duty
here abroad in a business of much moment, which sound you both
have from the same Bell;[1] but what should cause that to ring
after that manner I cannot imagine, for sure I am nothing hath
been omitted here, from the first to the last, to advance his
majesty's desire of having a new envoy into England, which in
the end will be effected, though it hath already passed many difficulties and doth yet meet with some; but to make this company
dance as soon as ours pipe, it is not in my power. And whosoever
were in my place would quickly find that resolutions of this nature
(in matters where so many have interest and in a state where all
goes by inducement, nothing by authority) are not *volentis* or
currentis; but that time must be allowed to endeavors, which hath
brought the business to this issue, that deputies are like to be sent
into England about the end of the progress. God send them better
luck than here is imagined, where most men suspect this earnest
pressing of a sending into England doth proceed from some dis-
affected persons to the conjunction of the two companies,[2] who
will labor to overthrow with one hand what was built with the other,
and by calling things into new question *factum infectum reddere;*
which consideration, with an account of the charge of the journey
(valued at no small rate by example of the last) and question who
should hear it (the generality or the company), hath held the business back all this while, and so would still have done and there men
have continued restive if they had not been suffered to bite on the
bridle and then rather be led than driven, as they now have been
by the prince of Orange and such of the States as prefer his
majesty's satisfaction before the interest of this company, of which
some of the chiefs remain [paper torn] obstinate, but in the end
they will [paper torn] overruled; and so I now write to Sir Dudley
Digges,[3] which I should have done sooner if things had been

[284]

brought to any ripeness; for I owe him much more service than such an advertisement comes to; and though I find myself bitten in this business I cannot suspect him of so much malignity, to whom I should refer myself for a good testimony, if there should be need, before any other and therefore must impute it to some (God knows whom) who neither know me, the nature of the business, nor the men I have to deal with. I have had somewhat to do of late in another matter concerning our merchants, wherein all men, I am sure, will not be well pleased, which is our company's [4] remove from Middelburg to Delft, where they now are settled and have had (by his majesty's commandment) my best furtherance. Some of our men, who had no mind to the remove, thought the business went by my means too fast forward; others were as much troubled to see it stick so long as it did. Now it is done, God send them good luck, for hitherto they have no cause to brag of their change, save only for the convenience of their residence; and for the chief point of utility time may mend their trade, as I believe it will. Meanwhile we have good neighborhood of them, of which I am very glad, and particularly of their preacher Mr. Forbes, a Scottish man, one of excellent parts of learning and utterance and of fair conversation. He is likened by most to Mr. Burgess, and for the doctrinal part, I think, he exceeds him far.[5] The king and queen of Bohemia have heard him twice here in our English church with much good liking of him; but he and all others they have heard since their coming into these parts still beat their ears with so many arguments and persuasions to support with patience their afflictions that (though they are in hard state enough) they make them think they are worse than they are and in place of comfort augment their sorrow. Mr. Paget [6] of Amsterdam went so far as to make affliction an argument of happiness, saying that therein we were more happy than angels and concluding with a prayer to God to increase our afflictions that thereby we might be known to be his children, to which none but his own parish said Amen. Yet I have heard of the like prayer of one sick of my disease. *Domine adauge dolores, ada* [paper torn] *etiam et patientiam.* Our deliverance we expect from lord Digby,[7] who having put himself upon the Danube at Ulm with purpose so to fall down to Vienna, we hear his secretary Simon Digby (who went before) was dispatched back towards him to turn him towards Prague, there to meet the emperor, who made account to part from Vienna thitherwards the 5th of this present, new style, having swept all clean before his coming by an execution of a great many of the best Bohemians, who innocently stayed behind when the king came away, and some of them have done the emperor service since that time by persuading obedience unto him as well in that kingdom as the confederate countries. Those we have here (as the burgrave, the chancellor, and vicechancellor of Bohemia, with some other men of quality whose fathers [men of 70 and 80 years of age] and nearest kinsmen are executed) were much afflicted with the first news, but afterwards took comfort in seeing one anothers' heads on their shoulders and in believing that God will not leave such cruelty unpunished. There is a fearful scourge hangs at this present over Christendom, the Turk (a young violent spirit)[8] being marched out of Constantinople towards Adrianople with an army of no less (if we may believe the States' ambassador's letters) than a million of men. Here we remain looking one upon another, with fairer armies on both sides than they had at any time during the wars. Yet this being the weaker and our war defensive, we shall stay till we see what the enemy will do, who, we believe, will not move until the affairs of Germany are settled and, it may be, until it be better known which way the Turk will bend, whose way as far as Adrianople lies indifferent betwixt Hungary and Poland. We have news that the archduke died this week,[9] after which we are the less inquisitive because he hath been *moribundus* this many a day, and no mutation can follow his decease. All other things which are stirring you will find in your gazettas, and thus have I endeavored to make appear unto you that when I can steal an hour's time I can better bestow it on you than any other of my friends, who must all excuse me for letters at this time, when my attendance on these princes takes up all I can spare from the necessary duty of my charge, and as *hoc oportet fieri,* so *illud non omitti,* and because I have of late days given a diligent account of both to those who can inform the lords [of the council] better of my endeavors, I pray you satisfy yourself and me too by what you can learn of my lord of Winchester touching Mr. Bell's report,[10] or of Sir Dudley Digges, who (I am sure) knows as much as he, and thereby deliver me of the melancholy (to which men in foreign employments are ever subject) which springs out of service *et non gradire*. My wife returns you many kind remembrances, and I ever rest

Yours most affectionately

Hague the 7th of a stormy July where hath been
yet seen no summer. 1621.

1. Chamberlain had written that several members of the council had expressed the view that Carleton had not been forceful enough in representing the grievances of the East India Company, *L. J. C.* II, 385. Thomas Locke became one of Carleton's business agents and regular correspondents late in 1618; Sherburne, who had filled the post previously, was secretary to Lord Chancellor Bacon and found himself unable to handle both jobs. Locke and Chamberlain had both heard the story from the same source, Robert Bell, the East India merchant.

2. As arranged by the treaty of 1619.

3. Chamberlain had written that Digges, who was a prominent shareholder in the East India Company, was upset because Carleton had not written recently; he "begins to suspect your affection towards him upon some sinister information may be given you from hence." *L. J. C.* II, 385. Digges had recently been in Holland with Maurice Abbot in an unsuccessful attempt to resolve the East India Company's disputes with the Dutch company.

4. The Merchant Adventurers. The move was made in part on Carleton's recommendation. December 10, 1620, Thomas Locke to Carleton, *C. S. P. Domestic 1619–1623,* p. 198.

5. John Forbes had been minister of Alford, Aberdeenshire. In 1605 he was chosen moderator of the Aberdeen assembly, which was held contrary to James's orders. For this and his subsequent denial of the Scottish Privy Council's jurisdiction in what he considered a spiritual matter, he was convicted of treason and banished for life. Eventually he settled down in Middelburg and, in 1621, removed to Delft along with the Merchant Adventurers. His exile was never revoked; he died in Holland in 1634. For Burgess see above, letter of September 12, 1617.

6. John Paget, who was ejected as rector of Nantwich for nonconformity in 1604. In 1607 he became minister of the English Presbyterian Church in

Amsterdam, a post he held for thirty years. Like Forbes, he died in Holland, in 1640.

7. John, Lord Digby, previously ambassador in Spain, was on his way to negotiate with Ferdinand II, on the basis of the abandonment by the elector palatine of his claims to Bohemia, in return for Ferdinand's agreement not to punish Frederick. Ferdinand was polite, but the mission failed, in large part owing to Frederick's unreasonableness. There is a full account in Gardiner, *History,* IV, chap. 38.

8. Osman II, who was an avaricious and cruel teenager. His military failures in the Cossack area of the Dniester led to his murder by the Janissaries in 1622, at the age of eighteen.

9. Archduke Albert died on July 3; his widow, the Infanta Isabella, remained as governor, but the nominal independence of the southern Netherlands was now over. For a discussion of the actualities of independence under Albert see Carter, *Secret Diplomacy,* pp. 77–87.

10. Chamberlain checked with Bishop Andrewes, who assured him that Bell had been in error. James was angry at Sir Noel Caron because Caron had assured him that commissioners to negotiate about East India questions would be in England by Midsummer Day, and they had not yet arrived. Thus the strictures on "the ambassador" were meant for Caron; Bell mistakenly believed they were for Carleton. *L. J. C.* II, 392–93.

The Hague, March 9, 1621/22

S. P. 84/105, ff. 221–23

Good Mr. Chamberlain, my nephew Dudley¹ returned about a fortnight since with a full report of all things (at least such as I am curious to know) in court, city, and country, and amongst such as gave me contentment (as there were both sorts), your well being and continuing unto me your wonted good affection (which did reflect upon him in your kind usage and free and friendly conversation), I assure you is none of the least; for I pray you believe there is no man's good and contentment (without exception of any my private friends though never so near) which I lay nearer my heart than yours and in whose love I more desire to keep possession. Wherefore you must make no cross construction of my long silence, which hath proceeded only of a new accession to my wonted affairs by a troublesome office of receiving and disbursing £30000, sent about three months since to the king and queen of Bohemia out of England, which was put upon me by his majesty's commandment. And I leave it to you to imagine that this sum being wholly expected on the one side by Count Mansfeld for his troops in the field, on the other by my lord General Vere for his garrison,[2] and here being many gaping after it for payment of debts, how hard it was to feed so many pigeons with one bean. Now the cash is empty, I begin to be at better leisure, the benefit whereof I first make use of in saluting you, with thanks for your often remembrance by letters, the last of which were of the 16th of the last, wherein I was only sorry to see you grow weary of well doing and resolved to leave writing, which I see not why you should do in regard of the times, because you know very well how to keep yourself within compass; and the uncertainty and variety of reports doth rather minister subject of often writing than otherwise. Wherefore, as far as may stand with your convenience, I would be glad we might continue our wonted correspondence; in which when I cannot by my own I will seek by my nephew's hand to make reparation of my long interruption. In one of your former you require of me Mr. Hare's picture for Captain Harvey, which he may take at Imworth [3] (to which effect I write to Mr. Lock) and copy it by what hand he likes best there; for the principal, I am loath to part with it, and therefore I pray you take order it be restored. It was a happiness for that unfortunate gentleman to have so honest a friend as Captain Harvey about him; otherwise his hypochondriacal humor might have carried him some such way as the lord of Berkshire is gone and as our strange bishop is going, through ambition and avarice,[4] who doubtless will speed no better than a certain French abbot de Boys, executed at Rome whilst I was at Venice for having used more liberty in his sermons at Paris than agreeth with the strict tenets of popery, though he went with employment from the queen mother during her regency and had a safe-conduct sent him to Florence, without which, mistrusting his safety, he refused to advance further.[5] But, I believe, he thinks the times are changed and grown to more mildness, as, indeed, they are to all strangers, who pass freely to and fro in the Pope's dominions and all other parts of Italy without search or inquisition; though the mesh be made wider the net hangs still, which if this great fish escape he will deceive my skill in that profession. I must confess I am much apprehensive of the mischief he runs willingly and wittingly unto (for he cannot be ignorant of the danger) as well for his own sake as for some other, who had a hand in his transmigration and conversion and may suffer by consequence; and, though all things else were pasted over, his book of the Council of Trent will never be forgiven him in this world nor the next as far as Popes have power; and I doubt he will be forced to discover the mystery of his *Pietro Soave Polano*. I know not *quo fato* our differences with these men by one accident or other are still kept unreconciled; notwithstanding that I very well know the orders given by the States to their former ambassadors, and those now sent, are to give all reasonable satisfaction, but public good intentions are many times embroiled by private interests, and there is questionless some secret *rèmora on* both sides, which must be discovered and removed before the business can come *a buon pòrto*. I am sorry Sir Dudley Digges hath so small part in this dispute about the East Indies, which he understands very well and might do much good in it. Touching our affairs on this side the sea, what betwixt the confidence of all with whom I hold correspondence who have their ears open to Spanish ministers and diffidence of others in the point of restitution of the Palatinate, I know not what to judge,[6] but seeing the same language held in Spain touching that business with his majesty's ministers as hath been two years together with the French concerning the Valtellina and longer with the Venetians about the galleys taken by the duke of Ossuna in the gulf [of Venice] (that is, promise of restitution of all, yet all held fast when execution is pressed), I must confess I lean to the diffident party and believe nothing will be recovered but by arms,[7] which are well, for numbers of men prepared by the Count Mansfeld in Alsace and the Duke Christian of Brunswick in Westphalia to an army (when they all assemble) of 50000; but how they can be well paid or disciplined without pay, I must confess I see not, unless, as they

[290]

hold here, *la guerre nourrit la guerre;* they, being masters of the field, can feed and maintain themselves upon the enemy's countries, which will make a hot summer of the next in Germany, when *summa rerum* lies at the stake. We have here Pittam the governor of Juliers in hold and in question about his rendering that town, which he answers but weakly for his part, though no small blame lights upon them who should have provided it better.[8] There is a new supply of men sent to Sluys in Flanders, towards which place the works the enemy doth advance do threaten an intention to besiege it this next spring. The marquis Spinola is gone that way since his return from Juliers, and the count Henry Vandenberg prepares with the help of the baron of Anholt's and the bishop of Cologne's troops to remove the duke of Brunswick out of Westphalia,[9] who requires but three weeks' time to make his troops 12,000 foot and 4500 horse. With your accustomed gazettas I send you a book styled *Cancelaria Hispanaica* in imitation of *Cancelaria Anhaltina,* which will give you some entertainment. We have here the ill news of my father Savile's decease;[10] which I much lament for the esteem I had of his virtue and merit and interest in his fatherly and friendly affection; but I know he lived and, by report, died well, which is the accomplishment of happiness in this world, which God send us all and have you in his holy protection.

Yours most assured

1. Carleton's namesake, the son of his brother George, was being employed as a courier by his uncle, who was eventually to make him one of his secretaries.

2. Ernst von Mansfeld, one of the best known and least competent of the soldiers of fortune of the Thirty Years War. He had been commander of Frederick's forces in Bohemia; he had engaged in negotiations with Maximilian of Bavaria to betray the Upper Palatinate to him and was now in Alsace, ostensibly preparing to defend the Lower Palatinate but actually plundering the bishoprics of the upper Rhine and intriguing with an agent of the Brussels government with a view to changing sides. Sir Horace Vere had been Frederick's commander in the Lower Palatinate for about a year.

3. Nicholas Hare, whom Carleton knew at Padua, had recently died. His executor, Captain John Harvey, wanted to have his picture, which Carleton owned, copied for use as part of a memorial. January 19, 1622, Chamberlain

to Carleton, *L. J. C.* II, 422. Imworth was an estate in Surrey whose lease Carleton had recently acquired.

4. The reference is to the archbishop of Spalato; see above, letter of November 26–December 2, 1616. The archbishop was intellectually arrogant; he found the English episcopate unwilling to follow his theological lead. The king had given him benefices worth £400 a year; he was continually seeking more. Carleton's use of the word "avarice" was based on personal experience. The archbishop had behaved greedily in the matter of a land lease; see the letters from Thomas Locke to Carleton for 1621 calendared in the *State Papers, Domestic.* The archbishop's dissatisfaction grew, and with the death of Paul V and the accession of his friend Gregory XV, he resolved to return to Rome, which he was now in the process of doing. Carleton's forebodings about his eventual fate turned out to be justified. Shortly after the archbishop reached Rome Gregory XV died; the new pope, Urban VIII, handed him over to the Inquisition, and he died in prison. For Francis Norris, earl of Berkshire, and his odd behavior, see above, Introduction, p. 6. He committed suicide in January 1622.

5. The reference is probably to Jean Dubois, one of Henri IV's favorite preachers. After Henri's murder Dubois publicly accused the Jesuits of complicity in the crime; for this he was imprisoned when he incautiously went to Rome. He was not in fact executed.

6. Tilly had conquered the Upper Palatinate in 1621 and was now preparing his campaign against those cities of the Lower Palatinate which Spinola had not already captured. Mansfeld and his associate Christian of Brunswick were raising forces for their defense—provided of course, that Mansfeld got no better offer elsewhere.

7. The Valtellina was the key to Habsburg military strategy, since it afforded passage for Spanish forces from Italy into the empire. In April 1621 the Spanish government had made a treaty with France agreeing that the forts they had built there would be razed and sovereignty restored to the Protestant Grisons, on condition that the Catholic religion be legally recognized. The treaty had not been implemented. The duke of Ossuna was the Spanish viceroy in Naples; he ran his administration with minimal attention to instructions from Madrid. He was eventually removed and died in prison. Sometimes there was good reason for Spanish procrastination; sometimes the government in Madrid was not at fault.

8. Juliers had been in the hands of the Dutch at the resumption of the war; it was too isolated to be easily defensible and was in effect written off.

9. Spinola had recently captured Juliers. Vandenberg was one of his fellow

commanders in Flanders. Anholt, not to be confused with Christian of Anhalt, was one of the commanders of the forces of the Catholic League.

10. He died on February 20. Carleton's episcopal cousin George Carleton wrote on April 1 that he was buried by torchlight to save expense. *C. S. P. Domestic 1619–1623,* p. 371.

The Hague, April 30, 1622

S. P. 84/106, ff. 129–30

Good Mr. Chamberlain, since my last to you by Mr. George Kevett I have received your two letters of the 30th of March and 13th of April, for which I return you many thanks; and now I will proceed to entreat you to rejoice with us at the good success lately arrived in the Palatinate, where the seasonable arrival of the king of Bohemia, after divers dangers of being discovered, hath already brought such strength and confirmation to the doubtful and wavering minds of his friends, ministers, and people there as you will easily perceive by the relation which now I am about to make unto you.

The marquis of Baden, without further delay, declared himself by an actual joining his troops to the count Mansfeld; Raville, the infanta's agent to Count Mansfeld, suddenly vanished; Mansfeld, having with a great expedition gotten over the Rhine, encountered the baron Tilly near Wesselock, put him to rout, taking divers colors, coronets, a colonel, with many other men of note, slew a good quantity (some letters say 1500) and the remainder being without retreat and far from succours (Leopold in Alsatia, and Gonsalo on the other side the Neckar, the troops expected out of Hungary not yet arrived, and those with Baron Anholt entertained by the duke of Brunswick), we hope to hear by the next of the prosecution of this victory and utter ruin of the Bavarian army.[1]

The queen of Bohemia's child was christened on Friday last by the States of Holland, Count Henry, the princess of Portugal, and the countess of Nassau. The States made an act of 1000-guilders' pension to the young princess for term of life, to begin at the day of the christening; and in relation to her godfather the States and the king's mother, she is called Louise Hollandine. The ceremony was performed in this manner. First, marched all the captains and gentlemen, after whom, next before the child, went the little prince Henry, and the prince of Orange, *quorum pars ipse fui*. The child was carried by Mademoiselle de Portugal under a canopy borne up by 4 of the queen's gentlemen; she, led by her brother Don Guillaume and the duke of Holstein, a *Rhingravine* with her sister Mademoiselle de Solms holding up the train of the bearing cloth; after, followed the States of Holland, Count Henry, the princess of Portugal, the countess of Nassau, and the rest of the ladies.[2] In this equipage they went to the cloister church, which is within three houses of the queen's lodgings, where was a Dutch sermon, and afterward ensued the baptism; which done, they returned in the like order as they came.

Although I am sure you will have heard of the process of Cavalier Foscarini, yet for your more particular information, I will put down what I have concerning the same in a letter from Sir Henry Wotton of the 21st of April.[3] Foscarini on Wednesday last (the 13th after his imprisonment) about six hours of the night was strangled in prison and all the next day till sunset was hanged up by one leg betwixt the two fatal pillars, in a gown furred with martens, a black satin doublet, and a pair of old wrought-velvet hose, his face, by dropping of wax lights and dragging on the ground, pitifully but perchance purposely deformed. His public execution they seem to have remitted either in respect of those dignities [paper torn] had borne abroad or those at home, where he was actually a senator in ordinary. Of his true imputations I cannot yet speak warrantably, which have been so corrupted with false noise that I was fain this morning to wait on my lady of Arundel to College for clearing of a malicious conceit artificially spread that he had suffered for secret meetings with some other public minister in her house, where she received a great satisfaction from the prince.

We have as yet no certain news of the duke of Brunswick's marching; neither of Count Henry Vandenberg; though by some circumstances we do conjecture the duke to be set forward on his way, and some letters report that the count was to pass over the Rhine the 25th of the present.

I send you herewith a printed copy of the emperor's declaration given to the Pope's nuncio concerning the electorate.[4]

The commendation you give of Bartley's book makes me look after it, but I cannot yet light on it.[5] Henry the 7th commends the writer so much that it is much pity all his petty printings have not been employed upon such worthy works. Now I wish, being at so good leisure, he would go on where he leaves, and he being a man who (as all the world knoweth) doth *famae servire,* since his own deeds succeed no better, may do well *res gestas scribere.* Thus I rest as ever

Yours most affectionately

1. Carleton's account is substantially correct, although Tilly's situation was by no means as desperate as he makes it sound. The engagement between Mansfeld and Tilly was fought at Mingolsheim on April 27. "Leopold" is the Habsburg archduke Leopold, bishop of Strasburg. Gonsalo Fernández de Córdoba was a descendant of the Great Captain of the days of Ferdinand and Isabella. He assumed command of the Spanish forces in the Palatinate at the expiration of the Twelve Years Truce, when Spinola returned to the Low Countries to take up the war against the Dutch.

2. The princess of Portugal was a sister of Maurice and Frederick Henry's; Sophie of Nassau-Dietz, the sister of the duke of Brunswick, was Elizabeth of Bohemia's first cousin. "Mademoiselle de Solms" is Amalia von Solms-Braunfels, who later married Maurice's half-brother Count Henry. Carleton obviously enjoyed his part in the ceremony. He would have been less pleased had he known that, thirty-five years hence, Louise Hollandine would take the veil.

3. From this point to the end of the paragraph Carleton is quoting Wotton's letter. It was Wotton himself who had told Lady Arundel of the stories about Foscarini's use of her house; she was very angry and insisted that he make a public statement of her innocence to the doge and senate. See the account of the affair in Smith, *Wotton* I, 183–90. For Foscarini's earlier difficulties see above, letter of September 8/18, 1615.

4. Ferdinand was preparing the transfer of Frederick's electoral title to Maximilian of Bavaria, a plan which, for various reasons, most German

princes opposed and the Pope supported. There is a good account of the complicated political factors involved in C. V. Wedgwood, *The Thirty Years War*, Penguin edn. (London, 1957), chap. 4, esp. pp. 141–45.

5. Carleton's nephew Dudley served as amanuensis for the bulk of this letter, which may account for the fact that the letter is paragraphed; only the final paragraph is in Carleton's hand. The book in question is John Barclay's *Argenis*, a satire which Chamberlain called "the most delightful fable that ever I met with" in his letter of March 30. *L. J. C.* II, 428. "Henry the 7th" is probably Henry Wotton.

The Hague, January 17, 1622/23

S. P. 84/111, ff. 16–17

Good Mr. Chamberlain, you are so well acquainted with the manner of these parts that I need not excuse my seldom writing in the depth of winter, when affairs are as cold as the weather; nothing more than preparation against next spring (a thing of course) and talk of doings elsewhere, which I should but molest you with, since our chief talk is what you do at home: upon the *belle parole* you have out of Spain and *cattivi fatti* you hear of in Germany. For the marriage, *Deus bene vertat,* which your letters of the 4th of this present say is concluded; but for the restitution of the Palatinate the proceedings of the Imperialists and Spaniards, both after the same manner in fortifying what they have got and gaining the poor town of Frankenthal (which only remains), put us here in much despair.[1] Mr. Burlamachi,[2] newly come from Frankfort with purpose to go with my lord General Vere into England, gives us but small comfort, for he saith both of them concur in winning the place, though there is some odds betwixt them which of them should have it. Our countryman Borough[3] doth his duty in the meantime in hearkening to neither till he have order from hence and England, whither the town is sending an express to know what to trust unto. My lord General Vere hath had some trouble here about his troops, which, being divided in their desires, some to go into England, others to stay on this side the sea, fell into a mutiny in north Holland but were appeased by the officers before my lord's coming to them, who went expressly thither and returns this night to this place. The troops are to be licensed at Tergow [Gouda?]. Some of them took their passage directly into England from Delfzyl by Groningen before they knew they were to be licensed in these parts. My lord general hath been somewhat afflicted with this accident, but more with the ill countenance the king of Bohemia hath used towards him since his coming hither, which he need not much take to heart. The prince of Orange hath been dangerously sick of a languishing disease but is upon the mending hand and gathers strength daily. Mansfeld and Brunswick begin to increase their army in East Friesland and to enlarge their quarter, having taken in Cloppenburg and some other places in Münsterland; but I see not *cui bono* that preparation, in terms as it stands being owned by no prince or state; only they have help from hence of arms to the value of 50000 florins and fair promises of more.[4] You have herewith Colonel Naui's manifest,[5] the expectation whereof made me before send you only his challenge. The man in a word is *miles gloriosus,* and his quarrel being with his superiors in command they are not bound to answer it. Yet is he gone to Bergen op Zoom in opinion to meet them at Roosendaal. All I hear of the archbishop of Spalato you will find in an extract of a letter from Rome, which, if it saith true, I believe by this time he wisheth himself again in England, for he is like to find his homicide at Rome. Heinsius,[6] our chief man at Leyden, hath published a book much commended unto me for the conceit, and I send you one before I have had time to overlook it. So with my best wishes I commit you to God, ever resting

Yours most assuredly

1. The situation of the Elector Palatine was now desperate. Frankenthal was the only town remaining to him. The optimism of the English government about the possibility of recovering the elector's position as part of a bargain over a marriage treaty with Spain was very high at this point and was shortly to lead to the extraordinary expedition of Prince Charles and Buckingham to Spain.

2. Philip Burlamachi, the greatest financier of this period, was now about

to embark on those huge financial transactions for the government which led Robert Ashton to write that "In the matter of government borrowing, the 1620's may, with little exaggeration, be called the era of Burlamachi," *Money Market,* p. 21.

3. Sir John Borough was the commander of the garrison at Frankenthal.

4. Mansfeld and his fellow *condottiere* Christian of Brunswick had been in Dutch service briefly during the summer of 1622. In October they had been discharged and sent over the frontier; they were now ravaging East Friesland, after an attempt on the bishopric of Münster.

5. An Italian soldier of fortune.

6. Daniel Heinsius, a prominent Contraremonstrant, was the successor of the well-known textual critic Joseph Justus Scaliger at the University of Leyden.

The Hague, March 21, 1622/23

S. P. 84/111, ff. 204–205

Good Mr. Chamberlain, I have too long deferred my thanks for your ample letter of the 22 of February by which you advertised our prince's posting journey into Spain [1] and judged rightly at the strangeness of the news here amongst these people, who have always entertained and so do still more distrust and diffidence of the reality of Spanish proceedings than any else whosoever; and unless their judgments fail in this point we shall have little reputation of ours, for putting ourselves so far and so freely into the hands of that nation: but I have observed that the Spaniards have of late years gone a new way to work and by fair and civil means won more good will in the world than they were wont, whereby they have advanced their affairs exceedingly, and I will hope that by the like dealing with us they will make these men see the error of their jealousies; but when I consider that Spain and these United Provinces are at this present the two most diametrically opposite and hostile countries of the whole world and that the two only children of the king our sovereign are, one with the one, the other with the other, it passeth my capacity how they can be long well looked on in both places. Wherefore I leave all politic speculations and fall to theological, knowing that God hath his hand in all things and can turn all to the best and so will, when he seeth his own time to be most for his glory. I have formerly advertised you of the treason against the prince of Orange [2] and the execution of four of the hired executioners thereof, three of whose bodies are set naked and upright as in so many chairs upon wheels, with their heads on poles like long necks (betwixt this and Ryswick) turned to the place where they should have committed the fact, and it is a very dismal sight. The fourth, who was quartered, hath his head and right arm set up and hung nearer the highway in the same place, the rest of his limbs being hung up in the three chief avenues of this town. On Wednesday last three of the chief conspirators were executed in the same place as the former, which is the common place of justice in this town, but with some more ceremony, here being two companies of soldiers fetched from Delft and added to his excellency's guard, who stood all in arms in three several quarters, somewhat remote from the place of execution. The first which died was Barnevelt's eldest son (the Heer Van Grondeville) who much deceived the world, in that he being known to be *meticulosus* did notwithstanding put on a good and manlike countenance, both at the reading of his sentence and upon the scaffold, where he used but few words to the people, saying that desire of revenge and ill counsel had brought him to his end, to which he made the most haste that ever I saw and had his head as soon and clean taken from him, which the States at his wife's suit have suffered to be buried in the French church and in the same vault with his father. The other two, Secretaries of Berkel and Bleiswiik (two villages betwixt Rotterdam and Tergow), after they had used some words both to the same effect, confessing their fault and asking forgiveness of the people for the ruin they had brought upon them if their enterprise had taken place, were both beheaded and quartered and their heads and limbs set and hung up upon several poles and gibbets with the former, who was executed after the same manner; as Slatius (the Arminian minister) and the two brothers, the Blanckarts of Leyden with another, are like to be the next week. Barnevelt's younger son escaped to Goch in Cleveland, is there sick, and not altogether free from being sent back hither, in that the enemy doth much condemn this fact; and the States have offered to ransom him and Vanderdussen his companion with money or in exchange of prisoners, of which they have one of good value fallen casually into their hands (the prior of the Dominicans at Antwerp), a man much esteemed on the other side, who out of a foolish presumption of his force of persuasion undertook, upon a pretended passport for another occasion, to come to Huseden and there to practice upon the governor (the Heer Van Kessel) for the rendering of that town and the new forts he hath built by Boslduke [s'Hertogenbosch] to the enemy; which the governor answered by laying him by the heels, where he lies fast at Huseden and is much lamented and looked after from Antwerp and those other good towns. The fair weather makes the prince of Orange begin to look about him, not to be behindhand with the enemy, who hath already laid a bridge over the river by Antwerp and threatens to be early in the field, but the want of money, by reason of the failing of the West Indian fleet, may cool their courage. Tilly prepares a strong army about Frankfort with great equipage, being furnished with another year's contribution of the Catholic League, and he hath all Germany open before him, so as with former successes and his present force he is grown very fearful. He hath appointed his rendezvous in the land of Paderborn, which way he is upon his march against Mansfeld and Brunswick, the first of which is sent to by the French king to be entertained into his service for the war of the Valtellina; [3] the second is already entered into the oath and pay of the duke his elder brother, so as Tilly will find none in those parts to fight with but his own shadow; [4] and therefore it is feared he will fall upon these provinces in assistance of the Spaniards to recompense the help the Catholic League in Germany (which goeth now under the name of *la ligue sainte*) hath had of that nation, both in recovery of Bohemia and conquest of the Palatinates, which now they seek to settle by two years' truce in those parts, during which time they promise themselves the like success in these. But I hope they reckon without their host, though these poor men will have hard dealing with so many hosts at once, as they are now threatened withal. All is in the hand of God, to whose holy protection I commit you, ever resting

Yours most affectionately

1. Prince Charles and Buckingham had set out for Spain to woo Philip III's daughter on February 18, disguised with false beards and calling themselves Tom and John Smith. One of the false beards fell off at Gravesend, wrote Chamberlain, which caused some suspicion, and they were halted at least twice before they sailed from Dover. Chamberlain was not sanguine about the result of the journey: "Few believed it at first, because they could not apprehend the reasons of so strange a resolution, as being a mystery of state beyond common capacities." *L. J. C.* II, 479–81.

2. This was a plot to assassinate Maurice on his way from Ryswick to The Hague. The younger son of Oldenbarnevelt, who was the chief organizer of the conspiracy out of a desire to avenge his father, was able to avoid extradition and ultimately took refuge at Brussels. Some fourteen in all were executed. There is a purple description of the conspiracy in the last chapter of J. L. Motley's biography of Oldenbarnevelt, *The Life and Death of John of Barneveld* (London 1874) a beautiful example of a certain sort of nineteenth-century historical writing.

3. On January 28/February 7, 1623, the French government had signed a treaty with Venice and Savoy designed to restore the sovereignty of the Grisons in the Valtellina and get the Spanish garrisons out. They were now negotiating with Mansfeld for his service.

4. This prediction turned out to be rather less than accurate. On July 27 Tilly destroyed the army of Christian of Brunswick at Stadtlohn.

The Hague, July 11, 1623

S. P. 84/113, ff. 28–32

Good Mr. Chamberlain, in the whole time of our correspondence of letters, which is now very ancient, I never received any from you more opportunely than your last of the 28th of June, which found the way over and came to my hands on Saturday last, single and alone, without any company either to myself or anybody else. And we were then in a time of much expectation of news out of

England on all hands, which you did sufficiently satisfy in advertising what was stirring; but for myself in particular I had a lost wife to hearken after (from whom I had not heard in many a day before) and was glad to find by your letter she was lost in good company. Since, I have recovered her again, having had a letter from her by my nephew (who arrived here on Monday last), the chief subject whereof is the contentment she receiveth in the good usage of her friends and particularly in the kindness you do her, for which she requires my thanks; and I call to mind in one of your former letters you were as well pleased with some courtesy she did you, so as, without remitting the exchange of compliment hither, I think you will do well to pay one another; and I thank you both for being so good friends, which I pray you continue.

Touching our match, the Spaniards have us at too great an advantage, which it is not their manner to lose, who always make the best of their game, good or bad; and that which they now have in their hands was never so fair; yet I am nothing troubled with the noise of liberty of religion, of leagues, of cautionary towns, and suchlike as fill the world. That I most fear is the *aequum* covered under *iniquum,* which these extravagant reports may make seem plausible and hurt us much, both at home and abroad. For many things good and allowable in themselves have their natures changed by circumstance, and connivance in religion, absolute neutrality, and matter of assurance (which it is likely they will stand upon) will very ill concur with the constitution of our state at home or our alliances abroad. Amongst other things methinks I foresee a demand concerning these parts to have the rivers and ports of Flanders set as free and open to his majesty's subjects as those of Holland or Zeeland,[1] which cannot be denied but to be full of equity; yet such hath been the practice hitherto contrary to this course and such the interest of this state not to admit it that nothing is more unpossible to be effected but by force; and no force in this cause can be used by us without a bloody war at sea, from which God deliver us. And deliver us I hope he will; howsoever this conceit of mine I could not but put into your breast, of which I pray you make no other use than one day to remember betwixt us two how right or wrong I guessed.

All is yet quiet betwixt these two armies, either of them being sufficiently strong for the defensive and not powerful enough for the offensive, which makes them as yet stand looking one upon the other fair and far off in garrison. It is likely the marquis Spinola may besiege Meurs [2] towards the end of summer and carry it too, for reputation of the Catholic army, that being a Protestant town and county in the midst of the enemy's new acquisitions in Juliers and Cleve, where it raiseth great contributions, and the apprehension hereof hath caused the prince of Orange to thrust a strong garrison into it presently upon the expiration of the late neutrality, for the continuance whereof he hath been held in hand from day to day at Brussels; and the marquis Spinola wrote unto him there yet wanted a month's time to dispatch it, during which space he promised his excellency he would attempt nothing against the town; but his excellency, taking this as a stratagem to gain time till the marquis were ready to draw into the field, thought best to go a surer way to work than to trust to courtesy. And this being properly his town he governs himself concerning the same with the king of Spain as he doth at Orange with the French king, fortifying that castle daily and stuffing it with men and munition, by which means he doth much displease both those great monarchs yet saith that, knowing both their teeth water at those two places, he will have the honor to have a royal war made on him, in which he can lose nothing but the places, whereas, if he should be over-reached and thrust out by fair words and treaties, with the places he should lose his reputation likewise.

Mansfeld [3] plays the juggler with all the world, offering his service to all, threatening one and another to get money, bargaining with the count of East Friesland and the Emdeners to quit their country, yet sticks close by them, and so (I think) will do as long as he finds food. His entertainment for general of the Valtellina league was to begin the first day of his marching; whereupon he sent 3000 men the first of this month out of East Friesland to Meppen, a place in Münsterland, near Lingen, which raised a bruit as if he would beseige Lingen; but his intent was no other than under color of that march to begin his entertainment, of which he hath already received by way of anticipation 120,000 crowns for two months and distributed the same amongst his horse and old Dutch troops without suffering the French (from which nation the most part thereof comes) to partake any whit thereof; so as they being come unto him 5000 strong begin to melt away; and I do not think you shall hear of any great effects this year of that army. Yet it hath been the luck thereof to come opportunely in the nick of two occasions (one the levying the siege of Frankenthal, the other of Bergues)[4] and may do the like again if it subsist (as it may very well do) till the enemy be engaged. The whole strength thereof exceeds not 10000 foot and 2000 horse. The duke Christian of Brunswick, with the reputation of a young prince's valor (which is rare in this age) and no other means (for when he left The Hague he had but 50 ducats in his purse, which he showed me often), hath got together 20000 foot, 5000 horse and 18 piece of cannon, all well armed and with good equipage; but having no pay for his men and being to encounter Tilly (an old soldier with an entertained and disciplined army encouraged with many victories) it is *impar congressus,* though Tilly be fewer in number. For it is likely Tilly will entertain the time in places of advantage till his numbers increase (for which purpose he expects aid from Córdoba and Anholt, and the count the [*sic*] Collalto [in whose castle you and I ate melons once in as hot a day as this I am now writing in] brings him 4000 men out of Bohemia) and the duke Christian's diminish. Yet hath the duke Christian the advantage of the first blow, by a regiment of horse he hath cut off, commanded by two Dutch dukes of Saxe-Lauenburg, one colonel, the other lieutenant colonel to the regiment, who was present, but the colonel absent at Vienna.[5] We have here a Venetian ambassador of the House of Morosini come to reside with this state, who made his entry very youthfully in a habit and cloak of white silk stuff, which had more *del soldato che del senatore* and takes away much of the opinion these burgomasters had of the gravity of that senate.[6] His first audience he had in the assembly of the States General, with liberty for who would to enter, for so he would have it, after the Venetian manner; and he kept himself in his speech within the compass of Venetian generalities: of amity, friendship, and good correspondence; but Aerssens, who was prepared to encounter him, gave downright blows, saying the chief end of this confederation betwixt these two commonwealths was to defend the common liberty against the House of Austria, the common enemy, and concluding that the poverty of this state which now bears the burden of a war must in reason be sustained by the wealth of Venice, *ad quod non fuit responsum*.

Monsieur Chastillion [7] is come hither with a great number of glittering Frenchmen, who grow impatient and angry with the prince of Orange that he will not go into the field for their sakes, that they may show their valor.

Your old acquaintance, Sir John Sammes, is in a fair way of a company in Sir Edward Horwood's regiment, *en payant*. Poor Peter Manwood is upon a *bon voyage* from Bergen, where he hath lived long on Captain Applegate's purse, to Brussels, to do Mr. Trumbull the like courtesy. [8]

Thus have you a large volume of all our doings, by which I would gladly make you amends in one entire payment, for my letting slip many messengers without letters. But besides my many businesses I must excuse myself upon my indispositions, which have of late much afflicted me and now are somewhat abated but without hope of any but the last remedy.

God send you health and all happiness and me the contentment of seeing you and the rest of my friends before I die.

Yours as ever most assured

This will be delivered unto you by one of my youths (John Nicols), who came a poor lad unto me but hath done me good service, and I give him this employment for his encouragement.

I hear of a new pretender for the provostship of Eton: Sir Henry Goodier, who to show his abilities hath made a long elegy in English upon the prince's journey into Spain, as if the place were to be won with a song. Howsoever his wit appears therein I cannot much praise his judgment in sending it to the queen of Bohemia (as he hath done transcribed by his own hand), since he therein commends the Spaniards for having effected so much in the Diet at Ratisbon that the emperor hath only excluded the king of Bohemia from the electorate and left a possibility for his children to recover it.[9] And for religion he likes not a hard-hearted one but rather commendeth a waxen religion pliable to the times. No doubt you [paper torn] have it printed or get a sight of it, and I shall be glad to know your opinion as well of the poet for his pretention as the poem.

Since the writing hereof I find this matter of Sir H. G. is made a great secret; wherefore I pray you speak not of it unless you hear of it by others.

1. At this time the annoyance of the English government at the behavior of Dutch men-of-war was at its peak. In May a Dunkirk privateer which the Dutch had cornered in the harbor at Leith tried to escape; it ran aground on a sandbank and was destroyed by the Dutch. Another privateer trapped in Aberdeen was threatened with the same fate. Furthermore, in April, the Dutch had seized one of their own ships, suspected of piracy, in Cowes Roads. Carleton had been ordered to protest; the Dutch thus far had offered very little satisfaction. They admitted that they had erred in the Cowes incident; but they had not agreed to allow the ship blockaded at Aberdeen to go. Hence Carleton's predicion about freedom of trade in Flanders. This was already announced English policy; what Carleton feared was that Spain would stipulate, as part of a marriage agreement, that England use force to implement it. Far worse was in fact in contemplation: on July 21 James instructed Charles and Buckingham to reopen with Spain discussions of an old scheme to partition the Netherlands. There is full account in Gardiner, *History*, V, 79–88.

2. Meurs was a town south of the Spanish-held fortress at Wesel; it was part of the Orange patrimony, and Maurice was busy fortifying it.

3. Mansfeld was now briefly in French pay for service in connection with the question of the Valtellina. Before the end of the year the French dropped him.

4. The references are to Mansfeld's forcing the Spanish general Córdoba to raise the siege of Frankenthal in October 1621 and to his helping to compel Spinola to raise the seige of Bergen op Zoom, which Carleton here calls Bergues, a year later, while he was in Dutch pay.

5. Franz Albrecht, duke of Saxe-Lauenburg, was one of the many princely soldiers of fortune in Germany who changed sides as their interests dictated.

6. Marc Antonio Morosini was a professional diplomatist, in spite of his

apparently frivolous garb; he had been ambassador in Savoy, and in 1624 was to move from The Hague to Paris.

7. Gaspard de Coligny, count of Châtillon, a peripatetic anti-Habsburg soldier.

8. Sir John Sammes had gone to Bohemia in 1620, both to fight for Frederick and to escape his creditors. See *L. J. C.* II, 322. Sir Peter Manwood, an antiquary-friend of Carleton's and Chamberlain's, was another Englishman who had found it necessary to evade his debts by going abroad.

9. For Sir Henry Goodier see above, letter of August 2, 1616. His tactless reference was to events at the electoral meeting at Ratisbon, where in February 1623 the emperor solemnly transferred Frederick's electoral privileges to Maximilian for life; the question of what was to happen after Maximilian's death was left open. There was no English representative at Ratisbon; the Spanish ambassador made the only public protest against the transfer of the electorate. Goodier's blunder was the more remarkable in that he was now the father-in-law of Elizabeth of Bohemia's indefatigable agent in England, Sir Francis Nethersole.

The Hague, September 14–16, 1623

S. P. 84/114, ff. 69–71

Good Mr. Chamberlain, I received this last week your letter from London, written in your passage betwixt your two retreats, which I am glad to find you continue, because change of air—and recreation sometimes—cannot but contribute much to your health; and withal I am not a little pleased in my mind to see that in this wanton and mutable world (which appears so, more now than ever, in all sexes and ages) two women [1] can be found out of so much temper and patience to live as their husbands left them and *menage faire* estates to the good of their children; and, whereas wives commonly hate those whom their husbands love, these are so free from that natural imperfection that they still cherish the remembrance of their husbands in their friends, for which I cannot but exceedingly honor them both, even at this distance. I do now every hour expect the return of my wife, who could never have been absent from hence in a worse time, both in regard of the queen's lying in (at which she hath been much missed) and likewise of her friends being here (the lady Hatton [2] and her daughter), who much wanted her company, especially whilst they lay wind-bound, as they did above a fortnight, and took it so unkindly at Aeolus' hands that my lady Hatton vowed she would never come more in his danger, having never in her life being [*sic*] so absolutely over-ruled, as she confessed herself. My lord of Warwick, with his brother my lord Mountjoy in his company, set forward this day towards England upon commandment I laid on him in his majesty's name for his return to compound the quarrel betwixt him and my lord Cavendish,[3] having been stayed longer than will be expected in England by an ague which took him at Rees and held him some while at Arnheim. There the prince of Orange hath remained all this summer hitherto, since he parted from hence, save only a start he made to Rees and Emmerich to visit those two towns and take a view of the duke of Brunswick's and Count Henry's armies, and there he will continue till the rivers be risen, when we shall expect him back here at The Hague. The French have swarmed about him but begin now to drop away, seeing there is no more doings. General Vere, with my lord Wriothesley in his company, young Wentworth, Sir John Ratcliff and Sir Thomas Dutton passed by this way the last week and are now with his excellency.[4] The enemy, with some troops drawn out of Córdoba's army and companies from the Spanish garrisons on the north side of the Rhine under the command of the younger count of Emden, is besieging of Lippstadt; upon the passage to which place Córdoba himself lies near the Lippe, with the gross of his army, ready to put over the Ysell, if his excellency should stir from the guard of that river, so as, having a double design, he is likely to speed of one and carry the town, which is all, in all appearance, will be done in these parts this summer. Spinola stirs not with his army for fear of mutinies (as we say here) if he should draw into the field without money, of the want whereof here is complaint on both sides; but on this, there is no danger of such disorder. Tilly, since his overthrow of Brunswick's army, hath marched fair and softly towards Mansfeld in East Friesland, having had passage given him through the county of Oldenburg, where he remains without advancing further, not willing (like a wise captain [as he is] and a fortunate) to engage his army in a wasted country. Mansfeld, having spoiled and consumed all about him, is retired with his whole army to Greetsiel and that corner of land betwixt that place and Emden, where he hath some help of victuals and munition from the States with no more money than will serve for his works, so as he hath wants sufficient of pay and other necessaries, with the plague in his camp (of which some principal men, besides four or five of his own domestics, are dead about him) and yet takes heart and encouragement, promising in his letters to Count Ernest (who is entered Emden with new garrison from hence) to hold out some months and to make Tilly retire; whereas all this summer, when he had no money near, the style of his letters to the States continually ran that unless he were plentifully supplied of all things, he could not keep his army together a week.[5] The States are more troubled with that man than they were ever with any, having indeed *lupum auribus;* meanwhile the Emdeners, to whom he hath been a *lupus* in earnest, do not jest with him, having taken in revenge of the spoils he hath committed in their country two ships he had lying upon the Ems, one laden with cannon, which he had taken from the count of East Friesland and new cast here in Holland with his own arms and made fit for the field to the number of 30 pieces with munition suitable, the other with arms, tents, pavilions, beds, rich apparel for himself, and liveries for 80 servants from head to foot, with which the chief workmen of this town and others in Holland have been busied the most part of this year past and is an equipage, indeed, for any prince—not much commended in him, for costliness in that kind whilst his army hath been often ready to mutiny for want of pay and to perish for famine; but that is the man's humor—rich and sumptuous in external appearance, though otherwise poor and beggarly, which, he saith himself, he learned at the court in Brussels amongst the Spaniards. I must tell you one story of his civil government in his camp, which suits with his military discipline. One Carpasson, a Dutch colonel of his, having a wife in his army none of the chastest, it fell out that

[309]

he in his jealousy asked one of the young marquises of Baden (of which there are two in those troops) whether he had not had to do with his wife; which being faintly denied by the marquis and Mansfeld, hearing of some quarrels about that woman, told Carpasson he could not do better than either to put her away or go away himself. Carpasson takes this for a sufficient warning and warrant to make her away; and carrying with him the common executioner to his quarter, with two Lutheran preachers and a surgeon, commands her to rise, when she was gone to bed suspecting no such matter, and, after the preachers had ministered the communion unto her, cut off her head about midnight, and sewing it on again upon her shoulders, by the help of the surgeon, buried her in the next churchyard, against whom he is now taking informations and framing a process, continuing in his charge of colonel as before; which, how it is understood abroad in the world, may be seen by one Bernardin Rota (a Venetian, who hath long followed that camp as a chief engineer) and coming through Leeuwarden in Friesland, a voice ran amongst the people that it was Carpasson; whereupon he was pursued by women and boys and almost torn in pieces before he could persuade them he was another man. The Italian, Colonel Naui, whose manifest and writings I heretofore sent you, having been with the duke of Brunswick sometime before and likewise at his overthrow, for overfree speaking and censoring men for that service hath raised to himself as many enemies on this side as on the other and is busy with new manifests and challenges, which make him notably ridiculous, though he be a man of good abilities. I send you certain papers touching the old Pope and election of a new [6] (whom Pasquin calls *filium lassitudinis*), which show plainly how little part the Holy Ghost hath in that business. When you have overlooked them (which you may do at your leisure), I pray you return them unto me. Thus having paid you (as my manner is, when I can light on leisure) in gross for what I receive from you in detail I confess, notwithstanding, much obligation for your often remembrances and ever rest

Yours most affectionately

Hague this 14th of September 1623.

It seems the wind is set this year to break women of their wills, because it is come opposite for my wife's return as it was to my lady Elizabeth Hatton's; and I persuade myself she desires as much to be here as the other lady with impatience longed to be gone; once more adieu. The 16th of September.

The Venetians have chosen a new duke [7] as you will see by Sir Henry Wotton's letter, which I pray you return with the rest of these idle papers.

1. Chamberlain had written on August 30 that he was in London on his way from the house of Sir Ralph Winwood's widow to that of the widow of Sir Henry Fanshawe. Carleton esteemed both of them highly.

2. Sir Edward Coke's wife. Part of her motive in making this journey was almost certainly to get her daughter Frances, newly separated from Buckingham's mentally ill brother, John Villiers, Viscount Purbeck, away from Sir Robert Howard, son of the disgraced Lord Treasurer Suffolk. As is usually the case, such measures proved futile; in the following year Frances had a son by Sir Robert and later lived with him more or less openly.

3. Robert Rich, earl of Warwick, had quarrelled with William, Lord Cavendish, the son of the earl of Devonshire; they "fell so foul at a Virginia or Bermudas court," wrote Chamberlain, "that the lie passed and repassed and they are got over to try their fortune," *i.e.,* to fight a duel outside James's jurisdiction. *L. J. C.* II, 509. The king forbade the fight and was obeyed. Lord Mountjoy was Mountjoy Blount, Baron Mountjoy, the illegitmate half-brother of Warwick, the product of the liaison of Penelope Rich and Lord Mountjoy.

4. James, Lord Wriothesley, was the eldest son of the third earl of Southampton. He died of fever in 1624; for his death and that of his father, see below, letter of November 16/26, 1624. Ratcliff and Dutton were soldiers. I have been unable to identify "young Wentworth"; in the State Papers, Domestic, for 1624 there is a letter to Carleton from a Peter Wentworth thanking him for past favors. *C. S. P. Domestic 1623–25*, p. 230.

5. Tilly, after his victory over Brunswick at Stadtlohn, was instructed by Maximilian of Bavaria to attack Mansfeld in East Friesland and drive him across the Dutch frontier. Count Ernest of Nassau had occupied Emden with a small Dutch force. Mansfeld was not now in Dutch employ but was hopeful of being so again; he was now awaiting Tilly's attack.

[311]

6. Gregory XV had died during the summer and was succeeded by Urban VIII, who was to have a pontificate of twenty-one years.

7. Francesco Contarini, who was elected to succeed the recently deceased doge, Antonio Priuli.

The Hague, December 21, 1623

S. P. 84/115, ff. 142–43

Good Mr. Chamberlain, I have of late very ill merited your often kind remembrances (whereof the last I received in two letters by my nephew), my many affairs (greater or smaller, such as could not be dispensed withal) having taken up all my time. Now I come to wish you a merry Christmas, which we entertain the better here by Sir George Goring's [1] good company, who came soon after my nephew (from the duke of Buckingham to excuse his grace's and the duke of Richmond's [2] absence from the christening of our little young prince here, to which they were invited as *parrains* by the king and queen of Bohemia) and lodgeth in my house. He hath brought messages of much comfort to these princes touching their affairs in Germany, that the king is resolved to see them absolutely restored before he proceed in the match with Spain; and our ambassadors writing from thence that the match is in such terms of assurance that it is *piaculum* to fail in belief thereof, all might seem to be near a good conclusion. But one of these not being free from difficulties and delays as long as anything in it *superest agendum* and the other subject to apparent impossibilities (other princes being actually invested of their dignities and estates) I must be pardoned if I believe neither, especially considering that nothing but necessity can sway such affairs with the men we have to deal with; and a new accident of which they were much afraid, being turned to their advantage, will rather increase their pride than otherwise, they having their accustomed happiness continued in Gabor's [3] sudden and unexpected retreat into Transylvania from the frontiers of Moravia, where he held the emperor's army besieged and ready to perish for famine; so

[312]

as all was full of despair at Vienna itself, from whence the emperor
sent away his children to places of more security; and fair language
was used to all the princes and towns of Germany by way of
supplication for succors; which is already converted into *volumus
et jubemus*; and if we had any hopes to fare the better for that
diversion (as here much triumph was made for it by these provinces) they are already at an end. Tilly's troops, in opinion they
should be called away after their fellows some while since marched
upwards to the war, have utterly spoiled and consumed the landgrave of Hesse's [4] country, where they have lodged ever since they
left Westphalia. Mansfeld's continue in much extremity in East
Friesland, being afflicted at once with the three sharp scourges,
war, pestilence, and famine. For now those poor men thought to
have looked abroad upon the freezing of the rivers and lakes of
those parts, Córdoba's troops and Anholt's, joined together, will
be too strong for them, especially they being forsaken by their
French, who made a third of the foot and are come away for
want and wearisomeness of that hard service. We have had here
a petty mutiny amongst our English at Breda [5] upon the mistaking
of a new placard of musters published by the States, the suppress-
ing whereof hath cost four of our poor countrymen's lives, who
were executed this last week, and so all quieted. But the discontent-
ment is great and general through the whole land, so as there is
doubt what the soldiers will do when they come again into the
field, though they are easily bridled in garrisons. Our West Indian
fleet set sail from Texel the 11th of this present; but the vice
admiral's and another of those ships, by loitering after their
fellows, are catched by the ice and frozen in at Gore. My arrearage, which I confess in the beginning, is increased now whilst I
am writing by your ample letter of the 6th of this present; for
which I render you many thanks. I pray you congratulate Sir
Isaac Wake's match [6] from me and remember my service to my
lord General Vere, if he be well arrived, as I hope he is, but as
yet hear no news thereof. Thus with my own and my wife's wonted
good wishes, I rest

Yours most affectionately

1. George Goring, the future earl of Norwich and father of the royalist general of the Civil War (who predeceased him) was a friend and favorite of Prince Charles's, and had accompanied him to Spain. He had an eccentric sense of humor which endeared him to the king.

2. The duke of Lennox was now duke of Richmond in the English peerage. The "little young prince" was named Louis, in honor of Louis XIII; he did not survive infancy.

3. Bethlen Gabor, prince of Transylvania, was a good Calvinist, and a wily and unpredictable enemy of the Habsburgs. He had invaded Hungary with a very large army in the summer of 1623, after coining money which gave him the title of king of Hungary. Had he pressed his planned attack on Vienna in November, he might well have captured it. He did not, partly because of the unreliability of his Turkish allies, and in the following year he made peace with the emperor.

4. Maurice, landgrave of Hesse-Cassel. He is remembered, among other things, for having founded a temperance society, whose first president died of drink.

5. The riot apparently developed on account of a decree by the States which attempted to cut down on the ways in which officers were fleecing their troops financially. *C. S. P. Venetian 1623–1625,* p. 176.

6. Carleton's former secretary had long been courting Anna Bray, stepdaughter of Sir Edward Conway, the secretary of state. In February he had been given leave to come home and marry her, and now he finally had done so.

The Hague, February 26, 1623/24
S. P. 84/116, ff. 172–73

Sir, I was lately surprised with my nephew's sudden departure, who was a speaking letter, and therefore my silence might be better excused. Now I am in the like state again for haste but cannot forbear thanking you for your letter of the last of January, which came late to my hands now within these two days but was full of news, the frost having closed our havens and kept us from all letters since that date. We have had here a winter war (as you will have heard) not much unlike our English boys' play of bidding of base;[1] for when Count Henry Vandenberg, having crossed the Ysell into the Veluwe, heard of the prince of Orange's going to Utrecht, he retired to his passage and there stopped; when his excellency understood of his making a halt, he stayed likewise without going further; so as they did one another no great hurt. We are now subject to a second inundation by reason of certain dams and banks of ice as high as Tiel, which proceed of the waters' opening and the ice driving as high as Cologne, when all is fast below. And it may seem strange that what hath not happened in a hundred years before (as in man's memory no such things have been, but the like is found about that time upon record) should now fall out twice in one winter, and that inundation should be followed with invasions (which are likewise very unusual) upon the ice; but mischiefs seldom come alone. Count Mansfeld is going into France, so to Savoy, after to Venice if he find no employment by the way. The duke of Brunswick is already weary here of doing nothing and speaks of taking the same course.[2] The old count de la Tour is come hither in company of an ambassador from Bethlen Gabor, who hath not yet settled his affairs with the emperor. The old prince of Anhalt,[3] being the prime *butte-feu* of these German troubles, having hid himself in a corner in Denmark since the loss of Prague, doth finally submit himself and goeth to Vienna upon the emperor's safe conduct. All other news you will have of this honest gentleman Sir Edward Conway (eldest son to Mr. Secretary), my very dear friend and one well worthy of your acquaintance, who will deliver you a book from me, touching which I shall be glad to hear Sir Isaac Wake's opinion, to whom I pray you let me be kindly remembered. So with wonted good wishes I rest

Yours most assured

1. The issuing of a challenge in the game of prisoners' base.
2. Mansfeld, having devastated East Friesland, attempted in December 1623 to break out of a blockade which Tilly had set up around his army. After his vanguard was wiped out at Friesoythe, he got money from the Dutch to pay off his troops in exchange for turning over to the Dutch the fortresses he held. Christian of Brunswick had also disbanded his army. Carleton was quite wrong in his speculation as to Mansfeld's movements; he went

to England, where he found that employment which was to do so much to ruin the prestige and credibility of the government of Charles I.

3. Christian of Anhalt, whose recklessness and ambition had contributed greatly to the elector Frederick's ruin. Ferdinand eventually pardoned him.

The Hague, November 16/26, 1624
S. P. 84/121, ff. 98–99

Good Mr. Chamberlain I was soon put out of the way of my late resolution to double my diligence in writing by a long and sharp fit of the stone, followed with more weakness than usual; but now being come to myself again I return to you, rendering you many thanks for your often letters, which come to my hands very seasonably when from none of my private friends I can have a word, my nephew Dudley being as silent as others, or else he hath ill luck with his letters, for since his leaving London to go to Royston I have not heard from him. I know not who it is you hear named to the secretary's place;[1] but if it be one I guess at, you need not much doubt him, for he is no suitor for it, and such places require that diligence and more. True it is that he lent a willing ear when he was called upon by a friend (as you know) and was putting himself forward but had soon his *quietus est* and so rests. And anything you since hear is but the sound of that bell which then rung louder than I could have wished. I am exceeding glad of my lady Smith's good fortune, and so will my wife be when she knows it, who loves her so dearly that she was passionately affected and troubled at a voice was here spread that she should marry her cousin Tom Carew.[2] She is now in Zeeland at an *incanto* of Italian and Spanish goods taken by a freebooter of that province from a viceroy of Naples as they were transporting into Galicia (where it seems his habitation is) by the cape St. Vincent; and having seen the list of them, I more commiserate his family than himself, whose gains of the whole time of their service in clothes and trinkets are lost in that one prize, wherein is much waiting-gentlewomen's ware but withal store of hangings and

[316]

good household stuff, Spanish and Italian books (which are my merchandise) and pictures of the best hands, about which my wife hath chiefly undertaken this journey to do service to our chief persons at home, who look after them. And it is well if she can purchase thanks answerable to her pains, for she hath had an ill passage thither, being four days and three nights on shipboard in tempestuous weather; and there the air is grown ill and contagious, as may appear by the directors of this East Indian company there lately assembled in full college, of the 17 of which the most part returned sick, 4 or 5 are since dead, of which two of mean beginnings have raised in short time and left to their heirs, the one 7, the other 8 ton of gold, which raiseth a general clamor against the rapine of them and the rest of their colleagues. I cannot yet get out of the thorny business betwixt them and our company, but it is now brought to this pass, that unless they will yield to reason for our men's satisfaction the States will leave them to themselves and so have plainly told them; wherewith they are much troubled as with a great change and alteration of their affairs, which heretofore, right or wrong, were ever supported by the state; to which their will and decree served as a law.[3] Our camps and the enemies' with the besieged town [4] are at a vie which can suffer most, there being sickness and incommodities on all sides and so many fugitives from one to the other that a Spaniard told one of our trumpets the two generals would be left before long alone to try the quarrel by single combat. The prince of Orange, having failed of a second attempt upon the citadel of Antwerp (wherein English and French were employed to stop their mouths from reproaching the Dutch for the former), is come hither to seek health, being so much afflicted with cold and pain and weakness of his loins that he goeth for the most part about his chamber on crutches and taketh not above an hour's or two hours' rest in a whole night.[5] But his doctors make his disease rather dolorous than dangerous. You will have heard of the death of my lord of Southampton and my lord Wriothesley; the son first at Roosendaal, and the father four days after at Bergen, both of the same disease, fevers with convulsions. They are both much lamented here of strangers; and we should think we had a great loss of such eminent persons, but I doubt we are not so kindhearted as we were wont. My lord Mountjoy and Sir John Borlase stand for the vacant regiment, which I have moved the prince of Orange, being a prime place, to bestow with advice from his majesty, who payeth the troops, and till that be known, to suspend it. But Sir John Borlase is a diligent solicitor here, as he hath reason, my lord Mountjoy being gone into England; and I do not stir nor stand much in it, though *ex officio* I could not but do as I have done, to have his majesty acknowledged, but this Sir John takes somewhat unkindly.[6] My lady of Oxford is fallen dangerously sick at the leaguer at Waalwijk, a very unfit place for a fair lady.[7] Count Ernest commands in his excellency's absence at Roosendaal, sick and crazy and not like to last long. This general mortality hath carried away a great part of our few learned men in these parts; as Arpenius, a famous linguist, Vorstius, a chief physician, and Colonius, all professors at Leyden and all dead of the plague (as is Scultetus[8] at Emden), which rageth still in that town and Amsterdam; but ceaseth, when it was hottest, at Delft, where hitherto God hath preserved all our English merchants, both masters and servants. It hath been much scattered in this town and is now within three houses of mine; but custom makes none start at it, and therefore I stir not. Thus I wish you health with all happiness and rest

Yours most assured

1. Sir George Calvert, who opposed the breach with Spain, was on the verge of resignation. Chamberlain reported on October 23 that Sir John Coke was to succeed him. This prediction was slightly premature. Calvert was succeeded early in 1625 by Wotton's nephew Sir Albertus Morton, who died before the end of the year; Coke then got the appointment. He was a bad choice; he was regarded as a tool of Buckingham's, and relations between crown and Parliament were exacerbated by his ineptitude.

2. Carleton's cousin Judith Lytton, the widow of Sir George Smith, who had died in 1620. Her new husband was Sir Thomas Barrington, son and heir of an Essex country gentleman; Chamberlain described him as well suited to the lady, among other things, in "conformity of studies (somewhat poetical)." *L. J. C.* II, 572. Tom Carew was Lady Carleton's scapegrace poet-cousin.

3. News of the massacre of Amboina, which effectively gave the *coup de*

grâce to the English position in the East Indies, reached England in May 1624. James insisted that justice be done; but the news caused very little stir in England at a time when anti-Spanish feeling was at fever pitch, and in the following month England signed a treaty with the Dutch agreeing to pay 6000 English volunteers in Dutch service for two years. The Dutch government's disavowal of their company was a standard diplomatic ploy which ensured that the incident would not disturb the good relations between the two governments.

4. Breda. Spinola's famous siege began in July 1624; he captured it in May 1625.

5. Maurice died early in 1625. His younger brother, Frederick Henry, an equally talented commander, succeeded to his position in the state.

6. Sir John Borlase was a veteran soldier who had served with Vere in the Palatinate; Mountjoy Blount, Lord Mountjoy, the future earl of Newport, was a courtier. Borlase got the regiment.

7. Diana Cecil, daughter of the second earl of Exeter, wealthy and beautiful, had married Henry de Vere, eighteenth earl of Oxford, in January 1624. He was now serving as a colonel in the Low Countries, and it was he who in fact was to die of fever in the following year. She subsequently married Thomas Bruce, earl of Elgin.

8. Abraham Scultetus had also been a professor of divinity at Heidelberg; he went to Emden after the Habsburgs' army captured Heidelberg.

INDEX

Abbot, George, archbishop of Canterbury, 80, 82, 158, 160, 235, 247
Abbot, Maurice, 271, 287
Aerschot, *see* Croy, family of
Aerssens, François van, 257, 258, 261, 305
Ahmed I, sultan of Turkey, 43, 114, 123, 125, 143, 147, 176
Albert of Habsburg, Archduke, 10, 17, 38, 41, 63, 78, 81, 146, 194, 196, 234, 236, 264, 265, 282, 286, 288
Alexander III, pope, 141, 142
Amboina, massacre of, 8, 318
Amsterdam, 195, 198, 218, 227, 228, 231, 237, 285, 318
Anderson, Sir Edmund, 38, 46
Andrewes, Lancelot, 15, 48, 91, 93, 110, 111, 119, 120, 128, 151, 161, 162, 181, 247, 253, 254, 262, 263, 268, 280, 282, 283, 287, 288
Angennes, Charles d', marquis of Rambouillet, French ambassador to Savoy, 171, 172, 174, 175, 180, 182–184, 186
Anhalt, Christian, prince of, 293, 315, 316
Anholt, Johann Jakob, baron of, 291, 293, 304, 313
Anne of Denmark, queen of England, 34, 36, 37, 54, 60, 62, 66, 67, 82, 90

Antwerp, 22, 210, 212, 218, 225, 234
Aremberg, Charles, count of, 36, 38, 40, 41, 43, 45, 61
Argyll, Archibald Campbell, seventh earl of, 35
Arminians, 18, 19, 226, 242, 243, 250, 251, 253, 260, 269
Arundel, earl of, *see* Howard, Thomas
Ashton, Roger, *see* Aston
Asselinau, Jacques, 14, 128, 130, 232, 233, 239, 248
Asti, treaty of, 16, 174, 175
Aston, Roger, 39, 46
Austria, House of, *see* Habsburgs
Auvergne, Henri de la Tour d', duke of Bouillon, 30, 31, 33, 34, 75, 78

Backhouse, Samuel, 106
Bacon, Sir Francis, 76, 79, 84, 98, 145, 146, 233, 235, 247, 252, 255, 287
Badoer, Anzolo, 129, 130
Bager, Sir Thomas, 67
Bancroft, Richard, archbishop of Canterbury, 57, 59, 99, 111
Banks, Mr., 54, 59
Bar, Henri of Lorraine, duke of, 31, 89
Barbarigo, Gregorio, 148, 153, 154, 188, 189
Barclay, John, 295, 296

Cosimo II, grand duke of Tuscany, 114, 136, 143, 146, 266
Coventry, bishop of, *see* Overall, John
Cranborne, Viscount, *see* Cecil, Robert
Cranfield, Lionel, 21
Croft, Sir Herbert, 100, 101
Cromwell, Thomas, fourth Baron Cromwell, 168, 169
Croy, family of, dukes of Aerschot, 212, 215
Cueva, Alfonso de, marquis of Bedmar, Spanish ambassador to Venice, 119, 120, 129, 144, 148, 167, 171
Cumberland, George Clifford, third earl of, 36

Darcy, Sir Francis, 88
Delft, 207, 282, 285, 287, 299, 318
Della Rovere, Francesco Maria II, duke of Urbino, 89, 225
Denny, Sir Edward, 62, 63
Derby, Elizabeth Stanley, countess of, 54, 67
Devereux, Frances, countess of Essex, 35
Devereux, Robert, 2nd earl of Essex, 7, 37, 247, 248, 261
Devereux, Robert, 3rd earl of Essex, 152
Devonshire, earl of, *see* Blount, Charles
Dewhurst, Sir Bernard, 248, 249
Diego (servant of William Cecil, Lord Roos), 154, 180
Digby, Sir John, later first earl of Bristol, 241, 285, 288
Digby, Simon, 286
Digges, Sir Dudley, 273, 276, 284, 287, 290
Dingwall, Lord, Richard Preston, 214, 215
Diston, William, 236, 238, 239
Doddridge, Sir John, 76, 79

Dohna, Baron Achatius, 275, 276
Dohna, Christopher, 276
Dominis, Marc Antonio de, archbishop of Spalato, 224, 226, 227, 229, 230, 245–247, 253, 289, 292, 297
Donato, Leonardo, doge of Venice, 129, 130, 134, 158
Doncaster, Viscount, *see* Hay, James
Donne, John, 93, 211, 233, 235, 275, 276
Dormer, Sir Michael, 5, 9, 63, 65, 98, 101, 103, 104, 106, 114
Dorset, earl of, *see* Sackville, Thomas
Dort, synod of, 227, 260, 262, 263, 265
Dort, United Provinces, 194, 213, 257
Dove, Anne (Sir Dudley Carleton's sister), 258
Dove, Bess (Sir Dudley Carleton's niece), 258, 274
Dove, Reverend John, 258
Drummond, James, first earl of Perth, 81
Dubois, Abbot Jean, 289, 292
Dudley, Robert, earl of Leicester, 75
Dudley, Sir Robert, 74, 75, 135
Du Maurier, Aubrey, French ambassador to The Hague, 224, 231, 234, 257, 258
Dunbar, George Home, earl of, 89, 92, 105
Duodo, Piero, Venetian ambassador to England, 43, 46
Durham, bishop of, *see* James, William; Matthew, Tobie
Dutch East India Company, 17, 218, 220, 264–266, 284, 317, 319
Dutton, Sir Thomas, 308, 311

Earth, Joseph, 113
East India Company of England, 17, 218, 220, 264, 265, 270, 271, 274, 276, 284, 287, 317
East Indies, 19, 268, 277, 290, 319

Hele, Sir John, 38, 40, 46

Henri IV, king of France, 6, 7, 11, 12, 29–31, 33, 36, 42, 54, 70, 73, 74, 78, 84, 184, 189, 292

Henry, Prince, son of James I, king of England, 35, 36, 37, 66, 86, 96, 131, 135, 137, 167

Herbert, John, 43, 46

Herbert, Mary, countess of Pembroke, 44–46, 67, 209, 211

Herbert, Philip, fourth earl of Pembroke, 44–46, 54, 66, 69, 77, 110

Herbert, William, third earl of Pembroke, 35, 54, 56, 64, 66, 81, 247–248

Hertford, Edward Seymour, earl of, 68, 69

Hicks, Sir Baptist, 84, 85

Hobart, Sir Henry, 76, 79

Hoby, Sir Edward, 66

Holstein, duke of, *see* Joachim Ernest; Ulric

Holy Roman Emperor, *see* Rudolph II; Matthias; Ferdinand II

Home, George, earl of Dunbar, 89, 92, 105

Hoogerbeets, Rambout, 256, 258, 260

Horne, Thomas (Sir Dudley Carleton's chaplain), 121, 124, 157, 161

Horsey, Sir Jerome, 98

Horwood, Sir Edward, 305

Hoskyn, John, 124

Howard, Alathea, countess of Arundel, 144, 145, 294, 295

Howard, Anne, Lady Effingham, 67

Howard, Charles, first earl of Nottingham, 8, 35–37, 56, 90, 93

Howard, Elizabeth, countess of Nottingham, 39, 93

Howard, Frances, 152

Howard, Henry, first earl of Northampton, 38, 56, 57, 61, 81, 86, 131

Howard, Katherine, countess of Suffolk, 39, 54, 67

Howard, Sir Robert, 311

Howard, Thomas, second earl of Arundel, 13, 48, 74, 75, 144, 146, 148, 149, 151–153, 155, 247; wife of, 144, 149, 294, 295

Howard, Thomas, first earl of Suffolk, 38, 45, 46, 81, 201, 203, 264, 278, 311

Howard, William, third Lord Howard of Effingham, 62, 63

Ingram, Sir Arthur, 209, 211

Inoiosa, Juan de Mendoza, marquis of, Spanish governor of Milan, 142

Isabella, Clara Eugenia, wife of Archduke Albert, 10, 196, 215, 234, 236, 288

James I, king of England, 4, 8, 10, 12, 13, 17, 18, 20, 35, 36, 37, 42–44, 49, 51–53, 57, 61, 62, 64, 66, 75, 82, 86, 99, 105, 109, 110, 121, 124, 154, 164–166, 172, 177, 178, 180, 194, 196, 205, 216, 233, 236, 238, 250, 251, 253, 255, 265, 267, 272, 273, 275–277, 282, 284, 306, 318, 319, and *passim*

James, William, bishop of Durham, 91

Jermyn, Sir Thomas, 44

Jesuits, 12, 34, 122, 124, 125, 187, 188, 204, 209, 213, 271, 275

Joachim Ernest, duke of Holstein-Sunderberg, 229, 230, 294

John George, elector of Saxony, 240, 270

Johnson, Sir Robert, 82, 83

Jones, Inigo, 69, 101, 145, 146, 211

Jonson, Ben, 69, 121, 124, 211

Juliers, 17, 157, 202, 203, 206, 228, 291, 292, 303

Kemys, Captain Lawrence, 58, 60

Kennedy, Sir John, 113

Kevett, George, 293

[329]

Norris, Lady Elizabeth, 59–60

Norris, Francis, earl of Berkshire, 69, 71, 289, 292

Norris, Henry, first Baron Norris of Rycote, 5, 6

Norris family, 5

North, Dudley, third Baron North, 69, 71

Northampton, earl of, *see* Howard, Henry

Northumberland, earl of, *see* Percy, Henry

Norton, Sir Dudley, 111, 226, 227

Nottingham, Elizabeth Howard, countess of, 39, 93

Nottingham, earl of, *see* Howard, Charles

Noue, Odet de la, 231

Nys, Daniel, 195, 196, 254

Ogle, Sir John, 58, 60, 204, 205

Oglethorpe, Sir Owen, 95

Oldenbarnevelt, Johan van, 18, 19, 46, 194, 196, 232, 236, 242, 247, 248, 256, 258, 262, 299, 301

O'Neill, Hugh, second earl of Tyrone, 88, 92

Onslow, Sir Francis, 227

Orange, prince of, *see* Philip William; Maurice

Orange, dowager princess of, *see* Coligny, Louise de

Osman II, sultan of Turkey, 286, 288

Ossuma, Pedro Giron, duke of, 290, 292

Ostend, 5, 58, 63, 65

Overall, John, bishop of Lichfield and Coventry, 253, 255

Owen, Hugh, 78, 79, 81

Owen, Sir Roger, 101

Oxford, Henry de Vere, eighteenth earl of, 319

Packington, Sir John, 84

Paddy, Sir William, 11, 102, 104, 110, 113, 114

Padua, 15, 118, 122, 127, 131, 132, 138, 140, 170, 172

Paget, John, 285, 287

Painton, Sir John, 44

Palatinate, the, 280, 299, 293, 296

Palatinate, elector of the, *see* Frederick, king of Bohemia

Parham, Sir Edward, 38, 45

Parliament, 8, 9, 75, 93, 100, 106, 161, 318

Parry, Henry, 91, 93

Parry, Sir Thomas, 6, 44, 46, 72, 73, 74

Parsons, Robert, 105, 107

Paul V, pope, 89, 92, 122, 129, 151, 162, 171, 177, 179, 254, 292

Pecquius, Pierre, 282

Pembroke, countess of, *see* Herbert, Mary

Pembroke, earl of, *see* Herbert, Philip; Herbert, William

Percy, Allen, 43, 67

Percy, Dorothy, countess of Northumberland, 110

Percy, Henry, ninth earl of Northumberland, 6, 8, 9, 36, 42, 46, 56, 61, 72, 74, 85, 90, 91, 93, 96; wife of, 110

Percy, Thomas, 8

Perth, James Drummond, first earl of, 81

Pescina, Giovanni, senator, 179

Philip II, king of Spain, 215

Philip III, king of Spain, 5, 6, 10, 88, 89, 92, 109, 146, 153, 265, 272, 283

Philip IV, king of Spain, 303

Philip William, prince of Orange, 221, 229

Philips, Sir Thomas, 38, 207

Pindar, Paul, 123, 125, 129, 130, 177, 178

Playfere, Dr. Thomas, 91, 93

[332]

Widdrington family, 101

Willaston, William, 72, 73

William, duke of Cleves, 114

William Louis, Count of Nassau-Dillenberg, 257, 274, 277, 278

Williams, Alexander (Sir Dudley Carleton's brother-in-law), 9, 45, 80, 139, 140, 159, 160, 165, 185, 191, 275

Williams, Anthony (Sir Dudley Carleton's nephew), 145, 146, 232

Williams, Sir David, 105, 106

Williams, Elizabeth (Sir Dudley Carleton's sister), 80, 100, 105, 108, 232

Williams, Will, 246

Willoughby, Richard, 66, 67, 133, 151, 152

Winchester, bishop of, see Andrewes, Lancelot; Bilson, Thomas

Wingfield, Richard, 268, 270, 273, 274

Wingfield, Sir Robert, 113

Winwood, Lady Elizabeth, 196, 217, 247, 268, 307, 311

Winwood, Sir Ralph, 6, 8, 10, 15, 16, 21, 22, 33, 37, 43, 58, 84, 95, 109, 111, 113, 114, 121, 132, 134, 138, 140, 142, 148, 151, 153, 154, 156, 159, 160, 163, 164, 167, 170, 173, 175, 177, 180, 181, 182, 185, 196, 198, 200, 203, 205, 210, 214, 216, 217, 222, 226, 229, 230, 235, 240, 244, 246–249, 251

Woodrows, Captain Henry, 220, 221

Worcester, Edward Somerset, fourth earl of, 36, 56, 110

Wotton, Edward, first Baron Wotton, 36–38, 61, 165, 167

Wotton, Sir Henry, 13, 16, 20, 57, 58, 112, 118, 120, 125, 127, 136, 137, 152, 156, 157, 165–170, 173–175, 186, 196, 201, 206, 219, 221, 229, 235, 236, 240, 246, 249, 251, 253, 276–279, 294–296

Wriothesley, Henry, third earl of Southampton, 35, 37, 41, 46, 56, 64, 81, 311, 317

Wriothesley, James, 308, 311, 317

Wymark, Edward, 76, 79, 88, 97, 99, 113, 122, 263

Xanten, treaty of, 228, 230 278

Yelverton, Sir Henry, 76, 79

York, archbishop of, see Matthew, Tobie

Young, Peter, 165, 167

Zamet, Sebastian, 43, 46

Zen, Ranier, Venetian ambassador to Savoy, 171, 183, 187

Zouche, Edward, eleventh Baron Zouche, 88, 92

Zuniga, Don Pedro de, 71, 89

ABOUT THE AUTHOR

Currently a professor in the Department of History at Douglass College, Dr. Lee has been on the Rutgers University faculty since 1966. He taught seven years at the University of Illinois and nine at Princeton University, where he received his B.A., M.A., and Ph.D. degrees. His previous publications include *James Stewart, Earl of Moray* (1953), *John Maitland of Thirlestane* (1959), *The Cabal* (1965), and *James I and Henri IV* (1970).

The text of this book was set in Caslon Linotype and printed by offset on P & S Special Book manufactured by P. H. Glatfelter Co., Spring Grove, Pa. Composed, printed and bound by Quinn & Boden Company, Inc., Rahway, N.J.